Suffer the Little Children:
Urban Violence and Sacred Space

Suffer the Little Children : Urban Violence and Sacred Space

EDITED BY
Kay A. Read and Isabel L. Wollaston

THE UNIVERSITY
OF BIRMINGHAM
UNIVERSITY PRESS

First published in the United Kingdom by The University of Birmingham Press, Edgbaston, Birmingham, BI5 2TT, UK.

ISBN 1-902459-11-3

British Library Cataloguing in Publication data
A CIP catalogue record for this book is available from the British Library

Printed in Great Britain by MPG Books Limited, Bodmin.
Typeset by Book Production Services, London,

Contents

Preface

Kay A. Read

In spring 1995, a youthful gentleman with short cropped hair, wearing sports shoes and a leather jacket, knocked unannounced on the door of Dennis McCann, then chair of the Religious Studies Department at DePaul University Chicago (USA). McCann thought he was a student, but that proved not to be the case. Gareth Jones wanted to know if the DePaul department might be interested in a collaboration with the Department of Theology at the University of Birmingham (UK), of which he was a faculty member. After all, Birmingham and Chicago were twin cities; moreover they shared similar strengths and problems of diversity and violence, which might provide fruitful ground for some sort of shared endeavour. This somewhat modest and serendipitous meeting proved the starting point for several collaborations, including this volume of essays.

A joint colloquium on 'Religion in an Urban Context', held at DePaul in February 1996, became our first event. During that week of meetings exploring various facets of our shared urban and religious characters, we paid a visit to St James Episcopal Cathedral, and listened to Janet Campbell and Todd Smelzer tell us about the Children's Cross Memorial that then stood in the Cathedral plaza.[1] Many of us found ourselves taken with the simple, even crude handmade cross made by Sunday school pupils to remember the children who had died in Chicago in 1993 and beyond. It seemed to all that its creation and presentation in a very public plaza raised a host of larger questions concerning the cross, sacred space, urban violence, suffering, memory, memorialization and multi-vocality. It therefore offered a unique opportunity for a joint exploration. By the week's end we had decided that a volume of essays addressing some of the many questions raised by the Children's Cross would be our first collaborative project. A number of us developed our individual essays, which we then presented to each other the following year during a second colloquium, this time in Birmingham UK.

As with many academic projects, the volume took rather longer than at first any of us wanted or anticipated. This, however, also proved fairly serendipitous, for by the time we had finally gathered everyone's papers together in February 2000, the Children's Cross and the public plaza in which it was displayed had each lived through at least one complete life cycle, which we would not have seen had we been more efficient. Such observations allowed several of us to reflect upon the Cross's and plaza's entire lives in our essays, thereby nicely enriching our efforts. Briefly then (for other essays tell the story with more depth and eloquence than I can), here is a synopsis of the lives of the St James Episcopal Cathedral's Children's Cross and the plaza in which it dwelt for several years.

In 1993, the *Chicago Tribune* ran a year-long, award-winning exposé of the children killed in the city in just that one year. Sixty-three children lost their lives to violence in 1993, and the very public recording of this on what seemed like almost a daily basis deeply affected people across the entire urban area. Feeling like they wanted to do something about the city's violence against its children, parishioners of St James Cathedral, among other things, formed a prayer group, created a special altar commemorating the children, and decided to dedicate 1994's Sunday school Lenten project to a cross memorializing the city's dead youth. On one side of this simple wooden cross, broken mirror pieces reflected the fractured nature of the observers and their city; and on the other side, the names of all sixty-three children along with those killed thereafter called people to witness and remember. When finished, the Sunday school children erected their Cross in a modest planter in the cathedral plaza, right on the corner of Rush and Huron streets, lying just off Chicago's Magnificent Mile. It became the focus of some press attention, a couple of influential observers and many of those who hurried past the very public and very busy corner.

There it remained until 1998, even though the Cathedral had originally intended to take it down not too long after its erection in 1994. Somehow the rather fragile wooden and painted Cross had taken on a life of its own, and continued to stand out in the elements, growing a little older and more tired with each passing year. In October 1998, death (or at least the end of one of its life phases) came to the simple Cross. One of Chicago's infamous winds blew it over. Cathedral members picked up the pieces, reconstructed the Cross inside, and hung it name-side out on a large wall above the stairs leading to the Sunday school rooms. The focus now shifted to what to do with the plaza space, which seemed so empty and devoid of public meaning without the Children's Cross. For a while, some parishioners wanted to construct a meditation labyrinth on the plaza's floor (a plan they eventually abandoned); the opening of a photographic exhibition of the suffering caused by landmines occurred on the plaza; and then in 1999, the Episcopal Peace Fellowship chose the plaza as the site for a permanent statue dedicated to world peace. And so the story of the Children's Cross and its plaza ends.

The essays in this volume respond in various ways to these two life stories because the authors themselves vary. First, our two departments are different. Not only do we find ourselves in distinctive educational systems separated by a large ocean; but one of our departments, Birmingham, is a theology department; while the other, DePaul, is a religious studies department. Each therefore has tended to take a somewhat different approach to the issues of religion in an urban setting. Our collaboration thus continues to serve as a helpful source of cross-fertilization in a variety of ways ranging from this volume of essays to the kinds of programmes we foster in our institutional homes. Second, the faculty members themselves come from diverse perspectives and disciplines, representing among them the fields of cultural studies, theology, sociology, ministry, Christian history, Jewish studies, anthropology, practical theology, history of religions and social work. These various approaches also often cross-fertilize each other in interesting ways throughout the volume.

But diversity does not necessarily mean chaos. The book's differing authors chose to focus their attention around five major themes that weave themselves throughout their essays: (a) the cross, as both a symbol of protest against violence, and as the source of a possible ethics of violence. (b) Sacred space: its nature and role in places of both violence and sanctuary. (c) Suffering, as both a result of and a response to violence in the practical and theoretical spheres. (d) Memory, as both the persistence of, and a redemption from, violence. (e) Multi-vocality: both the ethical animosities and moral creativity of pluralistic environments in historical, contemporary, and cross-cultural situations. The collection thereby creates a tapestry of differing approaches, positions, and themes. Not all the essays agree, and many raise hard questions that are not always answerable. For all, however, the Children's Cross and its plaza home served as the impetus for explorations into the many-faceted character of urban religion and its often intimate relationship to violence.

The book itself is divided into three parts. Part One tells in more detail the story of the Children's Cross, exploring the motivations of those involved and the immediate responses to this initiative. Part Two contains more philosophical and theological reflections, focusing in particular on violence, memory, time and sacred space. Finally, in Part Three, the emphasis is upon the nature and role of memorialization. The Children's Cross is set alongside and compared to a number of other examples of memorialization, such as the Vietnam Veterans Memorial, the NAMES Project AIDS Quilt and the United States Holocaust Memorial Museum, as well as memory in other contexts, such as the African Diaspora.

Many people have helped facilitate this project. We very much appreciate Martin Marty's willingness to take on the difficult task of responding to the diverse essays in this volume. Special thanks go to St James Cathedral, who patiently put up with our questions, and agreed to continue going public with their 1994 Sunday school project even after its apparent demise. Rev. Janet Campbell, who served as Canon of Liturgy and Outreach at the Cathedral during the production of this volume, deserves particular thanks. If we had not had her patience with our diverse and often contradictory opinions, and her willingness to search her own sometimes intense feelings about the Children's Cross, this project would have been far poorer. In the course of production, I wager we felt, along with Campbell, the need to do more than we could about the suffering. In some ways, that perhaps is the most eloquent message of the St James Cathedral Children's Cross. Like all of us, that modest and finite symbol of death and resurrection accomplished way less than many hoped, and perhaps way more than anyone realizes. Besides the support of the Cathedral, both DePaul University and the University of Birmingham made possible our collaboration, which simply would not have happened without their repeated and generous financial support. Dennis McCann and Gareth Jones deserve recognition, for without them none of this would have even begun, much less been brought to fruition. Both of them have now moved on to new positions at other institutions, and others have taken over their responsibilities (rather as the Children's Cross has moved on and been replaced by something else). Finally, our thanks go to Vicki Whittaker at the University of Birmingham Press for her patience and help in seeing this volume through to publication.

Notes

1 Throughout this volume, for purposes of clarification, we have used upper case for the Children's Cross, and lower case for Jesus' cross, simply to differentiate between the two. No value judgement is thereby implied.

Writing and Rewriting the Cross

Isabel l. Wollaston

Violence, including violent and often random death, is part of the reality of life in a contemporary urban or inner-city context. Indeed, it is now so characteristic that it is only considered newsworthy in its more extreme forms, such as the death of the very young (as in the case of the murder of James Bulger or of sixteen five-year-old children at Dunblane), or because of its scale (for example, riots in Brixton, Handsworth, Crown Heights, or Los Angeles). The Children's Cross in Chicago represents the attempt of one Christian community to grapple with the challenges posed by sudden violent death, particularly the death of sixty-three children who were murdered in Chicago during the course of 1993. As such, it generates a series of questions. What precisely is being memorialized here? The violent, apparently senseless deaths of children in Chicago. Who is remembering whom? A largely white, affluent Christian community at St James Episcopal Cathedral, located just off Chicago's Magnificent Mile is remembering the deaths of children who were (a) not part of that immediate community, and (b) generally came from different social, economic, and ethnic backgrounds from those doing the remembering. How are these children being remembered? By the recording of their names, and by recourse to a relatively obscure day in the Christian liturgical year (the Feast of the Holy Innocents) and to the central Christian symbol – the cross.[1]

The Children's Cross thus serves as a microcosm of current debates, relating to both the way we talk about and represent evil and suffering, and the ambiguity inherent in that 'great symbol of all suffering, the tortured body of Christ on the cross'.[2] What is it about the cross that makes it a fitting medium for remembering such deaths in the present, while at the same time rendering such a choice so problematic? In addressing such questions, this paper begins with some initial remarks about representation, then considers some broad strategies adopted in talking about evil and suffering, before concluding with an analysis of the ways in which the symbol of the cross has been, and can be, written and rewritten.

Representation

A representation is a signifier, 'a sign – verbal, visual or aural – which contains meaning.'[3] That signifier symbolizes, stands for, or substitutes for that which it is representing. In doing so, it draws upon a wide range of cultural conventions and codes. Representations inevitably reflect the agendas and assumptions of their creators. Likewise, an audience brings a wide range of assumptions of their own to bear in responding to such representations.

To choose to represent something is both to acknowledge that thing's existence and to suggest that it has some relevance for our own situation, i.e. it is felt that that which is being represented does, or at least should, have an impact upon us in some way. To represent is therefore to render visible.[4] What is not represented is not remembered, at least not insofar as public or dominant memory in society is concerned; it remains invisible or marginal from the perspective of the mainstream. Remembrance and representation can therefore be seen in ideological and political terms. On the one hand, they can play a significant role in the repression of alternative or subversive memories. On the other hand, the recognition and/or recovery of such dangerous memories can play a key role in the process of conscientization: suppressed or forgotten memories ('dangerous memory') come to be articulated as a history 'from below', challenging the hegemony of history 'from above'. Hence the emphasis upon retrieving – or creating – alternative texts and traditions on the part of those engaged in challenging normative or dominant accounts of history.[5]

In commemorating the deaths of children in Chicago during 1993, members of St James Cathedral were making a public statement in acknowledging that these events were of relevance to them and demanded a response of some sort. They were also, significantly, responding to an initiative in the media: the *Chicago Tribune*'s decision to record the deaths of children in Chicago throughout 1993.[6] These members of the Cathedral were allowing their own self-understanding to be challenged by the experience of 'the Other'. However, the question then arises as to whether the Children's Cross in fact represents the experience of that Other, or rather appropriates and domesticates that experience by subsuming it within the terms of its own Christian metanarrative (particularly the cross and the Feast of the Holy Innocents). Is the Children's Cross an honest and legitimate response to the experience of the Other, or is it a means of rewriting that experience so that it conforms to the norms and expectations of its host audience? Or is it both of these things simultaneously? The variety of possible readings of, and reactions to the Children's Cross forms the subject matter of this book.

There are two key issues here. The first is the relationship between 'insiders' and 'outsiders' when it comes to the experience of suffering. It is now commonplace to hear that 'there is an understanding of suffering that only the sufferer can achieve.'[7] In other words, there is an experiential and epistemological gap separating the sufferer and the onlooker. Many of those involved in the project at St James clearly shared this belief, as is evident from Janet Campbell's account of the various attempts to bridge this gap. For example, members of the Cathedral met with mothers who had lost their children in gang-related violence, and consulted grassroots groups on the South Side of Chicago such as the Ark, the Rise High Project and the Green Program.[8]

The Children's Cross therefore raises in acute form the question of boundaries and of who is on the inside or the outside. The commemoration of these events existed on the fringes of the Cathedral's life. The initiative first came from a particular individual (Phoebe Griswold) and then a specific group within the Cathedral. This group's first initiative was to transform the Civil War Altar into a shrine remembering the child victims of urban violence, an altar that was itself marginal to the main body of the Cathedral, being set into the wall of the narthex (entrance). When erected outside, the Children's Cross was physically located on the margins of the Cathedral's precincts, and therefore on the boundary between sacred and profane space, in effect blurring the distinction between the two. The Cross's current location, on the wall above the stairs leading to the Sunday School rooms, further reinforces this sense of existing on the margins.[9]

As has been noted, the Children's Cross was a response to the experience of 'the Other'. Members of the Cathedral were conscious of being in the position of a spectator or bystander, responding to the *Chicago Tribune*'s reporting of the violent deaths of children in their city. However, they were not responding to the deaths of their own children, or the deaths of children in their immediate community. This is not to say that such a response is illegitimate. It is, after all, inevitable that any act of memory and/or representation will be influenced by who is doing the remembering and their own particular concerns, as well as the context in which they are remembering. Questions nevertheless arise as to whether such a response carries with it the risk of lapsing into voyeurism and mystification. The element of distancing raises questions concerning motivation. While not questioning the sincerity of Cathedral members, there is nevertheless the suggestion of a sense of worthiness here, of being seen to do the 'right thing' as a Christian, publicly demonstrating one's sensitivity and social concern in the face of events, such as those reported in the *Chicago Tribune*. From Janet Campbell's account, it is clear that some members of the Cathedral were well aware of this temptation.

Does the Children's Cross attempt to understand the experience of the Other and represent it on its own terms, or is it more preoccupied with the symbolic significance of these deaths, and their ramifications for an observing – and observant – Christian community? The process of representation, particularly when its authors are 'outsiders', inevitably brings with it a degree of universalization, of drawing wider 'lessons' from a particular experience. In the process, specific dead children killed at a particular point in time in Chicago are refigured as timeless slaughtered innocents. Hence the possible charge of mystification. Did those engaged in the Children's Cross project always maintain a strong sense of the difference between their experience, their grief, and that of those for whom events were more immediate? Or was there a tendency to overlook or ignore such differences in perspective? For example, is it of any consequence whether the children who died were Christian or not, practising or otherwise, when considering the appropriateness of the choice of these particular forms of memorialization?

In order even to begin answering such questions, we need to explore the motivations behind the creation of the Children's Cross. There was a sense of shock and horror at the statistics and stories reported in the *Chicago Tribune*. The decision to locate the Children's Cross outside the Cathedral suggests that there was also a desire to make a public statement, to engage in an act of public witness (as noted by Gareth Jones in his essay), and encourage others to participate in this. Phoebe Griswold was not alone in her belief that she was responding to God's call. In involving the children attending the Cathedral's Sunday school, the intent was to educate and foster a sense of solidarity and identification with the dead children. In initially incorporating this process of memorialization into the liturgical year, by associating it with the Massacre of the Innocents, the emphasis was also on remembrance and the provision of a ritual context for the expression of grief and anger. Thus, a whole range of motivations and intentions lay behind the Cathedral's initiative.

Having briefly considered the questions generated by the Cathedral's role as an 'outsider', the second issue – one already touched upon – is whether the cross and the Feast of the Holy Innocents are appropriate forms for remembering these particular events. The choice of the cross was, in many senses, an obvious one. It is the central, defining symbol of the Christian church and it was, after all, a Christian community that was committed to remembering the deaths of these children. There is a close association between Jesus and children, as depicted in the Gospels, in Christian art, and in numerous hymns. In both the cross and the Children's Cross, the victims are figured as innocent. In relation to the Children's Cross, there is no sense that these children were anything other than innocent victims. So, too, Jesus on the cross is often figured as the Innocent of innocents, the sinless Son of God suffering out of love for, on behalf of, or in place of, a sinful humanity.[10] Yet troubling questions remain. Without suggesting that these children in any way deserved their deaths, does it necessarily follow that they were innocent? For example, many were themselves involved in gang violence. This emphasis upon children's innocence is primarily a matter of convention, with its demand for clean-cut distinctions between good and evil, the innocent and the guilty, the victims and the perpetrators.[11] More often than not, media images of dead children offer us freeze-frames of innocence, of promise lost or unfulfilled.[12] Given such conventions, it is unsurprising that little attention is given to remembering that other children in fact killed some of the children being memorialized in the Children's Cross. Is it necessary for victims to be innocent for their deaths to be regarded as sufficiently newsworthy or 'tragic' enough to merit being remembered in this way? As will be argued below, the assertion of Jesus' innocence on the cross is also considerably more ambiguous and problematic than it might appear to be on the surface.

At this point, it is sufficient simply to note that the variety of meanings that can be ascribed to the Children's Cross, and the range of questions it gives rise to, serves to highlight the obvious: any representation or memorial can mean many different things to many different people. It can be understood either as containing a surplus of meaning, or as a blank canvas upon which we inscribe our own meanings.

Talking about Evil and Suffering

Questions relating to boundaries and perspective, appropriate forms of speech and representation, and of who is an 'insider' or an 'outsider' in relation to a particular experience of suffering underlie many recent discussions of the problem of evil. There is a preoccupation with what should and should not be said, and with who is entitled to speak about such things. The approaches in this discussion can be broadly characterized as either 'top-down' or 'bottom-up'. A 'top-down' approach begins with a preconceived theological and/or philosophical understanding of what God or the world is like. Evil, particularly in the form of innocent suffering, is then perceived to constitute a problem, a potential challenge, to this framework. From such a perspective, theodicy is a standard response to the problem of evil: it strives to demonstrate that the existence or possibility of evil is compatible with the existence of God (generally understood in theistic terms as all-powerful and all-good). A 'bottom-up' approach differs in insisting that we begin with human experience, with 'the plain fact of suffering', and then 'see what can be said theologically and religiously that is compatible with such a beginning.'[13] Each of these approaches tends to caricature the other. Adherents of a 'top-down' approach point to the relativism, logical inconsistency and sentimentalism often inherent in the appeal to experience. Adherents of a 'bottom-up' approach criticise theodicists for their optimism, rationality, and reliance upon an abstract, ahistorical concept of 'evil' when they should instead be grappling with the realities of concrete 'evils'.[14] Critics of theodicy insist that such metanarratives need to be interrupted, thus making it possible for the counter-testimony embodied in the voices of the victims of real, concrete evils to be heard.[15]

Representing the current state of affairs in this way serves to highlight the tensions between different approaches to the problem of evil. However, rather than portraying these two approaches as diametrically opposed alternatives, it is important to acknowledge that they are themselves characterized by plurality and ambiguity. For example, the Christian metanarrative incorporates a whole range of different strategies, of which theodicy is one, and theodicy in turn incorporates a variety of conflicting strategies and possibilities. Such plurality is inherent in the foundational texts of Christianity, for example in the presence of four gospel accounts, two creation narratives, two accounts of the ten commandments, and so on. We can respond to such plurality by attempting to rationalize it, by arguing that there is in fact only *one* story. We can interpret such variations as the textual remnants of earlier traditions, or argue that they were consciously and deliberately excluded as 'heretical' or deviant, and therefore lie outside that which should be regarded as acceptable and canonical. Alternatively, we can embrace such plurality as a reflection of 'the multiple possibility of alternative narrations', each of which embodies 'competing possibilities of what happened and why.'[16] In evaluating such multiple possibilities, the onus is upon the interpreter to be self-critical and adopt a hermeneutics of suspicion with regard to his or her own tradition. The process of deciding what is 'inside' or normative to a tradition, and what is 'outside', i.e. marginal or heretical, is seen in ideological terms, as much a question of power and authority as it is one of doctrinal 'orthodoxy'. In any given instance, we need to ask whose voice is being represented or privileged, and whose is being marginalized or excluded. Whose interests are being served by any particular 'version' of the tradition? What are the consequences of adopting one approach rather than another? From this perspective, to be part of a tradition is to 'own' that tradition in its entirety, in all its diversity and ambiguity, rather than 'cherry pick' and only acknowledge as 'authentic' those parts with which we agree. Such an approach is premised on the assumption that neither the tradition nor the interpreter can be considered entirely innocent: both are compromised by what has been done in the name of their tradition, in the past and the present. As David Tracy observes, 'there is no innocent interpretation, no innocent interpreter, no innocent text'.[17]

Writing and Rewriting the Cross

To apply such an approach to the way we interpret the cross means acknowledging its range of positive meanings and its shadowside. On the one hand, the cross represents Christianity's unflinching confrontation with the harsh realities of death, evil and suffering in the world – hence the insistence that it constitutes a 'practical theodicy', particularly when taking the form of an appeal to the suffering God.[18] The incarnation, culminating in the cross and resurrection, is the classic interruptive text: the divine entering into history and embracing the realities and limitations of human existence, even to the point of godforsakenness and death.[19] On the other hand, the cross can serve equally well as a strategy of evasion, a retreat or headlong flight into escapism and mystification, and/or as a symbol that perpetuates violence by both justifying and glorifying it.

A variety of positive constructive interpretations of the cross have been, and continue to be offered.[20] The cross is interpreted as, among other things, a victory over sin and death, the reconciliation of God and humanity, divine identification and solidarity with suffering humanity, and as a radical demonstration of God's preferential option for the poor and oppressed. Such interpretations appeal because they identify and address fundamental questions concerning human sinfulness, guilt and violence'. For Timothy Gorringe, the cross 'targets both guilt and violence, and offers a remedy to both through 'the "bearing" of guilt and the refusal to meet violence with counter-violence.'[21] For Jürgen Moltmann, while we await the new creation, 'the knowledge of the hidden presence of God in the godforsaken Christ on the cross already gives "courage to be", despite nothingness and all annihilating experiences.'[22] In a more traditional vein, Ian Bradley suggests that Jesus 'takes upon himself all the world's agony and pain as well as all its evil and offers it to God to be redeemed, transfigured and used in the divine economy.'[23]

Such diversity of interpretation has its roots in the New Testament.[24] On one level, the cross is presented as a judicial death at the hands of the Roman authorities (albeit one in which there are varying levels of involvement on the part of the Sanhedrin and Herod Antipas). On another level, we have a cluster of motifs offering a variety of interpretations of the death of Jesus of Nazareth on the cross. Theologically, this death is spoken of in terms of, to name but a few, expiation, justification, propitiation, redemption, reconciliation, and sacrifice. In dying on the cross, Jesus is presented as, among other things, the paschal lamb, the scapegoat, High Priest, a second Adam, and the Suffering Servant of Isaiah 53. The creeds continue this pattern by offering no definitive doctrinal definition or account of the meaning of the cross, instead they provide a narrative framework – Jesus suffered under Pontius Pilate, was crucified, died and was buried, descended into hell, and on the third day rose again from the dead.

Given such interpretations, it becomes clear why it was felt that the cross was an appropriate form for memorializing the death of children in Chicago. Linking the death of these children to that of Jesus on the cross emphasizes one's horror when confronted by such a reality. After all, for many Christians, there is no greater symbol of unjust suffering than the death of Jesus on the cross. In addition, as has already been noted, there is the close association between Jesus and children. Jesus is both figured as childlike and as the friend of children. Both Jesus and the children are frequently figured as 'innocent' victims. By linking the deaths of children with the death of Jesus on the cross, other possible meanings also emerge. Such a linkage gives grounds for hope: death is not the final word, but brings with it the promise of eternal life. Identifying the deaths of these children with that of Jesus on the cross suggests that such violence is not as meaningless or purposeless as it might seem: some good may come out of even the most radical of evils. The danger of linking the deaths of children in Chicago to that of Jesus on the cross is that it could suggest, however unintentionally, that the former should be understood in redemptive or sacrificial terms.[25]

Any suggestion that the suffering and death of Jesus on the cross is redemptive, let alone the extension of this to incorporate the deaths of children in the present, generates considerable unease. Having considered, albeit briefly, some of the positive interpretations of Jesus' death, we must also acknowledge the existence of counter voices that interpret this event in considerably more negative terms. Seen from the perspective of the latter, the choice of the cross to remember the dead children of Chicago is deeply problematic. While the cross has been 'written' in numerous and diverse positive ways, it has also been 'rewritten' in an attempt to highlight its inherent ambiguity and to point to its shadowside. Examples include artistic rewritings of the cross, such as Marc Chagall's 'White Crucifixion' or Edwina Sandys' sculpture 'Christa', as well as literary rewritings, such as Chaim Potok's *My Name Is Asher Lev*, John Steinbeck's *To a God Unknown*, or the child-hanging scene in Elie Wiesel's *Night*. The climax of *Monty Python's Life of Brian*, with its chorus of the crucified singing 'Always look on the bright side', serves as a satirical comment on the often facile ways in which the promise of 'greater goods' and/or eternal life are held out as a response to the problem of evil. On a more serious note, there is the close association between the cross and violence, and violent death, as typified by the symbolism of the Crusades or Reginald Blomfield's Sword of Sacrifice, found in all cemeteries under the auspices of the Commonwealth War Graves Commission. What meanings are conveyed by this symbolic synthesis of the sword and the cross in these particular contexts? The close association of the cross and the sword can also point to the violence done in the name of Christ, for example accompanying the missionary and colonizing activities of Western Christians.[26]

As the inversions or parodies of the crucifixion by Chagall, Potok and Wiesel demonstrate, the cross can have very different meanings when viewed from the perspective of non-Christians. The ongoing controversy about the offensiveness or otherwise of the presence of crosses at the site of Auschwitz serves to illustrate the ways in which the cross has come to symbolize Christian anti-Judaism and Christian triumphalism.[27] This point is made very clear by Elie Wiesel, addressing a Christian audience, when he notes, 'for you the cross is a symbol of love and compassion. Not for my people. For there have been times – naturally not today, but there have been times – when the cross symbolized, indeed incarnated, suffering and terror.'[28] One of the dif-

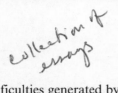 collection of essays

ficulties generated by the choice of the cross to remember the dead children of Chicago was that this very Christian memorial was erected in a *public* space in a thoroughly *multicultural* context.[29] Hence my question as to whether it matters if the children being commemorated were in fact all Christians. If, as has been noted, the Children's Cross was intended, in part, to serve as an act of Christian witness, does it matter that many of those it was witnessing to were secular or adherents of religions other than Christianity?

It is clear that the cross is a symbol laden with contradictory meanings. It can be problematic when viewed from the perspective of non-Christians. It can be equally problematic for many who continue to regard themselves as Christians. Liberation theologians have developed a critique of the close association of the cross and the sword, and its use to justify violence and the eradication, or suppression, of indigenous cultures and beliefs. Others, particularly feminist theologians, have been highly critical of various interpretations of the cross on the grounds that they glorify and perpetuate suffering and victimization.[30] It is undeniable that, in certain contexts, the story of the cross emerges as a text meriting Elisabeth Schüssler Fiorenza's warning label, 'Caution! Could be dangerous to your health and survival!'[31] A number of contemporary accounts of what was happening on the cross, such as those advocating belief in a suffering God, however well intentioned, nevertheless serve to blur the question of divine responsibility for the existence of evil and suffering in the world.

Placing the emphasis on Jesus' role as a victim, suffering out of love for humanity, is presented as an alternative to theoretical theodicies which justify the possibility of suffering as the necessary or inevitable 'price' of human freedom. According to such theodicies, if free will is to be meaningful, then there will always be the possibility that this freedom will be misused. If human freedom is to be meaningful, then we cannot expect God to intervene to stop such misuse or the consequences of such misuse. According to the theodicist, the possible existence of suffering is therefore compatible with belief in an all-powerful, all-loving God.[32] However, theologians such as Surin and Soelle suggest that such theodicies run the risk of presenting God as a victimizer, who is either directly or indirectly responsible for the existence of suffering. By contrast, they argue that emphasizing the fact that God shares humanity's suffering (i.e. God is a victim) serves as a practical theodicy: God is justified in creating a world in which the possibility of suffering exists because God shares in that experience of suffering. The inference to be drawn from Surin's argument is that a God who shares the suffering that is an inherent possibility in creation has more 'moral credibility' than a God who does not.[33]

Thus, while for some such as Surin, interpreting the cross as a trinitarian event focused around the suffering of Father and Son offers a way out of the difficulties generated by more theoretical theodicies, for others such a strategy generates considerable problems of its own. For example, Dorothee

Soelle criticizes Jürgen Moltmann's portrayal of 'the Crucified God' on the grounds that it serves to endorse 'theological sadism'.[34] Others, such as David Blumenthal, Rita Nakashima Brock and Bjorn Krondorfer go further in arguing that the cross portrays an abusive relationship within the Godhead.[35] Krondorfer suggests that 'by assuming the role of a victim, the parent evades and rejects guilt and responsibility.' As portrayed by Moltmann, 'the crucified God (or infallible parent) confuses ... the roles of abuser and abused.'[36] When a representation of what was happening on the cross such as Moltmann's is combined with an appeal to the resurrection, attention is deflected away from the realities of the violence inflicted or imposed upon the Son. Such violence is then considered acceptable because it is presented as the necessary means to a (good) end, namely the reconciliation of God and sinful or alienated humanity. Representing the act of violence that is the crucifixion as the necessary means to the ultimate good, and therefore as an expression of divine love, serves to mystify violence. The subtext of such interpretations of the cross is that the 'price' of reconciliation, of attaining God's forgiveness, is the torture or self-sacrifice of the innocent. Traditional interpretations of the cross thus serve, intentionally or otherwise, to reinforce patriarchal understandings of power and authority: the 'Father' makes salvation conditional upon the death of the innocent 'Son', who takes the place of an unworthy humanity. The 'cost' of our salvation is such that it demands unconditional obedience, with humanity locked into a state of childlike dependency. In such a scenario, 'sin' comes to be identified with the assertion of self, with attaining adulthood and independence.

Thus, while positive interpretations of the cross emphasize God's unconditional love for humanity, more critical, negative readings question the nature of the values and lessons embodied in such a story, particularly in terms of the 'conditions' that are attached. We are then faced with the question of how we differentiate between the two approaches. Which particular interpretations of the cross merit Schüssler Fiorenza's health warning, and which do not? One way of answering such a question is to consider the specific context in which such interpretations are being offered and applied, and the practical consequences of any particular 'version' of the cross. Simon Maimela adopts precisely this approach when he suggests that we should address three questions to any particular theology of the cross. First, who is speaking about the cross in any given instance? Second, to whom is such talk addressed? Third, whose interests is it serving?[37] The diverse, conflicting interpretations of the cross clearly indicate that it functions in different ways, depending in part upon how powerful or powerless those speaking and listening are, particularly in relation to each other. For example, presenting Jesus' death on the cross in terms of humility and self-sacrifice, in the language of Isaiah 53 and 1 Peter, can mean very different things and pose very different challenges to an audience that is empowered and one that is disempowered or the victim of oppression.[38]

The range of responses generated by the Children's Cross thus serves as a salutary reminder of the multiple, conflicting meanings inherent in the symbolism of the cross. It reminds us of the need to be self-conscious and self-critical of the way we deploy such symbolism, particularly in public contexts. Given that there is no consensus as to what this symbol and this narrative mean within a Christian framework, it is hardly surprising that the Children's Cross proved to be a highly provocative act to some, whilst being completely irrelevant to others. In many ways, it would have been much more straightforward for the Cathedral to have gone about the business of memorializing the death of the sixty-three children killed in Chicago in 1993 in private, within its own walls so to speak. By choosing to memorialize these deaths in a public space, the Cathedral invited specific responses of the kind recounted in the essays in Part I of this book, and more general reflection such as that found in Parts II and III. In doing so, particularly in such a multicultural context, it prompted debate concerning the relevance of both Christianity and Christian symbolism when it comes to memorializing this kind of urban violence. While we may agree or disagree with the strategies members of the Cathedral chose to adopt in responding to the realities of the city in which they lived, it is surely still possible to admire their courage in laying themselves open to this kind of critique.

Notes

1 For further discussion of the possible meanings of the cross, the Massacre of the Innocents and the relationship between this and the Children's Cross, see, in particular, the essays by Gareth Jones, Dennis McCann and Martin Stringer in this volume.
2 Albert Camus, *The Plague* (Harmondsworth: Penguin, 1960), p. 183.
3 Jill Nelmes, *Introduction to Film Studies* (London: Routledge, 1996), p. 437. For a more detailed discussion of issues relating to representation, see Stuart Hall (ed.), *Representation* (Open University, 1997), pp. 1–63; Umberto Eco, *Interpretation and Reinterpretation* (Cambridge: Cambridge University Press, 1992), and Paul Ricoeur, *The Symbolism of Evil* (Boston: Beacon Press, 1969), pp. 347–57.
4 To represent can be to render visible even when that which we are representing is the unspeakable, i.e. that which is beyond words. As Strain points out in his essay later in this volume, the experience of 'blinding pain' can mean that 'we literally lose the ability to perceive let alone remember.' (p. 85). Thus, the remembrance or memorialization of extreme suffering struggles to represent or give voice to experiences that claim to be, by definition, characterized by the loss of voice. The struggle to give voice to this loss of voice is a recurrent theme in many testimonies of atrocity. For more detail on the role of voicelessness as an essential part of the experience of extreme suffering, see Lawrence Langer's analysis of the video testimony of Holocaust survivors in *Holocaust Testimonies: The Ruins of Memory* (New Haven: Yale University Press, 1991), and David B. Morris, 'About Suffering: Voice, Genre, and Moral Community' in Arthur Kleinman, Veena Das and Margaret Lock (eds), *Social Suffering* (Berkeley: University of California Press, 1997), pp. 25–45. 5

It is therefore unsurprising that an ideological critique of 'mainstream' history and the recovery of alternative texts and traditions plays a central role in many feminist, Black and gay theologies. For examples of this process in practice, witness the creation of 'Black History Month' (October in the UK, February in the USA), the publications of Virago and The Women's Press, and the examples cited in the essays by Emmanuel Lartey and Frida and Roy Furman later in this volume. For a more general discussion of memory, see the essays by Charles Strain and Denys Turner.

6 The key role played by the *Chicago Tribune* in generating the response that ultimately resulted in the creation of the Children's Cross raises a number of pertinent questions. For example, did the deaths of children only have such an impact because the *Chicago Tribune* chose to report them in this way, i.e. did these deaths only become worthy of memorialization because they were deemed to be newsworthy? Were these deaths only considered newsworthy because the victims were children? The clear implication of this focus on children is that the death of sixty-three adults in Chicago over the course of a year would neither be newsworthy nor merit memorialization.

7 Nel Noddings, *Women and Evil* (Berkeley: University of California Press, 1989), p. 161.

8 For further elaboration of the motivations behind the Children's Cross, see the interviews conducted by Jule Ward and Jim Halstead.

9 For a more detailed discussion of this point, see the essays by Dennis McCann and Gareth Jones later in this volume.

10 The crucifixion can be understood as the death or sacrifice of the one perfect Child. A trinitarian interpretation of the cross, such as that of Jürgen Moltmann, inevitably emphasizes the role of the Son in relation to the Father, and hence draws heavily upon this familial imagery. In one sense, this image of the nuclear family is completed by the presence of the spirit and of the human Mary at the foot of the cross.

11 One need only think of the way children frequently figure in literature as the embodiment of innocent suffering. For some of the more frequently cited examples, see the child hanging scene in Elie Wiesel's *Night* (Harmondswoth: Penguin, 1981), pp. 75–7; the description of the death agony of a child in Albert Camus' *The Plague*, pp. 201–9; and Ivan's litany of abuses against children in Fydor Dostoevsky's *The Brothers Karamazov* (Harmondsworth: Penguin, 1982), pp. 276–88. In the context of the current argument, it is significant that Wiesel and Camus are deliberately parodying the crucifixion in their accounts. All Ivan's examples concern the suffering of young children drawn from the newspapers of his time (his *motivation* is therefore analogous to that of the members of the St James Cathedral who were responding to reports in the *Chicago Tribune,* even if his *response* is very different). For Ivan, the arguments of theodicists may be convincing in the case of adults but they are, at best, irrelevant where children are concerned: 'What have the children to do with it – tell me, please? ... I understand solidarity in sin among men, I understand solidarity in retribution, too, but, surely, there can be no solidarity in sin with children, and if it is really true that they share their fathers' responsibility for all their fathers' crimes, then the truth is not, of course, of this world and it is incomprehensible to me.' (p. 286).

12 It is significant that the most frequent media image of the victims of Dunblane was a school class photograph; and the two most frequent images of James Bulger

were a family photograph, and the still from the security cameras of him walking off with the two older boys who turned out to be his killers.

13 Stewart Sutherland, *God, Jesus and Belief* (Oxford: Blackwell, 1984), pp. 21–2.

14 See, for example, Noddings, *Women and Evil*, pp. 5–34; Terrence Tilley, *The Evils of Theodicy* (Washington, DC: Georgetown University Press, 1991), and Kenneth Surin, *Theology and the Problem of Evil* (Oxford: Blackwell, 1986), pp. 38–111. For a defence of theism against such criticisms, see David O'Connor, 'In Defence of Theoretical Theodicy', *Modern Theology* 5 (1988), pp. 61–74, and Michael Peterson, *God and Evil* (Boulder, CO: Westview, 1998), pp. 67–83, 111–30.

15 See, for example, Susan Shapiro, 'Hearing the Testimony of Radical Negation' in Elisabeth Schüssler Fiorenza and David Tracy (eds), *The Holocaust as Interruption, Concilium* 175 (Edinburgh: T & T Clark, 1984), pp. 3–10. Kenneth Surin consciously employs an interruptive strategy throughout his book *Theology and the Problem of Evil*.

16 Simon Schama, *Dead Certainties* (London: Granta, 1991), pp. 320, 323.

17 David Tracy, *Plurality and Ambiguity* (London: SCM, 1987), p. 79.

18 Typical examples of theologians arguing that the appeal to the cross serves as a practical theodicy include Paul Fiddes, Dorothee Soelle, Kenneth Surin and Frances Young. Surin asserts that 'the Christian who takes the atonement seriously has no real need for theodicy' (*Theology and the Problem of Evil*, p. 142).

19 This is very much the argument developed by Jürgen Moltmann in *The Crucified God* (London: SCM, 1974). He describes the cross as 'the very torment of hell' (p. 148), as a consequence of which 'all the depths and abysses of human history are taken up into the history of God' (p. 246).

20 For surveys of classical and contemporary interpretations of the cross, see F.W. Dillistone, *The Christian Understanding of the Atonement* (London: SCM, 1984) and Colin Gunton, *The Actuality of Atonement* (Edinburgh: T & T Clark, 1988).

21 Timothy Gorringe, *God's Just Vengeance: Crime, Violence and the Rhetoric of Salvation* (Cambridge: Cambridge University Press, 1996), p. 11. Gareth Jones makes a similar claim in his essay, 'Space to Pass By' when he asserts that 'in redeeming conflict, therefore, the cross redeems violence; through specific violence – to Jesus – the crucified God redeems *all* violence.' (p.80)

22 Moltmann, *The Crucified God*, p. 335.

23 Ian Bradley, *The Power of Sacrifice* (London: Darton, Longman and Todd, 1995), p. 256.

24 See, for example, C. den Heyer, *Jesus and the Doctrine of the Atonement* (London: SCM, 1998), Martin Hengel, *The Atonement* (London: SCM, 1981), Gerard Rosse, *The Cry of Jesus on the Cross* (Mahwah, NJ: Paulist Press, 1987), and Frances Young, *Sacrifice and the Death of Christ* (London: SCM, 1975).

25 The possible ramifications of understanding the Children's Cross in terms of sacrifice are explored in more detail in Kay Read's essay 'To Sacrifice Children'.

26 For a discussion of the close association of the cross and the sword in the context of mission and colonization, see the essays in Yacob Tesfai (ed.), *The Scandal of a Crucified World* (Maryknoll, NY: Orbis, 1994), and *Santo Domingo and After* (London, Catholic Institute of International Relations, 1993).

27 As a result of protests by various Jewish organizations, crosses were removed from the Field of Ashes at Auschwitz-Birkenau in 1997. In May 1999, the Polish government intervened to ensure the removal of a 'forest' of over a hundred crosses outside the Old Theatre Building at Auschwitz-I, formerly the location of

a Carmel which formerly housed Carmelite nuns, and as such, was the focus of much controversy from 1985 to 1993. Discussions continue concerning the future of a twenty-three-foot cross (used by John Paul II during a mass at Birkenau) which has been standing outside the Old Theatre Building since 1989.

28 Elie Wiesel in Ekkehard Schuster and Reinhold Boschert-Kimmig, *Hope Against Hope: Johann Baptist Metz and Elie Wiesel Speak Out on the Holocaust* (Mahwah, NJ: Paulist Press, 1999), p. 66. It is, of course, for precisely this reason that Denys Turner refers, in his essay, to the 'galling naïve and insensitive association of child murder and the cross of Christ.' (p.110) This association is one of the reasons why he concludes that the Children's Cross is 'a deeply problematic memorial'.

29 Dennis McCann's essay, 'Waylaying the Way of the Cross', offers a more detailed exploration of the problems generated by the erection of specifically Christian memorials such as the Children's Cross and the associated Stations of the Cross in public space, particularly in relation to the 'Wall of Separation' between Church and State. (p.103)

30 See, for example, Mary Daly's analysis of 'the scapegoat syndrome' in Christianity in *Beyond God the Father* (London: Women's Press, 1973), pp. 75–7; Ann Loades' analysis of the masochism that can arise from (over)identification with the crucified Christ in *Searching for Lost Coins* (London: SPCK 1987), pp. 39–60; and Joanne Carlson Brown and Carole Bohn (eds), *Christianity, Patriarchy, and Abuse* (Cleveland, Ohio: Pilgrim Press, 1989), pp. 1–30, 42–61, 139–47, 148–73.

31 Elisabeth Schüssler Fiorenza, 'The Will to Choose or to Reject: Continuing Our Critical Work' in Letty Russell (ed.), *Feminist Interpretation of the Bible* (Oxford: Blackwell, 1985), pp. 125–36, p. 130.

32 For examples of such a theodicy, see John Hick, *Evil and the God of Love* (New York: Macmillan, 1966, 1985) and Richard Swinburne, *Providence and the Problem of Evil* (Oxford: Oxford University Press, 1998).

33 For examples of such a critique, see Kenneth Surin, *The Turnings of Darkness into Light: Essays in Philosophical and Systematic Theology* (Cambridge: Cambridge University Press, 1989), particularly pp. 57–72; Surin, *Theology and the Problem of Evil*, pp. 142–64; and Soelle, *Suffering* (Minneapolis: Fortress Press, 1975). Soelle, in particular, suggests that we are confronted with a choice: we can either believe in an omnipotent God who is an 'executioner' (as, for example, in Genesis 22 or the Book of Job) or in a suffering God who is a victim (as, for example, in the crucifixion narrative). For a critical response to such claims concerning practical theodicy, see Marcel Sarot, 'Divine Compassion and the Meaning of Life', *Scottish Journal of Theology* 48:2 (1995), pp. 155–86, and James Wetzel, 'Can Theodicy Be Avoided?', *Religious Studies* 25 (1989), pp. 1–14.

34 Soelle, *Suffering*, pp. 26–8.

35 See, for example, David Blumenthal, 'Theodicy: Dissonance and Praxis' in David Tracy and Hermann Häring (eds), 'The Fascination of Evil', *Concilium* (1998/1), pp. 95–106, pp. 102–3; Rita Nakashima Brock, 'Losing Your Innocence but Not Your Hope' in Maryanne Stevens (ed.), *Reconstructing the Christ Symbol* (Mahwah, NJ: Paulist Press, 1993), pp. 30–53; Bjorn Krondorfer, 'Play Theology as a Discourse of Disguise', *Journal of Literature and Theology* 7:4 (1993), pp. 365–80, pp. 373–6.

36 Krondorfer, 'Play Theology as a Discourse of Disguise', pp. 375–6.

37 Simon Maimela 'The Suffering of Human Dimensions and the Cross', in Tesfai (ed.), *Scandal of a Crucified World*, pp. 36–47, p. 37.

38 See, for example, Jacquelyn Grant's analysis of the way in which servant language has been employed to reinforce oppression, particularly that of Black women, 'The Sin of Servanthood' in Emilie Townes (ed.), *A Troubling in My Soul* (Maryknoll, NY: Orbis, 1993), pp. 199–218.

Part I
The Children's Cross:
Origins, Reactions and Reflections

Figure 1: The Children's Cross painted with the names of the 63 children who died violently in Chicago in 1993. The names of some of the children who died after 1993 are painted around the edge of the planter (photograph, Dennis McCann).

Reflections on the Children's Cross at St James Cathedral

Rev. Canon Janet Campbell

This story of the Children's Project and the Children's Cross at St. James Cathedral is told from my own experience of it. Other members of our group would probably find other ways to tell it and to frame the difficult, often painful questions with which we struggled as we sought to make a faithful response to a local tragedy. I offer my own reflections grateful for having been part of the conversation, challenged by the prayer and informed by the questions, most of all by those questions for which we did not find any answers.

In the Beginning

In 1993, the *Chicago Tribune* ran a front-page series on violence against children in Chicago. 'Killing our Children,' an attempt to raise public awareness and concern, kept a running count of children killed in 1993, reported on the life and death of each child, and explored underlying causes. Some of the murdered children were killed by a parent or other family member, some by another child, some were caught in the crossfire of gang shootouts. Many were children of poverty living in Chicago's deteriorating and gang-ridden public housing projects. The killings happened at home, on the way to school, on playgrounds and in the streets.

In the spring of that year, Phoebe Griswold, wife of the Bishop of Chicago and a member of St. James Cathedral, shocked by the articles, wrote to Cathedral leaders expressing her concern and need to 'recognize what is happening in the context of Cathedral and prayer ... I need to stop and honour these children. I need to see this as a whole picture. I need to pray about this. I need a place and the support of others in this great sad mystery.'[1]

'A place and the support of others.' A small group of Cathedral members responded to Phoebe's invitation to prayer and reflection, meeting in the chapel one evening. We prayed for the children and their families. We prayed about our dismay and sense of helplessness. We wondered what, if anything, we might do, this small group; about what, if anything, our faith community might do. Prayer and action. These two responses, not necessarily mutually exclusive, became for us two poles around which our conversations revolved. What was God saying to us, asking of us?

St. James, located in Chicago's prosperous 'Magnificent Mile' shopping and entertainment district, is the Cathedral Church of the Episcopal Diocese of Chicago. 'Cathedral' suggests size, prosperity and a certain presence in civic life. The Cathedral building itself is large and richly appointed. But the community of faith, the 'church' which makes St. James its home, is not large (about three-hundred people scattered across three Sunday services) nor particularly wealthy or influential. A constant turnover in membership reflects the mobility of urban and American society and affects the congregation's ability to develop lay leadership, ministry, a sense of community. The Cathedral as institution had recently gone through several changes in clergy leadership and was still seeking its identity as 'cathedral' and its voice in the affairs of the city.

An awareness of these limitations shaped our conversation, although we continually urged one another to hope and pray outside them. We recognized other limitations, including our own privileged and secure lives. How could we even begin to imagine the circumstances and experiences of Chicago's least-advantaged parents and children? We realized we did not know what kind of help or witness was most needed or what might be welcomed as a form of outreach. We became wary of acting impulsively out of an uneducated impulse to 'do good'.

Our meetings became times of prayer and discernment, listening for God's direction in silence and in conversation. The process which would guide us in the days ahead was shaped early in our time together: pray, wait, discern, follow.

The Children's Project

Perhaps God's first challenge to us was to enter into the experience of these others we wished to help, to move from uninformed sympathy to understanding. A member contacted grassroots groups already at work in neighbourhoods most afflicted by violence:

- The Green Ribbon Program, a campaign against 'gangbanging' started by the mother of a teenager killed in a gang-style shooting.
- The Ark, a youth outreach program housed at St. Sabina's Roman Catholic Church on Chicago's South Side.

- The Rise High Project, a poster campaign against gun violence directed toward youth most likely to use and fall victim to guns, begun by an emergency room doctor concerned by the number of young gunshot victims he was treating.

We spent several Saturday mornings meeting with these groups at St. Sabina's. We became painfully aware of the gulf between their lives and ours. We lived just a few miles apart and yet our daily experiences and concerns were vastly different. For them, violent death was a common, everyday occurrence. Living with courage and hope in the face of fear and grief, they were already 'doing something'. Our meetings with them were humbling and inspiring. How could we help?

The Children's Project continued our ministry of prayer. We sought to involve other Cathedral members through invitation to our meetings, articles in the Cathedral newsletter, sermons and intercessions about violence and children in the community's Sunday prayers. By summer's end, we had come to believe that part of God's invitation to us was to create a place of prayer for the city, a sacred space dedicated to the children killed.

The Children's Altar

At the entrance to the Cathedral, set into the wall of the narthex (the foyer or lobby), there was an altar dedicated to members killed in the Civil War. It already had the set-apartness and character of sacred space. It would be more accessible to the congregation and the public than any other discrete space in our building.

To use it, we needed the permission of the Chapter, the governing body of the Cathedral. As stewards of the Cathedral (its past as well as its present and future) they asked an important question. Would this rededication of the Civil War altar somehow 'eclipse' its original dedication to the soldiers killed or be unfaithful to the intentions of its donors? Through our exploration with the Chapter of this concern, we were able to agree that additional meaning could responsibly be given to the Civil War Altar if consonant with its original purpose of memorializing young lives cut short by violence. The Altar would give new life to the donors' intentions by being a witness to this contemporary tragedy, a new 'civil war'.

We considered several concepts for the altar, including incorporating objects owned by the children. Family members might be invited to participate in the planning. This was unknown and difficult territory. Would it be insensitive, even exploitative, to inject ourselves into the lives of these grieving and often troubled families? What did our once-removed grief have to do with their suffering? For whom were we creating the altar? The dead children? Their families? The city? Our faith community? Ourselves? What was its purpose?

Figure 2: Erecting the Children's Cross in 1993. The mirror side is showing (photograph, unidentified church member)

Exploring these questions brought focus: the altar should witness to the tragedy of young lives lost by reflecting who the children were and should offer an opportunity to grieve and pray for the children. These functions seemed addressed to Cathedral members, to challenge the Cathedral community and through them our city to be a force for life for Chicago's children. We decided not to involve the families but to ask Green Ribbon, The Ark and Rise High to help us plan the altar and to share in a service of dedication.

One member of the Children's Project drew an icon of 'Our Lady of Chicago' as a focal point for prayer. Against a background of newspaper pages with headlines about violence against children, Mary holds her own child Jesus. Around them, Chicago's children, 'our' children, are gathered; wrapped in bandages or bearing gunshot wounds, they gaze solemnly out at the viewer.

Another member built a wooden 'sand box' to hold devotional candles which could be lit by visitors. Another created a large album of the *Tribune* articles and the minutes and reflections of the Children's Project, with blank pages for visitors to write prayers and responses.

During Advent, a Cathedral member dropped and broke the infant Christ from his family's old and cherished nativity set. He brought the shattered doll in its manger to the altar as a symbol of the suffering of Christ in the shattered lives of Chicago's suffering children.

Dedication of the Children's Altar

We chose the Feast of the Holy Innocents, commemorating the infants slaughtered by Herod after the birth of Jesus, as the occasion to dedicate our memorial to innocents slain in present day Chicago. Rise High contributed anti-gun posters to hang by the altar. The Ark brought a quilt made by children to commemorate their own friends who had died violent deaths. The Green Ribbon Project brought its 'Think Life – Stop Gangbanging' green ribbons to be pinned to the service leaflets.

Together we planned the liturgy and wrote the prayers. We invited neighbouring churches to participate. We envisioned the Cathedral filled with people from across the city, praying for the children and their families, dedicating themselves to finding ways to help children at risk. Information about Green Ribbon, Rise High, The Ark and the Children's Project was printed in the service leaflet. Green Ribbon, Rise High and The Ark would share the collection.

The Feast of the Holy Innocents falls between Christmas and New Year's Day. Our choice was appropriate in terms of our liturgical year and the content of the feast but, in hindsight, unrealistic in terms of the secular calendar. Only about seventy people attended. How many who might have come were out of town for the holidays? How many who might have come did not want to confront the murder of children in the midst of the season of 'comfort and joy' (which is what the Church's placement of this feast within the twelve days of Christmas invites us to do). How many who might have come did not want to make the connection between those innocents in a faraway long-ago place and those in the homes and streets of our own city, for whose lives and deaths we must take our share of responsibility?

Liturgy does not find its ultimate meaning or effect in numbers, although its planners often make the mistake of looking for it there. In the nearly empty Cathedral, scripture was proclaimed, a sermon was preached, prayers were prayed, hymns were sung, the names of the sixty-three murdered children were solemnly read, candles were lit as a sign of hope, and the Children's Memorial Altar was dedicated and established as a place of prayer.

Prayer is answered in unexpected ways and so it seemed to us when our sparsely attended liturgy received extensive media coverage. There were spots on television news programs and articles and photographs in the *Tribune* and *Sun-Times*. The concerns of the Children's Project, the Green Ribbon Program, The Ark and Rise High entered, at least momentarily, into the lives of more Chicagoans than we had ever imagined reaching. Bishop Griswold's challenging sermon was quoted: 'The blood of our children, our own holy innocents … can become the seed giving birth to something new. May the grief … spur us on together to make our city a place where children are able to live out their days in safety and peace'.[3]

As a result of the publicity, telephone calls came from three mothers of the children thanking us for what we had done, voice-mail messages left while our offices were closed over the New Year holiday. The telephone number left by one had been, by the time we called back, 'temporarily disconnected'. We were never able to contact her. One mother wanted to thank us but did not want to see the Altar. The third visited the Altar, glad to see her child remembered, glad to have her grief honoured.

Our contact with these women was fleeting. Our Altar had offered something small, but perhaps something needed. Their child had been deemed important enough to be remembered by others. Their own grief had been noticed, acknowledged. Nothing had been changed, but something had been done. They returned to the realities and struggles of their lives.

The story of our liturgy was quickly replaced in the media by newer stories in our city's life. We don't know who might have been moved by our work to take action of their own toward making 'our city a place where children are able to live out their days in safety and peace'. What effect, if any, did our ministry have? What is the definition, the measure of 'success' and 'failure?' These would be our continuing questions.

The Children's Altar, encountered by everyone entering and leaving the Cathedral, became a constant presence in our life. Candles were lit. Messages and prayers were written in its book. Little offerings, flowers or an occasional toy, were left there. The Children's Project continued to meet at the Altar to pray.

A tension between prayer and moving into programmatic action on behalf of children surfaced and gave rise to struggle and disagreement. Minutes of our first meeting after the dedication express a 'desire to stop mourning, to do something'. 'Is our call to continue to stand with the mothers whose children have been killed, or with moms whose children continue to live?' If 1993 was the year of 'Killing our Children', could 1994 be the year of 'saving our children?' What was God saying to us, asking of us? Was there a way to make our witness more public?

The Children's Cross

We decided to involve our own children, their parents and Sunday school teachers in the conversation. As Lent 1994 drew near, the Sunday School staff and children planned their annual Lenten project of making a cross as a response to that conversation: 'How can we at St. James honour the memory of these children and at the same time reach out to the violent city surrounding us and give witness to the season and spirit of Lent that hopefully is reshaping our parish into a clearer identity as an Easter people?'[2]

The Sunday School decided to build a large memorial cross to be placed outdoors on the Cathedral plaza, at the intersection of busy Rush and Huron Streets. This would carry our concern out of the narthex and into the marketplace of the Magnificent Mile.

Lettered on one side of the twelve-foot cross were the names of the children killed in 1993 and those killed so far in 1994, for the *Chicago Tribune* continued to keep its painful count. Inlaid on the other side of the cross was a mosaic of broken mirrors. Looking into those mirrors, passers-by would see a broken reflection of themselves and of the city behind them, a reflection of fragmented lives and a flawed society which allows its weakest members to suffer.

On the Saturday before Palm Sunday, the Children's Memorial Cross was raised on the Cathedral plaza. On Palm Sunday, when Christians enter into Holy Week and the celebration of the Paschal Mystery of Christ's death and resurrection, the Cathedral community gathered at the foot of the Cross for the Liturgy of the Palms and the beginning of the palm procession.

> This cross now stands on our Plaza to remind us that it is our choice to change our city. This wondrous Cross reminds all who pass by that these children still live in the memory of our community here at St. James as they live in the Risen Christ. For in the end it is these children who compel us all to proclaim in word and deed – Alleluia! Christ is Risen![4]

The Children's Cross, placed in a public location to be a sign to the city, became paradoxically a sign for the Cathedral community itself. What was this Cross challenging *us* to do? On Sundays during the Fifty Days of Easter, the Sunday Adult Forum focused on children and violence. Opportunities for ministry were identified, from continued prayer to ensuring that our own

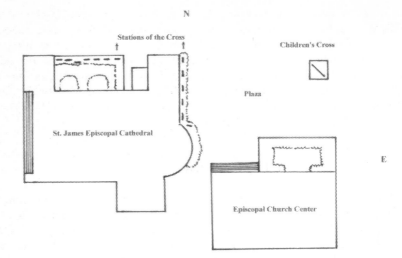

Figure 3: Map of the cathedral plaza in relationship to the Cathedral and administration buildings. The Children's Cross sat on the northeastern corner of the plaza, and the Stations of the Cross were lined up along the northern and eastern sides of the Cathedral (Drawing, Ceceley Fishman).

faith community was a welcoming place for children and parents; from sharing the ministry of the Children's Project with other parishes in our diocese to taking social and political action in some systematic way.

Through the ministry of our children and their Cross, the Cathedral was thrust into a ministry of public witness which seemed to grow organically from the presence of the Cross on the plaza. The Illinois Campaign to Ban Assault Weapons organized a news conference of Chicago clergy, held at the foot of the Children's Cross. On Pentecost, the day the Church celebrates the motive power of the Holy Spirit in its life, Cathedral members stood by the Cross gathering signatures of passers-by on petitions asking the Illinois General Assembly to enact legislation banning assault weapons. (This early attempt at a ban failed, but paved the way for later legislation.)

That fall, in conjunction with the Children's Defense Fund's National Children's Sabbath, a Children's Project member organized an art exhibition at the Cathedral. 'Good Works: Artworks, projects and proposals regarding Anti-Violence' gathered works of Chicago artists addressing violence in our city. Some projects were designed as intervention materials in neighbourhoods where violence is endemic (the Rise High Poster Project and a street sign project 'No Guns, Children Playing'). Others had as their stated objective changing patterns of thought and living as a way to end the cycle of destruction (a memorial garden for murdered children at the Cabrini Green public housing project and the Red Moon Puppet Theatre's pageants addressing the concerns of children in its West Side neighbourhood).

Response to these efforts was small. Very few clergy came to the news conference. Media coverage was minimal. Only a few people other than Cathedral members signed the assault weapons petition. The art exhibit was sparsely attended. Again the questions came. Does what we are doing matter? Is there any way to tell if this ministry makes any difference?

The Children's Project Struggles

The Children's Altar had continued to be a focal point for prayer. Five days after the erection of the Children's Cross, the Children's Altar served as the Maundy Thursday Altar of Repose. There the bread and wine consecrated at the Maundy Thursday Liturgy, the Body and Blood of Christ, are kept until the Good Friday Liturgy. It is a tradition in many places to watch in the presence of the Sacrament during that night, in response to Jesus' question to his disciples in the Garden of Gethsemane: 'Could you not watch with me one hour?'

For the small group gathered at the Children's Altar that Maundy Thursday, the sacramental presence of Christ on an altar dedicated to murdered children was a powerful image for contemplation and prayer. Christ offering himself, once on the cross, repeatedly in the bread and wine, for the life of the world, a world in which children, the world's new life, are abused and murdered.

The altar itself had been transformed by the Altar Guild. With a crisp white linen, crystal vases of springtime flowers, and the warm light of candles in brass candlesticks, they had created a lovely and peaceful 'garden-like' place. In a garden, most likely a grove of olive trees, outside Jerusalem on an early spring night nearly 2000 years before, Jesus had prayed in anguish that the suffering that awaited him might pass him by. Yet, he offered himself freely to whatever God's will for him was to be. Into the stillness of that garden, into the urgency of Jesus' prayer, burst an angry mob full of hatred, bent on murder. In yielding himself to them, Jesus chose to undergo suffering and death, a sacrificial act of solidarity with all those who have no choice. How are we called to do the same?

The Easter discussions of the Sunday Adult Forum had raised the hopes of Children's Project members that others would join our small group and assist in our ministry. But aside from the Pentecost Assault Weapon petitions, the only ministry which excited the Adult Forum as a whole was the desire to make the Cathedral a welcoming and safe place for children. In this, we had named a need of our own, to serve our children and to increase the number of families with children at the Cathedral. This was a laudable goal for growing the Cathedral as a community of all ages, but it had little to do with ministering to or on behalf of children trying to survive in the killing neighbourhoods of Chicago.

The Cathedral community did not seem able to respond prophetically to violence against children by taking a substantive leadership role within the religious or civic communities of Chicago. We did not seem to have the critical mass of people, time and energy to respond in a programmatic way to identified opportunities for ministry. We did not seem to have the visionary, passionate leadership that could move us beyond our sense of the possible into the realm of the holy impossible. Like many middle-class Americans, we were already stretched thin by the demands of busy, over-full lives. We had reached our limits.

The Children's Project was beginning to lose motivation and direction. Should we, could we take on the task of reaching out to the parishes of our diocese, carrying to them the witness of the Children's Altar and the Children's Cross? Our Easter faith proclaims that Christ has gathered all suffering, past, present and future, to himself on the cross, continually bringing forth from death new life. Pentecost, the celebration of the Holy Spirit's sending the disciples out from prayer to share the news of resurrection, would be a fit beginning for a new phase of our ministry, moving us from prayer to proclamation. We could share the spirit of the Children's Project with others, raise awareness and combine resources with parishes across the diocese. Perhaps from this effort some effective action would come.

Two members took the icon and book from the Children's Altar to one parish and shared with its Sunday Adult Forum the work we were doing. But our group was dwindling. No one had the time or energy to make more parish visits. Even these small actions now seemed beyond us. In frustration and with regret, one of the co-chairs left the group to volunteer with agencies working directly with children. For her, prayer without action was not enough.

As Christmas of 1994 approached, we decided to arrange the Cathedral's nativity set at the Altar. As they visited the crèche, perhaps Cathedral members would see God-with-us not only in the child born in Bethlehem, but in children at risk in Chicago. Perhaps they would be moved to join us in finding some way to serve them. We needed new hearts and minds and hands, new passion, new ideas, new energy.

After Christmas, we had to face the reality that our community had moved on. We could no longer sustain our own commitment even to care for the Altar. We tried taking monthly turns, but more often than not, the Altar was untended and, increasingly, began to look neglected. People seldom stopped there to pray or to write in the book. Eventually, because of increased attention from passers-by to the Children's Cross on the plaza, we realized that the ministry of witness begun by the Children's Altar had moved out onto the corner of Rush and Huron and was now centred in the Children's Cross. We put away the icon, the candle box and the book of articles and prayers.

A Businessman, a Nurse Practitioner, a Reporter

Since its installation, the 'home-made' Cross on the Cathedral Plaza had proved to be compelling. Shopper, tourist, skateboarder, school group, commuters hurrying to or from work, almost everyone who encountered it stopped to ponder its meaning and to read the signs around its base:

> The ultimate test of a civilization is not the power of its armies, not the size of its gross national product, but the condition of its children. If they flower a society deserves to be described as flowering.

> At the least children are owed food, clothing and shelter. If they are corrupted, if they suffer, if they die from abuse or neglect, an atrocity has been committed for which no other achievement can atone.

> All you who pass this way, look and see: Is there any sorrow like the sorrow inflicted on me? (Lamentations 1:12)

In the spring of 1995, one passing skater, a New Yorker on business in Chicago, found to his amazement his own last name lettered on the Cross – one of the children had the same family name. Shaken by this strange coincidence and moved by the message of the Cross, he met with the Children's Project, learned the story of our work, and wrote us a cheque for $10,000.

What were we to do with this windfall? How were we to use this money faithfully? Several in our group saw it as seed money. They wanted to start a foundation that would raise funds to support a grade school child at risk through private school and college. The idea was exciting. But others were wary about making such a long-term commitment, given our limited resources and the fluidity of Cathedral membership. Could we generate the additional funds and the sustained commitment to see it through? We had already had difficulty in sustaining our commitment to the Children's Project ministry. What would happen to a child taken out of poverty and introduced to a new life in private school if, after a year or two, we were unable to continue our support? When the more cautious among us prevailed, the more daring were disappointed. We were all left wondering if we had suffered a failure of nerve and faith or had made a wise and realistic assessment of our capacity.

Eventually we decided, with our donor's support, to give the money to St. Gregory's Episcopal School on Chicago's West Side, a small school that works with young boys from poor or troubled families. In response to our invitation, Cathedral members contributed another $5,000. St. Gregory's received a check for $15,000. For many of our members, money seemed a more possible response than a commitment of time.

That summer, another passer-by, a neonatal Nurse Practitioner from Florida, saw the Cross while attending a conference in Chicago. She works in paediatric intensive care and community health care and often treats children who live in violent environments. She is also a consultant and lecturer in children's health care and health care policy. She asked for slides of the Cross and the signs around it. The Cross and its challenge are now part of presentations she makes around the country.

In the spring of 1996, a reporter for *U-Direct Magazine*, a Chicago quarterly available free at drop sites around the city and also by subscription, was stopped in his tracks by the Cross on the way home from his teaching job:

> Only slowly, as you stand there in your trenchcoat, bundled against the weather, do you come to understand that this cross is the real thing, raw, stark, abrupt as a slap, posing a deeper question than anything or anyone else you will encounter that day will pose ... Why are children murdered? What kind of people do this? What kind of society allows this to happen? ... Are some children privileged and safe and others not? Is it enough to know that you and yours are on the safe side of this invisible line? ... What is my relationship and my responsibility to the children whose names are on that cross, and to other parents? What more is required of me?[5]

Looking at the Cross, thinking about the Cross, writing about the Cross, Bob Koehler found himself struggling with the questions besetting Children's Project members. What more is required of me? Bob did one thing he could do; he interviewed members of the Children's Project and wrote his compelling article. Thus our Cross began to ask its questions of his readers as well.

And so the Children's Cross, in its persistent witness in our bustling, upscale neighbourhood, found its voice, spoke to those who encountered it and through some of them, to others both near and far. It told of the tragedy of children being murdered; it questioned the values and priorities of a society which fails to protect the most vulnerable of its citizens. How many people were shaken, moved, discomforted, challenged, by the Children's Cross?

Of Time and the Cross

Originally intended to be taken down after the summer of 1994, the Cross claimed the corner of Rush and Huron Streets for its own. Persevering forlornly through the chilly, rainy days of Chicago's endlessly grey springtime; rising gaily out of the profusion of colourful summer flowers growing at its base; shaking, bending, groaning in late autumn's winds; glittering with ice and snow in stark silhouette against winter's steely sky, it steadfastly stood its ground.

Made to last only a season, the Cross began to deteriorate from the effects of wind and rain. It took on an alarming backward tilt. Its wooden base had begun to rot. One good windstorm might blow it down. In 1997, long after the Children's Project had ceased to meet, the precarious condition of the Cross brought us back together to consider what to do.

Had the Cross, like the Children's Altar, come to the end of its ministry? Should we take it down? If so, what would we do with it? Surely a memorial should not be, could not be, discarded? But where would we put it? Was there still important work for it to do on its corner? Some members of the group thought it was time to acknowledge that the Cross had never been intended to be a permanent fixture. Others felt it was still an important sign of the Cathedral's concern for the city's children.

We talked of the donation to St. Gregory's it had inspired; of the nurse who continued to use it in her lectures; of the *U-Direct* article; and of the inclusion of the Cross in the Birmingham Project symposium on religion in urban environments, a recent development. We talked of the countless people whom we did not know who might have been affected and influenced by the Cross, and others still to come who might be affected and influenced by it. Just when it seemed as if all interest had died down, the Cross would touch someone else and something new would develop. Surely, it should continue on its corner. One member donated the money for a carpenter to repair the base and brace the Cross with guy wires against further wind damage.

The repairs sustained the Cross through the winter, but the wind continued to rattle its joints and the rain and snow to rot its wood. We invited the parish council, a quarterly meeting of committee chairs and Chapter members, into the conversation. The Cross seemed to have worked its way into the heart and soul of the Cathedral community. What did the community want to do? Project members felt a responsibility toward the children it commemorated, toward the children who had made it, toward the Cross itself. And to the possibility that it might continue to move others. What did the larger community think we should do?

In the Council meeting, anger was expressed at what some saw as our own failure to heed the Cross's message. Violence against children continued unabated in our city, indeed around our country. Removing the Cross seemed a final, painful surrender of the Cathedral community to its inability or unwillingness to stretch itself on behalf of children at risk. The Parish Council found itself at an impasse. A small group was appointed to continue the discussion and report back.

The small group felt strongly that we should no longer put energy into maintaining the Cross unless we were also willing to reach out in some specific way to help children. There were ideas: participating in a tutoring programme at neighbouring Fourth Presbyterian Church or working with children's services in the juvenile justice system. But again, hope and motivation succumbed to busy schedules and over-full lives. We had little ability to follow through on our wonderful ideas. The Cross continued to stand stubbornly on its corner, perhaps in judgement not only of our city but of the community that had put it there.

Then, late in the summer of 1998, in a spectacular Chicago windstorm, the Cross was blown down and shattered to pieces. The matter had been taken out of our hands by the wind, and perhaps, in the wind, by the spirit of God. What was God saying? The small group now met to decide what to do with the pieces of the Cross. In one last effort to engage the Cathedral community, the pieces were put on a table in the Cathedral narthex along with a questionnaire. Should the Cross be preserved? Should we as a community be taking some action on behalf of children?

The broken Cross was a dramatic and sad presence in the narthex. People noticed it, talked about it; a few filled out the questionnaire. There was agreement among them that the Cross should be saved, although obviously it could not be returned to its corner. There was also agreement that the Cathedral should focus on ministry with and to children rather than on the Children's Cross alone.

A member of the Children's Project put the larger pieces of the Cross back together. He mounted it, along with its signs, on a large wall over the stairs that lead from the Cathedral to our lower level meeting hall. It was an enormous presence in this indoor space. It could also be seen, though not from any distance, through double glass doors that lead to the Plaza.

What was this Cross saying to the Cathedral community from its place of retirement? It hung by the sacristies, watching over our preparations for worship, commanding, overwhelming in that small indoor space. Yet, in the busyness of preparations and in our bustling from Cathedral to downstairs and back again, how many really noticed it, how many stopped to look, to listen, to wonder if there was still a call, an unheeded invitation?

The Cathedral leadership continued to emphasize and develop ministry with the children of the Cathedral community. No compelling vision emerged to urge the community beyond the boundaries of these concerns out into the city to minister with and to the rest of 'our' children, the children who are ours not because they are members of our family or of our faith community but because they are God's children as we are. Perhaps the Cross is biding its secret time, perhaps seeds planted by the Children's Project and this Cross have yet to germinate.

The Cathedral Continues to Go Public

The Children's Cross taught us that the Cathedral Plaza is an important place for public witness. Shortly after the Cross was blown down, the Cathedral was invited by the Canadian Embassy to host a photographic exhibition of the suffering caused by land mines. The opening reception, with speeches against land mine use and considerable media coverage, took place on the Cathedral Plaza.

In the summer of 1999, the Episcopal Peace Fellowship, a national organization working for peace and justice, chose the Cathedral Plaza as the site for the 'Angel of Peace' statue by sculptor Will Kieffer. The work was inspired by Psalm 46:10: 'It is [God] who makes war to cease in all the world; [God] breaks the bow, and shatters the spear, and burns the shields with fire'. Dedicated at a liturgy on Armistice/Veterans' Day, the statue is an urgent reminder of God's call for peace among nations and in societies.

In the years since the Children's Project began, the problem of violence against children, and particularly gun violence, has become a concern not just of big cities but of every community in our country. At the annual convention of the Diocese of Chicago in November 1999, the Cathedral's Outreach Commission (many of whose members were active in the Children's Project) sponsored a resolution calling for all Episcopalians in the diocese to remove hand-guns from their homes and vehicles. Commission members conducted a wide-ranging information campaign in the weeks preceding the convention and generated interest from the Chicago media. The resolution was passed and stories about it appeared in newspapers and on the radio. The Cathedral had taken a prophetic stance and led our diocese in making a public witness against the role of guns in violence, intentional and accidental, against children.

This growing understanding of the Cathedral's call to be a place where image and symbol might draw people first into contemplation and prayer, and then into witness and action, is a legacy of the Children's Cross.

Reflection

[Jesus] told them many things in parables, saying: 'Listen! A sower went out to sow. And as he sowed, some seeds fell on the path, and the birds came and ate them up. Other seeds fell on rocky ground, where they did not have much soil, and they sprang up quickly, since they had no depth of soil. But when the sun rose, they were scorched; and since they had no root, they withered away. Other seeds fell among thorns, and the thorns grew up and choked them. Other seeds fell on good soil and brought forth grain, some a hundredfold, some sixty, some thirty. Let anyone with ears listen!' (Matthew 13:3-9, NRSV)

The problem of violence against children was not new in 1993, nor was it something peculiar to Chicago, although Chicago had the terrible distinction of being the leader in violence against children. The articles in the *Chicago Tribune* brought this hidden disease to public attention in a new way. Scattered like seeds upon the ground of the city's heart, upon the ground of the Cathedral's heart, the articles brought forth grain and are undoubtedly, though secretly, still bringing forth grain.

The discernible harvest of the Children's Project and the Children's Cross seemed a small crop: heartfelt prayer, the Holy Innocents' liturgy, some media attention here and there, a few donations, some tentative steps toward a role of public leadership. We kept thinking we should and could do more. But perhaps our own ministry was itself more one of seed sowing than grain harvesting. The seed of the grant to St. Gregory's School, touching who knows what child with help, healing, a new beginning. The seed of the Nurse Practitioner's public talks, moving who knows how many other community health workers to advocate for children at risk. The seed of the Cross itself, bringing new awareness to Chicagoans and tourists alike, some of whom, seeing the Cross, may have gone on newly determined to make a difference.

When the Children's Cross began to deteriorate, the intensity of our struggles with what to do with it, with what the Cross meant to us and to the city, revealed that the Cross had rooted itself deep in the heart of our community. It said something about us – that we cared about children. It also said to some of us that we had done something about violence against children; to others of us that we had not done nearly enough. The Cross became a symbol of both these realities, a symbol of our success and our failure.

As individuals and as a community, we had been rocky ground and we had been good soil. Seed had fallen all over the place; some of it was snatched away before it could sprout, some of it had sprouted but not been sustained in its growth, some of it had taken root and flourished and brought forth grain and then more seed. The process, our own small part in the continuing growth of God's kingdom, was mysterious and secret. It finally escaped all our efforts to quantify and understand and judge it (and ourselves). Who can ultimately say if what we did was worthwhile, successful, important? By what measuring stick would such an assessment be made? Did the Children's Project matter? God knows.

Our natural concern with whether we are good or rocky soil may keep us from seeing the most important aspect of the parable of the sower. For the parable reveals a God of unbounded hope and generosity, a God who casts the seed of the kingdom with reckless abandon far and wide over all the world's ground, knowing that only some of it will take root and grow. This is a God whose ideas about waste and worthwhileness, success and failure are not our own. A God who dares to place God's hope of the kingdom in the hands of the tentative, the reluctant, the timid, the puzzled, as well as the confident, the enthusiastic, the courageous, the determined – in short, in our hands, trusting that in our struggle to be faithful we will mature as kingdom people and continue to bring the kingdom nearer. Small seeds planted in the expectation of the final, great harvest.

There was pride in the Children's Project, yes, and a sense of accomplishment. But many of us were left with a sense of inconclusion, dissatisfaction, frustration. Perhaps these are the fruit of facing into the impossible, of standing up against enormous injustice and violence in the small frailty of who we are. We had done only what we could do. Was it enough? No, it was not enough. It is never enough. But perhaps it was sufficient.

In Lent of 1994, a statue of Christ praying in agony in the Garden of Gethsemane appeared one day on the Children's Altar. I discovered it while on some errand to the narthex and was moved to write the following in the book at the Altar:

> Christ in Gethsemane has suddenly
> appeared at this altar.
> Yes, Father, let this cup
> pass from us
> if it be your will.
> Which cup is that?
> The cup of the suffering of children
> or
> the cup of
>   our responsibility?
> This is a cup
> that is difficult
> to drink.
> Can we drink from the
> cup of Christ?
> Can we share the
> cup of Christ?
> Are we willing to be baptized
> into the baptism
> with which
> he was baptized?
> Am *I* willing?
> O God – let this cup pass ...
> Christ in Gethsemane
> has suddenly
> appeared
> at this altar ...
> of course ...
>   of course ...
>   of course ...

Perhaps you are not reaching far enough unless you are continually worried about falling short.

Notes

1 Undated memo to 'the staff of St James Cathedral and relevant committees', (Spring 1993).
2 Homily, The Rt. Rev. Frank T. Griswold, Bishop of Chicago, as quoted in *The Chicago Sun-Times*, Thursday 30 December, 1993.
3 From a description of the 1994 Sunday School Lenten Cross project by Dean Niedenthal, Director of Children's Ministries.
4 Ibid.
5 Bob Koehler, *U-Direct Magazine*, Chicago, Illinois, (May–July) 1996, p. 8

When Children Are Killed, What Do We Do? One Community's Response

James Halstead and Jule D. Ward

In cities all over America, children go to bed frightened. Some kids are frightened because of the dark. Others are frightened because of a situation at school or within their own families. Still others are frightened because during the night, outside their bedroom windows, they hear the periodic burst of gunshots signalling death, perhaps the death of someone they know. In a letter to Marian Wright Edelman, president of the Children's Defense Fund, an eight-year-old girl wrote that one night she heard 'a lot of shooting'. On her way to school the next day, the little girl passed a blood-stain. That stain marked the spot where three people had been wounded the previous night. Earlier, the same girl had seen a young boy in her school killed by another student. As she and her mother took their weekly walk to church, they sometimes saw the gunfire of people shooting from neighbouring buildings. Yet, that little girl ends her letter on a note of hope, 'I believe in God, and I know one day we will be in a gooder place than we are now'.[1]

But where is that 'gooder place'? Until fairly recently parents believed that by moving away from the inner city and its problems of poverty, unemployment and overcrowding they could provide a 'safe' environment for their children. However, violence has spread to the suburbs and small towns. Children have been gunned down in suburban and rural high schools. Thus, children, even those growing up in 'safe' neighbourhoods become frightened when they become aware that other children have been murdered. They come to realize that these children were like themselves in many ways: they played with friends, went to school, and watched TV. Slain children had best friends and loved to play games. They had families. Children wonder if, like those other children, they might lose a friend to death or that they, too, might die violently.

Adults, especially parents, have different reactions to stories of childhood death. Fear, anger and a sense of powerlessness are primary reactions of those parents and adults who care deeply about children. They fear for the safety of their own children. They feel an undifferentiated anger toward killing, killers and toward those civic officials who are charged with maintaining the peace, and a sense of personal powerlessness and inadequacy. After all, a primary responsibility of adults is the protection and nurturing of children.

Reactions of the churches, mosques and synagogues to the stories of violence are complex. Religious communities have multiple tasks. In addition to the performance of religious rituals, churches, temples and mosques are to provide a safe home for their members. They are to educate their young members in a faith tradition and, for older members, interpret contemporary experience in light of their respective traditions. Many congregations see an engagement in various forms of social outreach and social transformation as part of their mission.

Some religious communities live their lives in the context of a ritual-liturgical cycle that raises specific themes for reflection at specific times of the year. The people of St James Episcopal Cathedral in Chicago are one such group; they pray, educate, and engage issues of concern in the city within the context of the Episcopal liturgical tradition.

Beginning on 3 January 1993, the *Chicago Tribune* published a front-page story about every child murdered in Chicago that year. As a result of this series, many children, adults and religious communities became painfully aware of the 'slaughter of the innocents' in their midst. As one would expect, reactions varied. The nine-year-old daughter of a St James Cathedral parishioner and Sunday school teacher, Bob Koehler, asked 'Do children like me ever get killed, Dad?' To protect his daughter and to quiet her nightmares (and 'my own'), Koehler quickly answered 'No, no, no. Not kids like you.'[2] The people of St James Cathedral, the cathedral parish of the Episcopal Diocese of Chicago, reacted in several different ways. Prayer, education, theological interpretation, social organization and outreach; and embarrassment and confusion were among the reactions of the members of the Cathedral parish. This chapter examines those reactions. It also asks what kind of ethic was at work here. Was there any moral value in the responses of the St James community?

The First Reaction

Throughout the summer of 1993, Phoebe Griswold, parishioner of St James Cathedral and wife of Bishop James Griswold, Episcopal bishop of Chicago, read stories of children killed in Chicago. After reading story after story of urban violence and death, Griswold's spirit resounded with an overwhelming 'NO.' She told herself, 'This has got to change. Or at least I must respond.'[3] Griswold publicly invited interested parishioners to gather in prayer. Those who responded to Griswold's invitation met for prayer at the cathedral's Civil War Altar. The Civil War Altar has a central significance in

St James' history. It stands in a tower that survived the cathedral's fire of 1972. Scorch marks of that fire can still be seen next to the altar. For Tom Patterson, father of two St James Sunday school children, these marks express his faith that the human struggle against the forces of devastation is ongoing.[4]

After gathering for several weeks the prayer group, with the Dean of the Cathedral's permission, transformed the altar into a memorial for the victims of urban violence.[5] The altar was embellished with an icon of the Madonna and Child, which included a newspaper front page behind the faces of Mary and Jesus with the headline, 'Mom Mourns.' Below was placed a child's drawing of a boy, a girl and a baby bearing the marks of violence – of beating, strangulation and gunshot. A baby doll was broken into pieces and placed nearby lying on swaddling clothes, lying in a manager. Near the icon lay a 'yearbook' enabling visitors to record their feelings or write their prayers.

Energized but still dissatisfied, Phoebe Griswold thought that the parishioners were beginning to feel the terrible tragedy of childhood violence. But they were not experiencing it deeply enough. She told *Tribune* reporter Michael Hirsley, 'When we feel this pain as a corporate grief, as a family tragedy, then maybe we'll know what to do.'[6]

By late summer 1993, members of St James parish began to meet regularly with mothers who had lost children to gang-related violence. They prayed and shared in the tragedy of urban violence. Not wishing to be perceived as merely voyeuristic, liberal do-gooders, they began wearing memorial ribbons for slain children. The ribbons were part of the Green Ribbon Program developed by Caroline Jimenez after her son was killed in a gang-related shooting. Jimenez told the St James parishioners, 'It is hard for parents like me to bring our grief out in public, but the interest of others confirms that we have to speak out, to do something, so our children's deaths might at least save the lives of others.'[7] Jimenez had quit her teaching job after her son was killed but she soon discovered that hiding at home only intensified her grief. She and several other mothers whose children had been murdered painted a mural in remembrance of their children. The mural covers the side of a currency exchange at Ashland Avenue and Forty-seventh Street. On the mural dozens of children's names are surrounded by a green ribbon. For the mothers green represents the lives they hope to save by bringing their stories to others. These mothers each had a strategy for keeping their children alive. Caroline was a protective mother until her son turned eighteen. She then relaxed because she felt he was an adult and able to care for himself. He died shortly after his nineteenth birthday. Another mother, Mary, thought that by giving her daughter a car she could keep her safe. Her daughter was killed by a man she knew from work who asked for a ride home. So now Caroline and the women of the Green Ribbon Project talk with everyone who will listen. They understand that we cannot save our children by ourselves. We must work as a community for the safety of all our children.

Griswold and her prayer group were deeply touched by Caroline and her friends. They felt that violence against children needed to receive broader attention in the parish. They planned a public memorial service on the Episcopal Feast of the Holy Innocents, 29 December 1993. The service began with a paraphrase of the prophet Jeremiah (Jer. 31:15), 'As Rachel wept uncontrollably for her children, so we weep for our children.' The prayers and symbols of the service entrusted the dead to God, and asked for the consolation of survivors, and safety for all children. The prayers also asked God's forgiveness for our tolerating the conditions that bred Chicago's urban violence. Those in attendance asked God for courage to speak and work for social change and to open their minds and hearts to the Holy Spirit. After the ceremony, one visitor wrote in the yearbook, 'King Herod is alive and well. We still murder the innocent.'

The Creation of the Children's Cross

The cross is an important element of the Christian (and Western) tradition – and an ambiguous one. What began as an instrument of Roman torture, terror and death has become, over the centuries, a reminder of the death of Jesus and a symbol of the Christian belief in the triumph of God over the powers of sin and death. The cross carries other, less theological meanings as well. Over twenty centuries, the cross has become a battle insignia for armies, a subject for the creativity of artists, and a signpost for rendezvousing tourists – 'I'll meet you over by the cross in the park.' The cross has a far different meaning for some non-Christians. For some the cross is a sign of religious intolerance, cultural imperialism and occasional genocide. Yet, for many ordinary Christians, the cross is a tool, a means for making personal meaning of the suffering, pain and death that haunts human life. The cross is a truly multivalent sign.

By 1994, the St James Sunday school, the parish's catechetical program for its children and youth, had a well-established tradition of creating a Lenten cross as part of its yearly educational program. Each year, for an unknown number of years before 1994, the dozen-or-so Sunday school students, along with their teachers and several parents, had hand-built a cross. Each time, students and faculty of the Sunday school had considered a different theology of the cross as they embellished its concrete representation in a different artistic mode. One year the cross was painted white, the colour of death in many cultures, and then throughout Lent, they continuously decorated it with colour using scraps of multicoloured cloth. Another year, clowns adorned the cross, leading students to consider the folly of the cross. The yearly, Lenten crosses usually were relatively small. About five feet tall, they easily fit within the Sunday school classroom. Up to 1994, the Lenten crosses were left standing in the classroom during the Easter season and then disassembled. The next year another cross was created.

Until 1994, everyone involved had been reasonably content with the educational and pastoral impact of the Lenten crosses. As is the Episcopalian theological and pastoral practice, the traditional Christian symbol had been creatively interpreted in new ways each year. The students who participated in the Sunday school program had been introduced to and deepened their relationship to the fundamental Christian symbol. But a chance conversation between Phoebe Griswold and a Sunday school teacher began a process that would transform the Sunday school project into an extraordinary experience for countless people. What began for Dean Niedenthal, Director of the Sunday school at St James Cathedral, as the continuation of the Sunday school Lenten cross project led him, his students, the parishioners of St James and countless unknown persons into varying degrees of solidarity with the murdered children and their families. It was a phenomenal journey, not a typical journey for north-side Chicago Episcopalians. As Bob Koehler later wrote, 'The Near North Side is not about sorrow. It's about having lots of money and buns of steel.'[8]

In January 1994, Phoebe Griswold met with Dean Niedenthal, to coordinate Lenten activities in the parish. Murdered children, the multiple causes of urban violence and ways to develop a community organization against violence were very much on her mind. But a uniquely spiritual concern also troubled Griswold. Especially disturbing to her was the fact that many of the slain children's families were so poor that they could not afford any kind of marker for their child's grave. It seemed to Griswold that these murdered children were doubly lost. Not only were they taken physically from the earthly community, but they were also in danger of being forgotten by that community. Griswold asked Niedenthal to consider dedicating the 1994 cross to the slain children of Chicago and making it large enough to be displayed on the plaza in front of the parish centre. In that way, Griswold reasoned, not only the people of St James, but all who passed the cathedral plaza would be called upon to remember the slain children.

In Lent 1994, Niedenthal and the children set to building the Lenten cross. Creating the cross was what Tom Patterson calls, 'a typical Dean project'. By that he meant it involved both the physical and the spiritual sides of the children. As they had before, the children sawed pieces of wood into the appropriate shapes and hammered them together. One student, Toby, remembers the cross building as requiring 'lots and lots of nails and lots and lots of holes'.[9] For Toby, the 1994 cross was both the same as and different from earlier crosses, 'it was a lot bigger'. After completing the basic carpentry, the children shellacked their cross. 'And boy was that a smelly job!' remembers Ian then five years old. When the shellac was dry, Niedenthal and the children took mirrors and smashed them. Becca, then three, recalls, 'It was really scary. There was broken glass everywhere. I was very little and I thought I might get hurt. Now I think Jesus must have been scared too.' The children then took the pieces of mirror and arranged them on the cross likes a jigsaw puzzle with missing pieces. Niedenthal explained, 'If you stand in front of the cross, you see a broken image of yourself. It is a remembrance that as Christ was broken on the cross, so we are broken. We are never our whole selves. Further, as you stand there, you see behind you images of the city – also broken, a place that murders its children.'[10]

The story of the construction of the Children's Cross contains an element of the mystical. An experience not uncommon in the religious traditions of the world is re-told in the context of Chicago's near-north side. Once the broken pieces of mirror were firmly in place, Niedenthal intended to paint the names of the children murdered in Chicago in 1993 on the opposite side of the Cross. He worked on this project late one night when no one else was in the Sunday school building. Niedenthal had seen photos of many of the murdered children in the newspaper. As he began to write their names, the children's faces appeared to him. Soon it seemed to him that the children themselves were running around the classroom in the same way his Sunday school students normally did. Slain children seemed to push forward and peer over his shoulders as he wrote their names on the Cross. To Niedenthal, it seemed that the children were making sure that their names were included, that they were clearly written, and that their names were spelled correctly. Niedenthal felt a spirit of joy infuse their faces because they had been included in the Cross project. They were remembered. Chicago's murdered children had not been forgotten.

By the end of Lent, the Cross was completed and ready for its public unveiling. On the Saturday before Palm Sunday, Niedenthal, the dozen children who had worked on the Cross, about a dozen parents, some other Sunday school teachers, Phoebe Griswold, and members of her prayer group processed with the Cross from their classroom to the cathedral plaza. The children carried the Cross from the Sunday school, into the cathedral, down the centre aisle of the cathedral, out the main door, onto Huron Street and into the northeast corner of the cathedral plaza. The twelve-foot Cross was heavy and awkward. Carrying it was no easy task for the children. Tom Patterson remembers how they struggled to carry the Cross, and that, even with adult help, it was difficult to raise the Cross and place it in the space prepared for it. The identification between Jesus carrying his cross and the people of St James carrying the Children's Cross was not lost on anyone.

Meanings of the Children's Project and Cross

Just as the cross is an ambiguous symbol, the placement of the Cross in the plaza of St James Cathedral – a large, public square, two blocks west of Michigan Avenue, Chicago downtown's most stylish street – also evoked mixed reaction. Not every parishioner was happy to see the Cross in the plaza. Some felt it was not sufficiently sophisticated. The Children's Cross was seen as rough, crude and aesthetically unrefined. Others were concerned about responsibility for maintenance of the Cross or its longevity in the plaza. Still others reasoned that, since the plaza was outdoor space and open to the public, the church might be legally liable if the Cross somehow injured someone. And some felt that religious beliefs and symbols are best kept private. The Children's Cross was seen as too public, too political. Cathedral parishioner Bob Koehler asked, 'Is the neighborhood even zoned for sentiment like this?'[11]

Throughout her work with the Children's Project and later with the Children's Cross, Phoebe Griswold felt called by God. She felt a new power as she spoke about violence in the city and as networks were formed by people, with little in common save religious faith and moral vision. As concerned Christians gathered to explore and develop a response to difficult issues such as gun control, sacred spaces, children's toys and the diocese's mission to children, Griswold felt herself an instrument of God's saving activity. She and the others with whom she worked identified with the cross. As the cross stood in public with its message of concern, so should and did they. They were prophets and the cross was their symbol and message. Griswold had been wounded by the knowledge of violence against children and by becoming involved in the world of violence. Through her work and through the cross, she had begun to heal. The wounds were not gone, but the pain of powerlessness was dulled as new life was experienced, new relationships were formed and new projects were initiated.

Four years later, Griswold worries about the lack of continuing support for the Cross and the projects it symbolizes. In retrospect, she especially hurts because she believes that the community missed an opportunity to effect a more practical change in Chicago life. She reflects, 'My energy was for prayer and for calling us all to be spiritually connected [and] from our faith and [from] our heart to speak out. That is all I could do. I wished I could have done more.'

As Dean Niedenthal painted the names of the murdered children on the Cross, he became aware of them as living children – as children as alive and as real, as the children he taught every Sunday. Their wounds and deaths became his wounds and death. In feeling assaults and deepening his insight, Niedenthal's own spirit grew and his concern for children deepened. The murdered children became a part of his life as both loss and gain. And through Chicago's slain children, other children's hurts and longing to be named and recognized became increasingly important to Niedenthal. He now felt called to do more for the children of the city. Shortly after working on the Cross, he left the business world and became a teacher in a Chicago Public School. He now works to stop the violence at its roots by offering children a vision beyond the bleak streets of their everyday world.

Niedenthal's work with Sunday school children and the Children's Cross reflects a double fidelity: fidelity to the God whose word Christians are called to announce, and fidelity to the needs of those with whom catechists and teachers share the Christian message. Tertullian realized that 'Christians are made, not born'. [12] Niedenthal agrees. His primary goal was to sensitize the children to the suffering of others in their city. And even though the children sometimes acted like they did not care about these children, he feels certain that he planted seeds. Being involved in the project involved the children in working, thinking and caring. He is convinced that the Children's Cross is such a successful catechetical tool that 'it ought to be marketed'. Niedenthal's convictions mirror the insight of religious educator Damian Lundy that, 'Symbols and symbolic actions are the ways in which the presence of Christ and his mystery is manifest to the worshipping community and the way in which the community's response to God is made evident'.[13] Because symbolic language is intuitive and non-discursive it touches our entire beings. Niedenthal is certain that the real impact of the Cross on the children awaits a further time. They need not be able to express its meaning now to be taught the community's faith.

The Children's Cross became a source of theological reflection and spiritual growth for many other St James parishioners. In time, Koehler came to believe that question-raising symbols are appropriate to public religious space. He also came to believe in the value of the Children's Cross as an appropriate symbol for the cathedral plaza. Koehler realized that if someone took the time to stand before the Cross, its stark reality would present them with deep questions: 'Why are children murdered? What kind of people abuse and kill children? What kind of society allows this to happen?' Koehler came to think that it was the role of the church to invite reflective people into chilling, perhaps self-indicting questions: 'Is there something more I should be doing than earning a living and protecting my own family? Is it enough to know that you and your children are on the "safe" side of some invisible line? Or is more required of us?'[14]

Nancy Patterson, a parent of two St James Sunday school children, now marvels at how the Children's Cross evolved. It was meant, she recalls, to be a temporary project, something similar to the crosses that proceeded it. Instead, she claims, 'The Spirit moved in an extraordinary way through this Cross. It became something much more than we could have imagined.'[15]

The impact of the Children's Cross on the St James community was felt by many not involved in the Sunday School. Betty Hedblom was seventy-five years old when the Children's Project and Cross was created. Her life had been one devoted to the care and healing of society's wounded. Hedblom had worked as a child-welfare worker when she was younger and volunteered as a caseworker for the Juvenile Protective Association in later years. From its inception, the Children's Project attracted her. Hedblom was among the first to join Griswold's prayer group. With other St James women, she met with mothers whose children had been murdered throughout the Fall 1993. Not surprisingly, Betty felt overwhelmed by the systemic nature of the problem of urban violence. Children continued to be murdered and not enough people cared.

Slain children are not the only victims of urban violence. The human spirit of the living was also affected. Hurt, sadness and even despair wounded the hearts and souls of many of the mothers of slain children, and a sense of powerlessness drained the hearts of those that met and spent time with the mothers.

Just as the ending of urban violence requires strategy, likewise, the healing of spiritual wounds also requires a strategy. One element of the strategy was prayer. As a response to the spiritual destruction caused by urban violence, Hedblom wrote 'prayer-poems' for use by St James women as well as by the mothers of the slain. These prayer–poems are both laments and statements of hope. Hedblom's prayers profess a faith that God is there for the parents who have lost children to violent death. Her poems call upon the 'God of Love' to hear the mothers who expect understanding from a God who lost 'your Jesus' to violence.[16] The prayers express the certain belief that God feels human hurts and sorrows. Understanding that 'Christ has no hands but ours', Hedblom prays, 'Light a fire in our hearts / To risk, to dare whatever / It takes to save our children.'[17] Hedblom and the women at prayer call upon God 'To hear the cries of the broken-hearted – / We are numbed by numbers.' They agonize, 'Is anger buried so deep / It cannot speak?' Then they petition, 'We cry for Justice / But are not sure / Where to find her.' The women of the St James prayer group and the mothers who lost children to violence pleaded with God, 'Bless these our children / We didn't love well enough to protect'. They joined with all other mothers seeking the wisdom, the healing, and the courage 'to search for Justice / And truth in our city'.[18]

Like Phoebe Griswold, Betty Hedblom began a spiritual journey by first recognizing her solidarity in woundedness with other women, by seeking active solidarity with other wounded members of the Body of Christ, and by participation with others in prayer and social activism. Hedblom identified with the mothers of the victims as Niedenthal had identified with the victims of violence. Their pain cannot be banished, but it can be borne and transformed into social action because of their belief and experience of God sharing in the pain of all parents and concerned adults who have lost their children. Hedblom's prayer speaks for many people involved in the Children's Project and the Children's Cross, 'In your love, there is Hope / In our shared brokenness, Strength.'[19] Griswold, Niedenthal, Hedblom and others who participated in the cross project believe that God is with them as they struggle with suffering and injustice. Further, they believe that God's final healing must await the Second Coming of Christ for which they hope. The Children's Cross is the symbol of their faith and hope.

The Children's Project revealed another face of Jesus to Phoebe and the women of St James who joined in solidarity with the mothers of the murdered children. Jesus said that when people give solace to those who are afflicted by the evils of the world, they are reaching out to him. The women of St James saw that face. And seeing the face of the suffering Jesus, they had another realization, one known previously, but experienced with new profundity. While called by a compassionate God to personify God's mercy, compassion and justice, Phoebe and her friends realized 'We are a race of sinners. We are people who fail.'[20] The women of St James had to face their failure to mitigate the tragedy. Betty laments, 'Sweet Jesus' they called you once / Will they still? / Or will those with hope lost? Wonder if you, too are powerless / In the white man's world of / Control, oppression and churchly trappings?[21] But they also continue to pray and continue to meet. For them, as for all Christians, God's sacred time is both already and not yet.

As for the rest of the St James community, the move from a quiet reticence to intrude upon the city around them to a bold evangelical and public proclamation of belief in the redemptive powers of the cross was troubled by doubts. Eventually, however, the Cross received the support of the administration and most of the community at large. They began, we believe, to see that the virtue of love is the deepest point of intersection between the private and the public. It is the ground of integrity, which helps us learn to judge each other not by our wounds but by our possibilities.

The children who made the Children's Cross in their Sunday school class do not articulate their inner experience or growing understanding of urban violence or the Christian tradition in the words of adults. Children speak of life and even spiritual experience in a more nitty-gritty way. The Sunday school class of 1994 remembers building the Children's Cross as a time of hard and dirty work, a project that was smelly and even dangerous. Five years later, the children who built the cross recall that they did not know whose names were going on the Cross or the precise relationship between the Cross and the names of the children written on the Cross. It is clear from talking with their teachers that this information was shared and discussed with them. Like other educational and religious educational projects, and in the words of Sunday school teacher Dean Niedenthal, 'you throw a lot of seeds, wait for years and maybe God will grow something'. Dean has faith that the Cross will return as a spiritual force in the lives of the children. He will most likely not be there, he says, because he expects the children will be young adults faced with some crisis or turning point when they suddenly remember the Cross and what it meant to them.

Yet, the children do realize something about the crosses they make every Lent and especially the Children's Cross of 1994. Laura remembers the first cross she helped create, 'It was scary'. On it they hung a papier mâché body of Jesus which they had made. They then wrote on long strips of paper, 'things that hurt Jesus' and wrapped the body with these. Laura remembers that the cross held her in awe both because 'it looked so real and yet you could tell it was made by kids'. Jesus became real for her when she wrapped his body with the wounds of her sins. Of the Children's Cross, Dale, now a young teen, states, 'I didn't know what those names were about – I didn't really get it until I was much older. Then, I felt sad.' He would share no more. Less reticent at eight years old, Becca shares, 'I know what the shattering of the mirrors means; it means someone is dead.' Laura, now twelve, recalls that she felt the purpose of the project was 'to fill an empty space' on the cathedral plaza. We are left to wonder if the emptiness was emotional as well as physical.

One of the important and debated questions in contemporary Christian religious education is the timing and manner in which children and other initiates into a tradition are introduced into its symbols. The symbol of the cross is especially problematic for Christians living in the midst of affluence and supposed security. A religion that finds eternal salvation in the midst of violence and death is difficult to teach two blocks away from Marshall Fields Department Store and the ever-changing advertisements of Bloomingdales and Nieman-Marcus. Yet, the impact of cross-construction on the children of the Sunday school program was not insignificant. Niedenthal who has constructed many Lenten crosses, remarked 'Who knows how hearts and minds are affected? What is sure is that it's successful. So successful that it ought to be marketed.'

Charles Wardell, a man from New York who saw his own name on the Cross, was a Vietnam veteran. Seeing the name Tatanya Wardell on the Cross may have evoked another 'There but for the grace of God go I' experience for him. St James parishioner and Sunday school teacher Bob Koehler believes the effect of the Cross is like that of the Vietnam War Memorial in Washington, DC, 'As you walk past the structure, the crescendo of the names, which you are reading silently, grows in intensity until eventually there is nothing else in your mind but the thunder of those names'.

According to Koehler, the Cross continued to be a force in the city calling people to a renewed reverence for life. The Cross has other evocative effects. Once a student of Koehler's told him this story. While waiting for a friend she had to quickly duck down into a doorway to keep from being hit by 'people [who] came by shooting AK-47s and Uzis'. As Koehler sees it, our governmental representatives who will not support gun control are 'the moral equivalent of the triggermen who nearly killed my student, who nearly got her name put up on the Cross'. But he recognized his anger as no different than that of 'the law-and-order crowd'. He sees the dilemma as a 'No easy answers allowed' situation. Retribution cannot, he concedes, be our first objective. Any child's loss is the community's loss. As he stood before the Cross three years after it was erected, he sees that his own grief was too small and too isolated. Children were still being slain 'because something in our midst is out of whack'. If he is to be honest with his daughter, he must tell her that children like her do get killed because all children are alike in their innocence and potential. 'We need to show our children that all our names are on the Cross'. [22] His cry is in a different language from Hedblom's, but it holds the same anguish. This is a broken world. We are all hurting and we are all healing. But complete health is out of reach in human time.

It is difficult, if not impossible, to know the impact of the Children's Cross on those who are members of St James Cathedral parish. Many Chicagoans and visitors to the city seem to rush by the cathedral plaza without noticing the Cross. The lure of Michigan Avenue's retail stores is more powerful than a Sunday school project. But not all passers-by were in such a hurry or so totally enthralled by shopping. When Wardell discovered his own last name on the Cross, he immediately entered the parish office and offered the parish $10,000. Phoebe Griswold wished to refuse the donation. Fundraising had not been the purpose of the Cross. In the end, the money was accepted and a high school scholarship for inner city boys was established. Another story is told of two persons who were members of no faith community. The two paused at the Cross. It so moved them that they went to the parish centre, joined the St James community and are active parishioners today.

The Accomplishments of the Children's Cross

Lent as a sacred time was one of the earliest established practices of the Christian church. The cross as a central symbol of Christian meaning is equally ancient, and commitment to the poor and the oppressed is a central message of the gospel. The St James community began nothing extraordinary when they initiated the Children's Project, but the Christian churches have also traditionally understood that the Spirit of God descended on Jesus' followers on the first Pentecost and remains with God's people today. Therefore, in a profound sense, the community of faith, in as far as it works to imitate Christ, cannot do anything ordinary. For each person involved in the construction of the Cross, and for all that were moved by it afterward the Cross had a particular meaning, each these repeats a traditional Christian theme.

As humans we yearn to have all pain removed from our lives or better yet to never experience pain at all. For many Christians, the mystery of why God allows suffering is one of the deepest spiritual challenges they face. The people of St James and others moved by the Children's Cross came to a place where, at least for a while, they could accept something less than a reversal of the present order. The story of the suffering and death of Jesus is retold every year during the Lenten season. Through this retelling Christians are reminded of a central precept of their faith, the belief that God can bring good out of pain and suffering.

Those involved in the various aspects of the Children's Cross Project were at times overwhelmed by feelings of anxiety and fear. The loss of the murdered children become a personal loss for them. Yet, several goods evolved from this pastoral project. The children and adults of St James became were more sensitive and thoughtful. The parish became more involved in the pain of its city. The Cross awoke an increased awareness on the part of those that passed by the Cross and paused to reflect. For some this led to community involved in action for social justice. But most importantly, the children who had died and may have been forgotten were remembered. Forgotten and lost to memory, they may have remained dead forever. Instead, they live today as full members of the community of faith because when their names are read they are known and recognized.

The Children's Cross and the Future

An important question remains. In what way can the Children's Project be incorporated as part of the ongoing pastoral process at St James? In Lent in each of the four years after the Cross was erected, a few parishioners, including the Sunday school children, had planted a garden around the Cross. The planting was accompanied by a memorial liturgy. As other children were murdered in Chicago, their names were inscribed around the base, which held the cross. But as 1998 progressed, parishioners began to wonder if the Cross had outlived its potency as a symbolic call to action and remembrance. It was becoming worn. The glass mosaic had fallen off in many places. The children's names were not as clear as they had been. The Cross had been vandalized with profane graffiti. Various church committees discussed the Cross's future as well as the future of the plaza as a sacred space. Then, one night in October 1998, Chicago experienced a powerful storm, which blew down trees and utility poles all over the city. It also blew down the Cross. One parishioner saw this occurrence as 'prophetic, as though the Holy Spirit were saying "It is time for the Cross to come down."' But neither she nor any other vocal member of the parish was willing to just store away the Children's Cross as the other Sunday school Lenten crosses had been in the past.

In November 1998, in solemn procession the Cross was carried back through the church and to the parish centre. Here both the Cross and the proclamations, which had surrounded it, were attached to the wall of the staircase that leads from the church to the parish centre. No one can enter the centre without passing the Cross. Many still pause to read the names, to reflect, and to pray.

What would happen with the plaza was more controversial. That it should remain a sacred space was uppermost in the minds of many of St James' most active members. How to do this was less certain. Wakening Women, a women's consciousness-raising group, wanted to build a labyrinth in the plaza. They made a case that doing so would allow both church members and those who pass by to take some time to meditate and pray. They pointed out that this has been successful both in other churches and in some public spaces like hospitals. Other members of the parish did not want to see the plaza lost as a space to remember the city's murdered children. Some were asking the parish to hire an architect who might plan the space to include a sculptural memorial to the children. When Ian (one of the Sunday school children) heard about this plan, he was incensed. 'How can they do it without us?' he demanded. 'It's for the children. We should be involved.'

Karen Hastrum, Ian's teacher, said, 'I must make sure that the children are heard. We must take into account what they would like to see on the plaza.'[23] Like Jesus before her, Karen invites the children forward. Another one of the children, Laura, expressed that she does not like to see the plaza empty. She missed the proclamation that she and her peers had made even if she did not always understand what it was about. For her, as for many who wandered about the empty plaza, she wondered with Mary Magdalene, 'What have they done with my Lord?' Both the adults and the children recognized that the only voice that God has in this city is our own human voice. If we remained silent, if the plaza remained empty, then we silence God.

In the end, the St James community decided to keep the plaza as a public sacred space. They did not, however, return to the theme of violence against children in the city. Rather, recognizing that reconciliation had long been a cornerstone of Episcopalian theology, they commissioned a bronze statue of the Angel of Peace. The angel stands tall in the plaza with broken weapons at its feet. It represents a hope for the future. Sadly, it says nothing of the children we continue to lose to violence every day of every year. As Griswold realized early in her endeavours, to hope for peace in the city is not enough. Action is called for even when its efficacy seems so slow as to cause us to question whether we ought to act at all.

The Children's Cross: Ethically Risky but Necessary

In her book, *A Feminist Ethic of Risk*, Sharon Welch asks, 'What does it mean to work for social transformation in the face of seemingly insurmountable suffering and evil?'[24] One possible answer is an ethical approach Welch calls an 'ethic of control'. This approach assumes that one can guarantee the efficacy of one's actions. Many St James parishioners are persons with a high degree of education who have attained both wealth and status in the wider community. They are used to thinking of themselves as persons who overcome obstacles by remaining in control. As Koehler noted, their neighbourhood is more about 'buns of steel' than about suffering.

Thus, it seems likely that, like most Americans in positions of relative power, St James parishioners approach any problem concerned to find some final, perfect solution. This is an approach that is often framed in absolutes such as 'end urban violence *now*'. Such notions presume that we can control the actions of others, a presumption that is both untenable and perhaps immoral. Further, when we pose our concerns in absolutes, it then appears that we cannot take smaller steps toward our goal because only a final solution is acceptable. The search for such a degree of certainty is a denial of the complexity of human existence. Other people make their own choices, which we cannot control. Yet, we long for total security. We seek the ideal of invulnerability. We respond to force with force calling for more police, stronger laws, longer sentences and capital punishment. This search for invulnerability understands moral responsibility to entail an assurance that one's goals will be met before any moral action is taken. It is part and parcel of a utopian dream that aims at a final defeat of all that is seen as evil.

Utopian dreams, however, are distorted by an inability to accept the long-term struggle. 'Seeking utopia, people turn to types of action that appear to offer immediacy and guarantees despite the dangers that may accompany these actions'.[25] Many times attempts to achieve a perfectly non-violent urban environment culminate in a severe curtailment of the civil rights of many of the city's citizens. Another hidden agenda of the utopian thrust is the hope for complete uniformity. We set the standards of moral action and demand that others conform. It seems not to matter that this demand comes not from the victims of violence themselves but from those who stand at some distance as they offer their solutions. Somehow we manage to convince ourselves that this is not arrogance but simply a realistic belief in the proven success of our ways.

Americans in positions of power tend to see pluralism and complexity as problems calling for solutions rather than as constitutive elements of the solution. 'Difference and disagreement are then viewed as the products of either ignorance or ill-will, unfortunate or dangerous factors to be eliminated'.[26] When such utopian endeavours encounter barriers, their supporters may abandon all effort. They fail to recognize that ambiguous and fragile gains are the norm in efforts toward transformation. Accustomed to demanding success, faced with possible failure they give in to despair.

As a possible alternative, Welch develops an ethic of risk, a transformative ethic that could be applicable to a wide range of social crises. The violent death of children is just such a crisis and the response of the parishioners of St James Cathedral was ethically risky. Therein lies its transformative power, its ability to change the way we see things and to change what we do about what we see. The small group of St James parishioners who were engaged in the Children's Cross Project were in many ways like others of their neighbourhood and class. They lived relatively safe lives. Their physical needs were met. An ethic of control could have tempted them. It was after all 'other people's' children who were dying. Yet, they were drawn to another approach, one that closely resembles what Welch describes as an 'ethic of risk'.

Those engaged in an ethic of risk begin where those committed to an ethic of control leave off – in despair. They chaff under their inability to wrest power away from those who have it and seem to abuse it. Phoebe Griswold and the other praying women felt powerless to keep guns out of the hands of children, to stop parents from abusing the children they should nurture, or to weaken the powerful gun lobbies. Niedenthal and Koehler knew they could not promise safety to the children they loved. Yet, despair did not break them down, rather it empowered them to renew their commitment to the transformative power of the cross by telling its story yet again, this time in a new way to meet the needs of their present struggle. In this moral tradition action begins with the 'recognition that we cannot imagine how we will win. Acknowledgement of the immensity of the challenge is a given.'[27] Betty knows that praying, writing and wearing a green ribbon will not end gang warfare but she must begin somewhere. Dean works with the children never knowing when the full impact of what they have done and what they learned will hit them.

Those who practise an ethic of risk necessarily labour within the limits of bounded power. There are no organized programs or particular strategies that can guarantee an end to violence or to the structures of exploitation that undergird it. Those who are propelled by an ethic of risk do not expect changes in the near future or even in their lifetimes. The St James community understands that change may not even occur in human time. For just as Jesus warned his followers that there would always be poverty, so too children have always been caught in the crossfire of human violence. At the same time this community realizes that resistance to the violence must continue even if they cannot imagine succeeding in their goal. According to Welch, 'the death that accompanies acquiescence to overwhelming problems is multidimensional: the threat of physical death, the death of the imagination, the death of the ability to care'.[28]

Therefore, for a time, the community of St James continued to meet, to pray, to build, and to hope for ways to reach out. Yes, there has been a temptation to abandon the whole project, to give in to the despair because children are still dying by violence and other children still live in fear. There has been also a strong resistance to such despair. While the majority of the parishioners have become involved in other projects, many still ask that the children not be forgotten. Foremost among these are the children themselves who asked not to be left out and who hoped so adamantly that the plaza continue as a place of remembrance to children who die violently. As a people committed to the Christian faith, St James parishioners have been asked to become like these little children. If they cease to protest against the violence in their city, they will lose the ability to imagine a community that is different from their present one. They will also lose the ability to sustain each other in the many struggles for justice, which confront them everyday. So, hope remains as long as Betty still prays with the women whose children were murdered, the Children's Cross still hangs in a prominent place in the parish centre, and Niedenthal works to show children a way out of violence.

Notes

1   M.W. Edelman, 'To Save Our Children', *Christian Social Action* (May 1994), p. 28.
2   B. Koehler, 'The Cross In Yuppieville: God's open-ended too!', *U-Direct Magazine* (May–July 1996), p. 7.
3   P. Griswold, letter to author, 12 September 1998, New York.

4 T. Patterson, interview by author, 24 January 1999, Chicago.

5 Some members of the parish were upset that the altar had been taken over for this purpose. They felt it should be preserved in its original form because Abraham Lincoln had once worshipped there.

6 M. Hirsley, 'Slain Children at the Heart of Cathedral's Nativity Scene', *The Chicago Tribune*, 30 December 1993, Section 2, p. 5.

7 Ibid.

8 Koehler, 'The Cross in Yuppieville', p. 7.

9 The remembrances of all the children quoted in this chapter were shared with author, Jule Ward, when she visited their Sunday School class on 23 January 1999 in Chicago.

10 The narrative of the building of the Cross and the impact it had on Niedenthal's life was shared by him in a conversation with the authors on 9 January 1999.

11 Koehler, 'The Cross in Yuppieville', p. 7.

12 Damian Lundy, 'A Vision for Catechesis in the 1990s,' in M. Grey, A. Heaton and D. Sullivan (eds), *The Candles Are Still Burning* (Collegeville, MN: The Liturgical Press, 1995), p. 42.

13 Lundy, 'A Vision for Catechesis in the 1990s', p. 42.

14 Koehler, 'The Cross in Yuppieville', p. 7.

15 Nancy Patterson, interview by author, 23 January 1999.

16 Betty Hedblom, 'A Prayer', 14 December 1993.

17 Ibid., 'A Prayer', October 1993.

18 Ibid., 'A Prayer (2)', October 1993.

19 Ibid.

20 Patrick Purnell, 'Reconciliation', in M. Grey, A. Heaton and D. Sullivan (eds) *The Candles Are Still Burning* (The Liturgical Press, 1995), p. 83.

21 Betty Hedblom, 'A November Prayer', November 1993.

22 Koehler, 'The Cross in Yuppieville', p. 8.

23 Karen Halstrum, interview by author, 23 January 1999, Chicago.

24 Sharon Welch, *A Feminist Ethic of Risk* (Minneapolis, MN: Fortress, 1999) p.1.

25 Ibid., p. 33.

26 Ibid., p. 35.

27 Ibid., p. 19.

28 Ibid., p. 20.

Part II
Philosophical and Theological Reflections

Introduction

Isabel L. Wollaston

For Gareth Jones, the creation and public display of the Children's Cross was motivated by moral outrage at the deaths of sixty-three children in Chicago, recorded in the *Chicago Tribune* during the course of 1993. He suggests that the Children's Cross should be seen as an act of Christian witness, embodying 'Christian duty in the face of appalling suffering'. Yet, for Denys Turner, the same memorial is 'deeply problematic'. Why such very different responses? There are a number of possible explanations. Clearly, the cross now means, as it always has done, many different things to many different people. As Dennis McCann points out, the cross is both a scandal (as in 'the folly of the cross') and an 'offensive weapon' (an expression of Christian triumphalism and exclusivism). Given such contradictory meanings, the question arises of whether, as McCann puts it, 'the cross is still retrievable as an authentic symbol of Christian faith and practice.' Such a question works on different levels. Can the positive meanings of the cross be separated from the historical uses (abuses?) to which it has been put? McCann himself suggests that it is naïve to assume that we can ignore the history and ramifications of the symbols we use. Turner goes further and criticises the Children's Cross for its 'gallingly naïve and insensitive association of child murder with the cross of Christ.' Such harsh language suggests that, at least in some contexts, it is not in fact possible to retrieve the cross as 'an authentic symbol of Christian faith and practice.'

On a second level, we can ask whether the cross has any meaning – that is, does it still 'work' as a symbol – in an increasingly secular and multicultural environment. Jones, McCann and Turner all note how easily such a symbol can be ignored, or passed by, in present-day Chicago. Turner goes so far as to question whether '*any* symbolic communication is possible in a "pluralist society"', let alone one as specifically Christian as the Children's Cross. For Turner, 'the very possibility of symbolic memorialization is problematic' in secular, capitalist societies, such as the UK and the USA. Charles

Strain's response, however, is of a different kind. Whereas, Jones, McCann and Turner are concerned with the possibility and relevance of Christian symbolic and theological discourse in a secular multicultural environment, Strain's essay demonstrates the resources such a context can offer to the Christian theologian. He looks outside the Christian framework to Engaged Buddhism and the theory of dependent co-arising for resources that might be helpful in articulating a Christian response to the challenges posed by urban violence and extreme suffering. The clear implication is that Engaged Buddhism provides a useful, even necessary corrective, to the emphasis of much Christian teaching.

Like the other essayists, Strain is also concerned with the possibility that Christian narratives help us to look away or overlook the realities of our complicity with violence. For McCann and Turner, such complicity is symbolized by the close association of the cross and the sword, the cross and Christian triumphalism. For Strain, the danger is that such narratives regard brutal violence as other than themselves, as acts committed by isolated individuals. We identify with the victims, whom we prefer to figure as innocent; an innocence that we can then extend to ourselves. The perpetrators of violence are presented as standing outside of, and as a threat to, this circle of solidarity. However, as Strain points out, the boundaries between 'them' and 'us' are rarely, if ever, so clear cut. It is precisely this blurring of boundaries between 'them' and 'us', victims and victimizers, that renders the Children's Cross so ambiguous and problematic. Is the cross a symbol of God's solidarity with victims, with the oppressed? Is it a symbol that God also suffers, as a victim? Is it a symbol of the long tradition of Christian victimization of others? Is it a divinely endorsed protest against violence and injustice or an act of violence and injustice in and of itself? The cross has been interpreted as all of these things. Any memorial that draws upon the symbolism of the cross can therefore also contain each and all of these meanings.

Strain goes on to speak of the problematics of giving voice to the voiceless, of speaking on behalf of those rendered silent by death or the experience of extreme suffering. The Children's Cross serves an important function in recording the names of those children who died in Chicago in the course of 1993. It ensures that their names are not forgotten. However, it can only do this if those who 'pass by' take the trouble to stop and read the names and understand their significance. Such attention was more likely during the public life of the Children's Cross than it is in its post-life, hanging on a wall inside the Cathedral. The suggestion that we can give 'voice to the voiceless' itself raises numerous questions, as Strain realises. Three questions are particularly pertinent: who is speaking? who are we speaking for? and who are we speaking to?

Who are we speaking to? Is our intended audience the Christian church? Or is it secular, and multicultural society? The language we use may well be different in each case. The suggestion appears to be that the language of the cross may well be appropriate and meaningful to a Christian audience, but that it is much more problematic for a non-Christian or nominally Christian audience.

Who are we speaking for? As a bare minimum, speech claiming to give 'a voice to the voiceless' must necessarily attend to the experience of the 'voiceless'. However, can those with 'voice' ever fully appreciate what it is to be rendered 'voiceless' by suffering or death? There is always the danger that rather than giving voice to the voiceless, we speak instead, that is, we substitute our voice for voicelessness. Strain warns of 'soothing and self-deceiving' voices that emphasize the transformative powers of suffering and/or that suggest that suffering serves as a means to bring about a better future (by, for example, prompting those who 'pass by' to work for social change). Such a warning stands in sharp contrast to Jones' suggestion that the Children's Cross is a 'prophetic' act of witness, one based on realism rather than sentimentality.

Who is speaking? Given the problematics of both Christian and symbolic discourse in a secular and multicultural context, and the complexities of the notion of giving a voice to the voiceless, it is essential that we are self-conscious as to what we are saying and how we are saying it. Such self-consciousness makes it imperative that it is made very clear who is speaking in such contexts. Is this institutional public speech, i.e. the Children's Cross is a public pronouncement in public/private, sacred/profane space by *the Church* (as Jones suggests)? Or is it a more modest statement by a group of concerned individuals within a particular church? The debate prompted by St James' Episcopal Cathedral's Way of the Cross suggests that there was considerable confusion and disagreement on precisely this point. As McCann points out, the presence of artistic representations of the Stations of the Cross on the sidewalk outside the Cathedral could be understood both as coercive and confrontational, and as an invitation to individual reflection.

These three questions can, of course, be applied equally well to the responses to the Children's Cross found in the essays in this volume. The diverse conclusions, and the varying styles employed, reflect the fact that a variety of people are speaking, each of whom speaks from a particular perspective, from within a variety of different contexts, and with a particular audience in mind.

Figure 4: One of the Stations of the Cross that lined the northern and eastern sides of the Cathedral (photograph, Dennis McCann).

Waylaying the Way of the Cross: A Dilemma for Practical Theology

Dennis P. McCann

St James' Way of the Cross: A Personal Encounter

Practical theology, as Charles Strain and I once defined it, is 'critical reflection on religious praxis.'[1] But critical reflection often begins with a narrative, this time a true story of my own encounter with the fourteen signs or Stations that made up the Way of the Cross at St James. The ambivalence that I experienced helped me understand the complexity of the signals relayed by this particular set of icons, and thus led me to consider the various levels on which it represents a dilemma for practical theology. That dilemma is not easily reduced to the truisms that, for me, usually govern mistaken readings of mixed signals. 'No good deed goes unpunished' is one such Irish witticism. Were it allowed to define my narrative, it would lead me to emphasize the sincere desire to do good that animated the Cathedral staff and to commiserate with them over the controversy they stirred as they went forward with the Children's Cross Memorial project and the Way of the Cross. But equally appropriate might be the pithy Christian realism that I first learned at my mother's knee: 'The road to hell is paved with good intentions'. For sincerity did not always anticipate the offences given and taken as the fourteen Stations were inserted in an extraordinarily complex field of religious and cultural meanings, that for a while threatened to cast a shadow on the Cathedral, its mission and its ministry.

Here, then, is what I saw and felt when I made my own pilgrimage to the Children's Memorial and the Way of the Cross, on what was for Chicago an absolutely perfect late spring afternoon, in June 1997. I had finished up some business at DePaul University's Loop Campus and then taken the 'El' to Chicago Avenue to visit St James Cathedral. As I strolled south on State Street toward Huron Street I passed the Roman Catholic Holy Name Cathedral just up the street from St James. 'This could be Chicago's Holy "Hood"', I thought, for in this near north neighbourhood there were a number of very powerful churches clustered near the Miracle Mile of Michigan Avenue.

The miracles performed on Michigan Avenue were mainly commercial, of course, with Saks Fifth Avenue, Bloomingdales and other upscale temples to American consumerism dominating the landscape. But these are just a stone's throw from the Cathedral Plaza, the Children's Memorial and the fourteen Stations. I had avoided the crowds of noon-day shoppers on Michigan Avenue for the time being, and approached the Cathedral as it was meant to be approached, from its frontage facing west onto State Street.

Like its Catholic sister up the street, St James Episcopal Cathedral is a relatively modest affair. It is less impressive than many parish churches I can think of, a monument to Chicago's late nineteenth-century's eclectic taste for the Romanesque, done in the same kind of softly ageing sandstone from which Chicago's Watertower Place was constructed. The sandstone makes the Cathedral anything but forbidding, but the overall effect is not exactly awe-inspiring either. A comfortable church, I thought.

As I turned the corner east on Huron, I easily spotted the Way of the Cross, already removed from the public sidewalk and relocated to the edge of the landscaping that separates the church itself from the street. The Stations were as close to the sidewalk as they could be, but now clearly on Cathedral property. At the time I saw them, they faced the sidewalk, hovering over the passers-by at an altitude of seven or eight feet. This is slightly higher than the many street signs that regulate the flow of traffic and the availability of parking spaces in the neighbourhood.

In order to recognize the Stations for what they are, one must turn and look up, and in looking up the bulk of the Cathedral's north wall loomed in the background. Each of the Stations was positioned roughly ten feet apart, and they drew one eastward toward the Cathedral plaza. The final four Stations, following the line of the landscaping, invited one into the plaza, with the fourteenth Station positioned in line with the corner of the terrace whose steps lead to the higher plaza, adorned by the emphatically modern building that houses the Cathedral and diocesan offices.

It is important, I think, to visualize what the lower plaza looked like at the time. The western side, as I've indicated, contained the final Stations against the backdrop provided by the eastern wall of the Cathedral. The southern side is the terrace leading to St James' modern office building. The east side is Rush Street, associated in Chicago lore with pub-crawling and other profane entertainments, and the north is formed by Huron Street, a narrow and all-too-busy thoroughfare linking the Cathedral with the upscale retail temples that grace the Miracle Mile. The plaza opens to the northeast, to the corner of Huron and Rush, at the intersection of which, stood the Children's Memorial.

On the day I visited the site, my overall impression was that of a congenial refuge, a place where tourists, day trippers, and Michigan Avenue sales clerks could find rest, sit and vegetate, meet friends, have a brief picnic, paint the sidewalk with chalk designs, or do their Tai-Chi exercises, as a group was doing under the gaze of Stations ten through fourteen. The Children's Cross, though rarely attended to by any of the passers-by, seemed to define a boundary for a sacrally protected space, where people in the city could just be themselves, if only momentarily. The Stations marked a trail into this protected space, but only if you had picked it up from the west, from the corner of State and Huron. Most of the pedestrian traffic comes the other way, from the commanding heights of commercial Michigan Avenue.

I was favourably impressed by the serenity of this noontime scene. Here was a successful blend of secular and religious architectures that gave definition to a people's park where strangers could set aside their agendas and put down their game faces. It was such a nice day, I decided to photograph the scene. Having made the trip without the necessary equipment, I legged it over to Walgreen's on Michigan Avenue and bought one of those disposable cameras, retraced my steps, and began photographing the Children's Memorial and the Way of the Cross. But then a funny thing happened. As I stood looking up at each of the Stations through the camera lens, I was taken back to my adolescent experiences as a Roman Catholic altar boy – pre-Vatican II, of course – when I used to accompany the priest in procession, who led us by the Stations as part of our parish's Lenten penances.

Those Stations from my youth were large, and anything but iconic: they were colourful, excruciatingly detailed, and morbid – realistically, though implausibly, portraying an all-too-delicate green-eyed Jesus, pierced and visibly bleeding with crown of thorns as well as distinctive halo, stumbling through jeering crowds of Jerusalemites, more Nordic than Mediterranean, toward his ritual execution at Golgotha. As I stood photographing each Station, I now remembered the names of each one, but more was remembered than the name. I was that altar boy again, still shamefully complicitous with the sinners who had caused the Lord's own suffering, and I heard again the sombre tones of Fr. Sullivan, 'Veronica wipes the face of Jesus ...; Jesus falls the second time..., Jesus meets the weeping women of Jerusalem ... Despite the warmth of a sunny June Chicago day, once again I felt the feverish Lenten chill of the cavernous parish church in which I had grown up. Once again, I was the cowering adolescent ('Yes, Father. No, Father ... Yes, S'ter. No, S'ter ...'), just beginning to grope his way out of the cramping devotionalism that marked those last days of an immigrant Catholic church.

This sense of déjà vu was rather unsettling, for it reminded me that the Way of the Cross had a well-deserved reputation for sending mixed signals, inevitably offensive, but often not intentionally so. If peering up at each individual station through the eye of a camera were enough to put me back in line as a guilty adolescent, what might these icons do for others who did not share my Catholic training in sin, guilt and ritualized expiation? How might the ritualized reproaches of the Christ abandoned by his faithless disciples be regarded by those who regarded the cross either as a curious obscenity or as a sinister expression of Christianity's unacknowledged will-to-power that, all too often, had become a will to punish those unbelievers judged responsible for His Crucifixion? The cross, after all, had been mystically transformed by Christian faith from a fiendishly sadistic Roman instrument for pacifying Jewish rebels into the sign by which Constantine would win an empire, the sign by which the Crusaders would recover the Holy Land, and the sign under which all sorts of atrocities would be committed against heretics, infidels, sceptics, and anyone else deemed to be a threat to the integrity of orthodox Christianity. The cross was not simply offensive, in the sense intended to summon pious Christians to repentance; it had also become an offensive weapon in the perverse struggle to maintain and extend Christendom as a global political hegemony. Just how much of the trauma of that history, I wondered, still lingered in the Way of the Cross that the Cathedral had chosen to erect on a public sidewalk in downtown Chicago.

Confrontation and Accommodation

Reflecting on my personal reactions to the Stations, I had begun to grasp the many different levels on which the Way of the Cross could still be regarded as controversial. The Cathedral's placing of the Stations on Huron Street was immediately noticed by Chicago's paper of record, the *Chicago Tribune*, whose offices were minutes away on Michigan Avenue. On 3 March 1995, the *Tribune* ran a front page story complete with photographs under the following provocative headline, 'Signs take Stations to the street: Sidewalk depiction of Crucifixion ordeal no pedestrian display.' A week later, a neighbourhood newspaper, the *North Loop News*, carried a photo of the Stations in its 9 March edition, with the caption, 'Yield for Salvation'. The photos accompanying these stories clearly show the Stations positioned as close to the traffic signs as possible in order to emphasize – the Cathedral staff may have thought – simply their artistic merit. The editorial comment, though favourable, is also clearly an open invitation to those civic groups who oppose religious displays on public property to get into the act; and so one of them did.

On 6 March, as if on cue, the 'Freedom from Religion Foundation' of Madison, Wisconsin, sent a letter to the Cathedral staff complaining that the positioning of the Stations was a 'violation', an abuse of 'separation of church and state', and requesting that the Stations be removed to private property. Apparently, the letter also was sent to the City of Chicago, for on 10 March the city ordered the signs to be removed, and so they were by city crews on Monday, 13 March, just ten days after the first story about them had appeared in the Tribune. As Nathan Mason, the curator of the Cathedral's exhibits, quipped 'It was the fastest I've ever seen the city respond … I guess if we want them to fix our streets we should paint crosses on our potholes.'[2] Later, the City of Chicago returned the Stations to the Cathedral staff and they were repositioned on church property in the manner I've described.

In hindsight, of course, the protest from the 'Freedom from Religion Foundation' and the city's quick response to it should have been foreseeable. For reactions such as theirs are quite common, as is the legal basis for their demand to have the Stations removed according to legal precedent based on the First and Fourteenth Amendments to the US Constitution. These amendments are commonly thought to enforce a somewhat porous 'wall of separation' between church and state in the USA, one which clearly restricts the use of public property for religious purposes. If routinely the courts have ordered Christmas cribs removed from public property, it would seem highly likely that the same fate would await the Cathedral's even more provocative display of the Way of the Cross.

Cathedral staff and some of the parishioners did not see it that way. Though the idea of positioning the Stations on the sidewalk had first emerged as part of the church's Lenten commemoration for 1995, any sensitivity to the Constitutional issues seems to have been submerged in an appreciation of the Stations' artistic merit. Nathan Mason had originally spotted them in a local art gallery, and persuaded the parish to buy and display them.

> 'When I saw the signs, I thought they were very cool and liked them a lot', Mason said. 'I liked their simplicity. A lot of religious art gets mired in sentimentality. But these images do not pander to emotionalism. They are a focal point for meditation without [specifically] directing you.'
> (*Chicago Tribune*, 3 March 1995)

Another parishioner, Sharrel Croswhite, gave the following comment for the same story:

> 'The nice thing about them is that the international symbols are so simple that anyone can figure out what's happening no matter what your religious, geographic or cultural background.... They're street signs for street people on the street. You can't miss them. Those yellow posts really grab you.'

After the city had acted, Mason continued to defend the appropriateness of positioning the Stations on the public sidewalk, primarily on artistic grounds:

> 'It's near a church, but it's not encouraging someone to follow a certain religion', says Mason [despite the fact that the original stories linked the Stations to a series of fifteen sonnets based on them, and posted in the Cathedral lobby]. 'Does a religious content obviate artistic merit? Can you not explore religious themes anymore? If that's so, should the Art Institute take down its copy of El Greco's *Assumption* because it has a religious theme and is hanging in a museum that's on public land and which receives public funds? What about the religious Native American artifacts and all the vestments and liturgical implements on display at the Art Institute? Is it a case where, as Andre

Malraux said, if you put something in a museum it's dead, but if you put them near a church it's living? Are they saying we can't have Easter processions in Pilsen where Christ is carried through the public streets? It gets ridiculous after a while.'
(*Chicago Reader*, 31 March 1995)

Mason's sense of frustration is understandable, and part of me wants to share in his grievances. But maybe there's a trap involved in assuming such an air of injured innocence. Religious art, whatever its artistic merit, has always played a role in Christian evangelization, as it has in the edifying activities of other world religious traditions. El Greco's *Assumption*, for example, didn't always hang in a museum. The fact that these Stations are, as Croswhite suggested, universally intelligible, does not render them inoffensive. If anything, intelligibility may have just the opposite effect. Precisely because 'you can't miss them', they are more likely to serve as more than a bland invitation to some form of generic meditation. Why else put them up for Lent, the holy season specifically dedicated to the grassroots renewal of Christian faith and practice?

Indeed, the Way of the Cross is a distinctively Christian devotional practice that cannot easily be separated from a history littered with a series of offences, some deliberate, some inadvertent, but none truly innocent. According to *The Catholic Encyclopaedia*, the Way of the Cross grew out of the Christian pilgrimages to the holy places in Jerusalem that began shortly after Constantine's conversion to Christianity. The practice was to retrace the path of Jesus' passion, as indicated in the Gospels, along what came to be known in later times as the 'Via Dolorosa'. The history of these pilgrimages is intimately connected with the Crusades, inasmuch as one of the religious goals of these Christian military exercises was to liberate Jerusalem, thus guaranteeing safe passage to the pilgrims from Europe. By the fourteenth century, the pilgrimages were sanctioned with Papal indulgences, that is, the Papal dispensation that released penitents from the punishments that otherwise would be due, either here or in Purgatory, for the sins that they or their deceased loved ones had committed. After the rise of the Turks virtually cut off all European access to the holy places in Jerusalem, the Papacy permitted and then encouraged the construction of symbolic Ways of the Cross, that would more or less replicate the pilgrim's spiritual experience on the Via Dolorosa. Many of these ersatz pilgrimage sites were established in the century prior to the Reformation, and at first the franchise for them was exclusively committed to the Franciscans.

After the Reformation, as was the case with many other popular forms of Catholic devotion, the Ways of the Cross tended to become increasingly uniform, both as to the number of Stations – finally set at fourteen – their iconography and the prayers to be said at each of them. In the context of Counter-Reformation piety, the Way of the Cross became especially popular, the *Catholic Encyclopaedia* reports, because of the Papal indulgences attached to them. Once the penitential practice of the Church had become focused on the need to shorten or commute one's sentence in Purgatory, popular demand for devotions such as the Way of the Cross steadily increased. The trend of Papal policy was to extend the privilege of erecting Stations, first to all Franciscan churches (1732), and later to all Catholic churches regardless of their foundation (1742). In 1857 the privilege was given specifically to the Roman Catholic bishops of England, who were empowered to erect the Stations anywhere in their jurisdiction. Thus they became a mainstay in the interior design of all Catholic churches, visually as indispensable and distinctive as the holy water font or, perhaps, the Eucharistic tabernacle.

This history suggests that certain ironies are inherent in the Stations' finding a home in the Cathedral of the Episcopal Church of Chicago. For the Way of the Cross devotion had virtually disappeared from many Roman Catholic churches, thanks largely to the general shift away from private *devotion* devotional practices following the Second Vatican Council (1962–65). The Anglican communion worldwide, however, has tended to preserve this devotion, consistent with its striking conservatism about most of its rituals, even as it continues to outpace Roman Catholicism in efforts to modernize its doctrinal teaching and its disciplinary standards. That the Way of the Cross should be promoted by those elements within the Anglican communion currently resisting the ordination of women to the priesthood and their inevitable consecration as bishops may come as no surprise. But it is remarkable to find this same devotion at St James Cathedral, which is so clearly committed to the mainstream of reform and adaptation within the Episcopal Church in the United States of America (ECUSA). In light of the historic link between the Way of the Cross and certain Counter-Reformation practices, such as the promotion of Papal indulgences, it may be easier to take Cathedral spokespersons, like Nathan Mason, at their word, when they insist that the Stations' artistic merits were what motivated their purchase and display on Huron Street.

Perhaps. There's no doubt about the artistry involved. The minimalist stick figures that represent each of the fourteen episodes commemorated in the Way of the Cross are a rather ingenious adaptation to the semiotics of modern urban traffic control. Like traffic signs they are meant to tell us where we are going, or at least where we might go were we to take up our Cross and follow Jesus. But traffic signs are part of the city's structure for maintaining law and order; there are penalties for ignoring ordinary traffic signs. They are intended and interpreted as an exercise in coercive authority, exercised in this case on behalf of the people of Chicago. But did the Cathedral deliberately mean to address the semiotics of secular power? Putting the Stations on the sidewalk suggests that at some, possibly subconscious level, they did. These Christian traffic signs could easily be construed as saying that Jesus is Lord, emphatically so, even on the street. Those who ignore His claim to power and dominion, do so at their own peril. Though part of what motivated the original placing of the Stations may have been a desire to make Christian ministry more relevant to the city, it is highly unlikely that the Cathedral staff harboured any notion of reconstructing a Christian America, or of legally supplanting the secular authority, if only by a clever cancellation of its routine semiotics of power. Otherwise, the Cathedral staff would not have so quickly given in to the demands of the Freedom from Religion Foundation and the City of Chicago.

Had they consulted a constitutional lawyer, they might have learned that they had other options besides accommodation. Despite the popular assumption that the First Amendment to the US Constitution dictates an unbreachable 'Wall of Separation' between church and state, and that religious displays on public sidewalks are clearly a violation of First Amendment rights, the fact is that case law increasingly has tended to poke holes in that constitutional 'Wall'. Indeed, at the time of the controversy over the Stations the US Supreme Court was hearing a case, 'Capitol Square Review and Advisory Board, *et al.*, Petitioners v. Vincent J. Pinette, Donnie A. Carr and Knights of the Ku Klux Klan', that would clarify the conditions under which unattended religious displays could legally be erected on public property. By a vote of seven to two, on 29 June 1995, the court defended the right of the Ku Klux Klan to display a cross at Christmas time in the public park, Capitol Square, adjacent to the Capitol building in Columbus, Ohio. Though the Klan has notoriously (mis)appropriated the cross as a symbol of their own white supremacist movement – a fact duly emphasized in the concurring opinion by Judge Clarence Thomas – the Klan's lawyers argued in court that the Review and Advisory Board's refusal to allow the display of the cross was a violation of the policy of neutrality toward all religious faiths, allegedly enjoined by the First and Fourteenth Amendments to the US Constitution.

The court granted a hearing of the case based on the issues raised regarding the interpretation of the First and Fourteenth Amendments and the exercise of civil rights enshrined in these. At issue is the basic tension inherent in the wording of the First Amendment, which prohibits the government from both legally establishing a religion and interfering with the citizens' freedom to express their private religious opinions. In other words, the First Amendment contains both an Establishment Clause and a Free Speech Clause, and neither is to be interpreted or enforced so as to nullify the other. The majority of Supreme Court justices ruled that the Klan's display of a cross was private religious speech, and despite the proximity to the Ohio Statehouse and its monuments, it could not be mistaken for any endorsement on the part of the State for the particular religious beliefs either symbolized by the cross or acknowledged by the Klan. To deny the Klan's request for a permit to erect the cross, the court held, would be discriminatory, since the Capitol Square had always served as an open forum where groups, religious and non-religious, would exercise their right to free speech, on behalf of a variety of causes. They also rejected the implication that private religious speech, however dear or obnoxious to a majority of the citizenry, was a particular threat to the common good, suggesting that it would be unseemly and distinctly odd to equate private religious speech with other forms of sanctioned expression in which the State had a particular interest, such as pornography or hate speech. So long as public forums were open to all forms of private religious speech, as clearly seemed to be the case at the Capitol Square, the State could not use its police powers to deny the Klan a permit. The fact that some of the citizens might take offence at the erection of a cross in Capitol Square was not a sufficient reason to interfere with the free-speech rights of the Klan. The decision would have been very different, obviously, had the court found that the cross in and of itself constituted a form of hate-speech, or if its erection had privileged the Klan's religious beliefs relative to any others that might be expressed in the Square, or if the cross were a direct interference with the public purpose to which the Square had been dedicated.

Had St James Cathedral decided to fight City Hall and reject the Freedom from Religion Foundation's demand, its legal case, in my view, would have been stronger than that made in defence of the Klan's cross. The Stations were clearly meant as a form of private religious speech. They were erected on public property, a sidewalk adjacent not to the seat of government, but to the church that sponsored the religious display. The precedents for using sidewalks for free-speech purposes are abundant and non-controversial. If the Klan's cross was not found to signify legal definitions of hate-speech then, surely, the Stations of the Cross could not be so construed. So why didn't the Cathedral defend the Way of the Cross and vindicate its First Amendment rights, as so many other groups are doing in their rush to litigate such matters?

I suspect that the Church had two reasons for making the quiet accommodation that it did. First, perhaps a technical point, the Church may have failed to anticipate the need for a permit to display the Stations on public property, and there may have been no clearly established procedure for obtaining one, even if requested. Second, and more tellingly, the Church may have wanted to avoid further controversy because it sensed that the Way of the Cross, despite their good intentions, had stirred up a hornets' nest of issues that the Cathedral at that time was not prepared to deal with. Those issues, I think, have to do with the Church's historic identity and the nature of its contemporary witness in the world. They are, in short, questions for practical theology.

Seeking a Way with Practical Theology

Practical theology is more than a slogan. It is 'critical reflection on religious praxis'. The praxis upon which it reflects is as diverse as the various ministries of the Christian churches, their mission and its histories, and their

impact upon the cultures and societies in which the churches have been organized. As Strain and I once argued, practical theology therefore is necessarily historical. For much of it will be seeking to construct a context, a useable
past, as it were, in which the churches' faithful witness to Jesus of Nazareth
can go forward. The narrative that allows a church to retrieve that useable
past cannot be triumphalistic, either in intent or in effect, for in order to
remain effective witnesses the churches must be able to face squarely their
own mixed record of success and failure, of faithfulness and betrayal, relative to the Spirit of Christ that they believe has animated their path through
our common history.

Critical reflection on St James' Way of the Cross thus must begin with a
disavowal of amnesia, in this case, the false pretence of innocence, as if any
of the Christian churches, but especially the mainline denominations, can
present their witness as though it were as fresh as that first Pentecost, as
though the signals they've sent out in seeking to bear witness, or the policies
— both ecclesiastical and governmental — that they have either enacted or
acquiesced in, have not already had an impact upon our common history,
for good or for ill. The conflicting significations generated by St James' Way
of the Cross certainly confirm just how counterproductive even false impres-
sions can be, especially when the Stations are presented as traffic signs in a
modern urban setting. '*Quo vadis?*' ('Where are you going?') is the question
that both traffic signs and the Way of the Cross are meant to help us answer.
But a spiritually renewing confrontation with Jesus' '*Quo vadis?*', such as the
Cathedral staff may have intended, must be built upon something better
thought through than a jarring, though aesthetically intriguing juxtaposition.

Practical theology, particularly as public theology, seeks to understand
the conditions required for establishing the credibility and authenticity of
the church's witness in the contemporary world. What is the situation of
Christian witness in such a world? Christendom long ago ceased to exist in
Europe and, arguably, never defined the polity that emerged under the US
Constitution. Nevertheless, all Christian churches operating in the USA are
or were at one time immigrant churches, and their religious praxis, their
institutional forms, their policies, their cultural values, and especially their
devotional practices still bear the marks of their ambiguous origins in Christendom. The Cross, alas, hasn't always been a symbol of repentance, of sin
and suffering overcome through grace and faith. It has also been the sign
with which to conquer an Empire, a Crusader's sword with which to smite
the infidel, a stake for burning heretics, and a pretext for pogroms, all of
which in a post-Christendom world can only be regarded as shameful
betrayals of Jesus Christ. Practical theology forces today's Christians to confront this legacy of mixed messages, but when one does so, as the staff at St
James Cathedral, no doubt, has been forced to do, one is left wondering
whether the cross is still retrievable as an authentic symbol of Christian faith
and practice.

poignant question

Practical theology, in short, may force Christians to consider whether the offence of the cross is still a stumbling block, the innocent *skandalon* in which preachers and theologians have gloried since the days of St Paul, a telling sign of sinful resistance to the Will of God. But today Christians must ask themselves whether they have so abused the symbolism of the cross that they themselves have laid down the stumbling block that others seize upon as sufficient reason for ignoring the churches' witness. Such a reading of the context for Christian witness suggests that the cross today presents the churches, less with a scandal, and more with a dilemma. How is it possible to invite non-Christians to participate in the mystery of Christ's passion without making them feel significantly diminished in their personal integrity? How is it possible to respect and celebrate religious pluralism and cultural diversity, without abandoning the churches' constitutive mandate for evangelization? How is it possible, in short, to overcome the unintended offensiveness of the cross without lapsing into total silence?

cross as symbol

There is no quick answer to these questions, nor is it the role of practical theology to provide quick answers. Practical theology is better used simply to help the churches understand the questions that they must address as they seek to serve as faithful witnesses. Though the question regarding the symbolism of the cross may be commonly addressed to all of the churches, practical theology, if it is done properly, will help each of them to formulate an answer that is distinctive and continuous with their own historic experience. In this particular case, once the staff at St James Cathedral were forced by the Freedom from Religion Foundation to confront their own amnesia, they moved almost as swiftly as the City of Chicago to remove the offence, apparently without much consideration as to why it may have been offensive. For a while, the Stations — as I saw them that late Spring afternoon in June — stood on church property, still facing all who pass by, inviting them to stop and think; lately, they have been removed from public view altogether. This outcome may strike some as itself an offence against the Gospel, a capitulation to the privatization of Christian faith that some theorists predict as the inevitable outcome of advanced modernization. Nevertheless, some kind of withdrawal for the sake of critical reflection may be the only authentic way forward so long as any semiotic residue of hegemonic power and coercive authority still clings to the churches.

Is there an alternative, a Christian religious praxis that would be authentically prophetic, appropriately confrontational without giving unintended offence? I would hope so, but I doubt that the mainline denominations, like Roman Catholicism, the Episcopal Church (ECUSA), and others, can grasp it yet. St James' bold attempt to retrieve the Way of the Cross may serve as a cautionary tale, reminding all Christians of the subtle ways in which 'cheap grace' ('cheap' because it is based on an all-too-convenient historical amnesia that allows Christians to claim an innocence that cannot be authentically Christian) undercuts the mission and ministry of the churches in today's urban environment. This tale is not, however, an invitation to take cheap shots against the Cathedral staff, or the mission and ministry of the ECUSA. It is, instead, an invitation for all churches to ask themselves, '*Quo vadis?*' If the Cathedral's well-meaning attempt at an innovative Lenten observance is not an appropriate way to honour the Way of the Cross, what is?

Notes

1 Dennis P. McCann and Charles R. Strain, *Polity and Praxis: A Program for American Practical Theology*, (Minneapolis, MN: Winston-Seabury Press, 1985).
2 *Chicago Reader*, 31 March 1995.

The Ambiguity and Promise of an Urban 'Cross-Road'

Gareth Jones

I have lost touch with the world
Where once I wasted too much time.
Nothing has been heard of me for so long
That they may think me dead.
Though I hardly care
If the world thinks me dead.
Neither can I deny it,
For I am truly dead to the world.
I am dead to the world's bustle
And rest in tranquil space.
I live alone in my heaven,
In my love, in my song.

Friedrich Ruckert[1]

I first saw the Children's Cross in 1994. I was in Chicago for a conference, and wandered by St James Episcopal Cathedral out of curiosity. The Cross was there in the open area on the north side of the Cathedral. It was easy to miss: only ten feet or so tall, it tended to disappear into the background. I was intrigued by it, by its apparent ambivalence to the world around it. Propped up in a city street like that, the cross as a Christian symbol seemed to be diminished. After all, the only other things one usually saw on Chicago's streets were mailboxes and trashcans.[2]

That was the way it was for me, at first. I intellectualized the situation, as academics tend to do. Some days later a friend told me the story behind the Children's Cross. Caroline was a member of the congregation, and understood the Cross's spiritual and devotional relevance for that community. Later still, as the relationship between De Paul and Birmingham was developing, the possibility of a group of colleagues writing about the Cross took shape. No doubt this was because of its suitability as a case study of reli-

gious expression within an urban environment. Certainly, *I* was still thinking about the Cross in very academic terms.

The evidence of this way of thinking can be seen in my title. Academics
love ideas like ambiguity. Theologians love to talk about promise, and when
it's 'the promise of the cross' one even has tradition on one's side. The physical space surrounding the Children's Cross, too, remains an object of philosophical fascination to me. The raw material is all there, in other words, to
write the kind of essay that in 1994 I would have written automatically. And,
in the process, I would have desiccated the Cross. Writing about the Cathedral's memorial to the violent deaths of children in that way would have
reduced everything to the level of an academic exercise. Space, ambiguity,
promise: these ideas have nothing *primary* to do with felt, palpable Christian witness.

So I am not going to do it: I am not going to write an academic paper
about the Children's Cross. I cannot claim that this volte-face is the result of
deep spiritual reflection, though it may indicate an awakening spiritual
crisis; I don't know yet. What I do know, however, is that the subject matter
here is too important to finesse away as some kind of exercise in conceptual
acrobatics. If there is any truth to be found in the Children's Cross, then it
will be found by the heart. The work of the mind may then come as an extra
dimension to that first encounter, but it is most definitely secondary.

Oversight 1

I said that my volte-face might be the result of an awakening spiritual crisis.
Well, that is probably too strong a way of expressing it, but it introduces an
autobiographical point that is relevant here. By the end of 1997 I had had
enough of university life. Not just Birmingham, but the entire academic
world. I had had enough of the endless self-obsession, the intellectual mas-
turbation that too often passes for scholarship, the petty yet very real obses-
sions most shared about status, promotion, income and publications (myself
included). I had had enough, too, of students who treated with cavalier dis-
dain a discipline to which I had devoted fifteen years of my adult life, and
which was the only career I was ever likely to have. So I called 'time out!' and
took three years secondment. I accepted a position with the Church of England as theological consultant to the House of Bishops, in the belief that
when I went back to Birmingham I would do so as a wiser theologian,
shaped and seasoned by my close encounter with the Church.[3]

The more cynical (or anxious) of my friends reasoned that this move was
an outlandish roll of the dice by a tired young man, one who needed a good
rest instead of endless wrangling with dozens of English bishops. And they
were probably right, in one sense. But I clung to the idea of a second sense:
that, through sheer exposure, I might yet come into fuller contact with the
primary reality of the worshipful Christian life. And I was right. Working

for the House of Bishops was endlessly bizarre, and now is not the time or place to explore the tragic and comedic dimensions of this reality (though deck chairs and very large boats immediately come to mind). But it was also endlessly *religious*, in the ordinary sense of that word.

All of this is a very roundabout way of saying that sitting in my office in the Church of England in 1999, I was much closer to the world of the Children's Cross than I ever was standing right next to it in 1994. I inhabited a world of oversight, of *episcope*, in which I helped to service the responsibility undertaken by others. Or, stated more bluntly: bishops are given the gift of pastoral oversight, which gift thereby makes them a bishop. And I worked as part of an office (the General Synod Office) that has responsibility for carrying out the wishes of the House of Bishops. I was a church civil servant, in other words.

It is easy to see oversight in very hierarchical terms, and since 'hierarchy' was originally a religious word before its politicization in the modern world, this is probably fair. But at the same time it would be wrong to understand hierarchy itself as something that inevitably stratifies Christian identity, so that bishops sit above priests, who sit above deacons, who sit above the laity. That makes no sense, a point that is easy to illustrate simply by referring to the Children's Cross in Chicago. No doubt at some stage the Bishop was consulted about the project, as undoubtedly the Dean was. But the Cross's erection was an expression of the will of the congregation *as a whole*, which tells us something important about oversight and its true meaning.

What do I mean by this argument? Think about the position of the Cross in relation to the Cathedral. The Cathedral sits on a city block, with a pavement all the way around it. The Cross was sited at one corner of that block, in the middle of the pavement, about seventy yards from the Cathedral in one direction, and the same distance from the diocesan offices in another. The physical dimensions of the situation are fairly evocative. Both the Cathedral and the offices looked over the Cross, but those seventy yards are significant, too. They establish a tension between the act of witness and its administrative and liturgical homes that one cannot help but notice. Maybe one thinks that the Cross is thrust out into the city, and that it is sustained by its relationship to Cathedral and offices. Perhaps one thinks the Cross is held at arm's length by the two, because they care not to embrace it too closely. Either way – or any other way – there is a gap between the buildings of the Church, and the Cross. And that gap dislocates the Children's Cross, in a very real and ordinary sense of the word 'dislocation'. The Cross might be on the same city block as the Cathedral and diocesan offices, but that is not how it is always *experienced*.

This takes us into sensitive areas, and I don't think it's right to speak here of anyone's intentions when the Children's Cross was erected as a memorial to the violent deaths of too many young people in Chicago. I do not suppose for one moment that anyone at the Cathedral or in its congregation wanted the Cross to be semi-detached from its surroundings, because that is not how one intends to exercise oversight of the faith's witness or its foundational symbols and events. Nevertheless, that is the reality of the situation, and it is one that is entirely fitting. Just as I do not think it is appropriate to judge the intentions of the people involved with the Children's Cross project, so I do not think one can judge the intentions behind the *real* cross. Without being trite about it, Christ too was thrust out into the world; Christ too was dislocated, and remains constantly dislocated for the sake of those who may or may not be saved in and by his name (such dis-location being the point of the Incarnation, so to speak). Whether by brilliant design, or accident of circumstance, the Children's Cross evokes something that is fundamental to our encounter with Jesus Christ, if we claim to have such an encounter.

Whether or not it evokes something that is deemed *appropriate* is, however, another matter. Traditionally, the siting of crosses in or by churches has tended to follow certain set patterns. One would expect, therefore, to find crosses above the altar, inside a church; or on top of a spire or tower, outside. One would expect to find quite a lot of crosses in a church yard, certainly (though this is not the case at St James), and it is definitely considered appropriate to have crosses present around a church's walls at certain key times of the liturgical year (Easter, for example). To have a cross thrust out into the world, however, as the Children's Cross was, is an exercise in distanciation that creates new tensions for Christian witness in that situation. Simply provoking the city populace, or courting controversy with non-Christian citizens, important though such things might be, is not the point as far as I am concerned. Rather, I am concerned about what this situation tells us about the truth of the cross. And I think what the positioning of the Children's Cross tells us is that oversight is not about something called 'pastoral care' in any generalized, insipid sense, but is rather about something strong and forthright and confrontational.

It would be easy at this stage to quote Dietrich Bonhoeffer's *Letters and Papers from Prison*, to the effect that God's being pushed out of the world, onto the cross, is an expression of God's overwhelming love. A few years ago I might well have pursued such a course, which comes so naturally to a student of modern theology. What I am more struck by today, however, is the sheer anger and indignation that the Children's Cross depicts. This Cross memorializes the names of children struck down by violence, and there is nothing peaceful or innately comforting about that process of remembering. Oversight in this sense is motivated by moral outrage, so that the presence of the Cathedral and diocesan offices, literally *over seeing* the Cross, should be the presence of something more than ecclesial bureaucracy. It should be the presence of prophetic indignation, in which respect we should recognise the Children's Cross for what it really is: a vivid tableau of New Testament witness, several blocks west of Michigan Avenue, Chicago. To put it bluntly, when we read Jesus saying in the New Testament, 'Suffer little children to come unto me', we should be struck both by the bitter irony of the literal truth of this sentiment, and its appalling *wrongness*.

If this sounds like a somewhat long-winded way of saying that I think the cathedral was right to authorise the erection of the Children's Cross, then that is only a very small part of the story. Erecting or not erecting the Children's Cross was a moment of decision, of *kairos*, of the kind that the Church faces every day of every week. What makes it also into an *episcopal* moment is the conviction of the bishop and the congregation to share their outrage and witness with the world around them, in as straightforward a way as possible. For in the final analysis, when one speaks of oversight one also needs to ask, 'What is actually being *seen*?' In the case of the Children's Cross, the answer to this question is very clear: Christian duty in the face of appalling suffering.

Oversight 2

These last few thoughts start to take me into areas where others, for example Janet Campbell or Jule Ward and James Halstead in this book, are better qualified to comment. I do not live in Chicago, and I do not live in the neighbourhoods where the victims remembered on the Children's Cross were killed. There is something voyeuristic about coming too close to their names and faces, if all one comes to do is look. And if one comes to do more than look, then such activity rightly begins closer to home than the Mid-West. If one finds the Children's Cross in any way compelling, then it should be a compulsion that has practical results in one's own local community or church.

At the same time, however, that tentative suggestion of relocation, of taking the Cross, at least in terms of its meaning, and transplanting it into new ground, raises a fundamental difficulty which as theologians and interpreters we are forced to face. In one respect, the Children's Cross is firmly rooted in certain local, Chicago streets: even on the level of speculative Christian doctrine, there is nothing much more concrete than the death of children and their memorialization on the limbs of the cross. In another respect, however, the act of distanciation whereby St James thrust the Cross out into the streets and sidewalks of the Gold Coast created the very conditions whereby people could pass it by. To put it in the simplest language: by creating gaps around the Cross in the Cathedral plaza, people could simply walk by and ignore it. And they did, every day.

This brings me to the second sense of 'oversight' that I want to consider, namely, 'overlooking' as avoidance. It is, after all, easy to overlook the Children's Cross. Even if one is standing quite close to it, it is still easy to miss the fact that children's names are written on its surface. By stretching the distance between the Cross and the Cathedral and diocesan offices as far as they could, the people who erected the Cross took a calculated risk, whether they realised it or not. They risked the fact that people would *walk between* the Cross and its sponsoring institutions. Again, this was either a masterstroke or a mistake, depending upon how one looks at it. Either way, however, it raised for discussion an aspect of oversight that requires every bit as much attention as the more traditional variety.

If one thinks about the degree to which Christianity is overlooked in the modern world, the results are shocking. At the latest count, there were over 20,000 different Christian denominations in the world. And yet, at least in modern western society, we now live in a world where Christian symbols are either corrupted by extensive commercial pressures – for example, the sponsorship and thereby manipulation of Christmas decorations in central London – or else widely ignored. Certainly, this is far truer in the UK than the USA, where there is a more honoured tradition of churchgoing. But it remains a general characteristic of the western world/northern hemisphere, to such an extent that in the eyes of many Christianity and capitalism are inextricably, and detrimentally, interwoven. Whether this world is now viewed as a series of commodities, one of which is Christianity, or indeed as a post-Christian tableau of competing narratives and rhetorics, the fact remains that churches are substantially challenged by the world of late modernity.

This is precisely the world, of course, in which St James Episcopal Cathedral finds itself in Chicago; indeed, that world forms a large part of its congregation (the previously mentioned Gold Coast). One could argue, therefore, that by erecting the Children's Cross in the way that it did, in full sight/oversight of the world of late capitalism, the Cathedral was throwing into relief its own relationship with that society. That this was done in such a way as to make as ambiguous as possible the character of that relationship – the Children's Cross, after all, is not *sponsored* – simply serves to highlight the fundamental tension; i.e., that modernity has created a 'space' in which one can 'pass by' Christianity. Going to the trouble of erecting one's most basic symbol in the midst of that space, as St James did with the Children's Cross, throws into sharpest relief the nature of the problem I am trying to wrestle with at this juncture, namely, the distance between the Church and the modern world.[4]

It is certainly true, of course, that such an action has missiological value, even if, as I would contend, far more people simply passed by the Cross without noticing it than were drawn into the Cathedral. The deeper question, however, is to what extent *any* missiological witness is effective in the modern world. When even two-thousand years old institutions like the Christian Church can be reduced to the level of commodities, to be bought and sold in the marketplace (witness the Alpha Course in the UK), mission *per se* is reduced to near total ineffectualness. This may not be the case in South Korea, or Latin America; but it certainly is the case in the UK and the USA, and probably in a lot of other places, too. If the distance between the Church and society is made so great because, paradoxically, it is made infinitesimally small by the massive engines of commercialism, then the two simply become separate, rather than distinct. Then one needs to speak not of a constructive though tense relationship between the two, but of the replacement of the latter by the former. Once this has taken place one either has to go with the flow – which has been the resort of far too much theological liberalism – or reject the game entirely, a strategy that is advocated by John Milbank's Radical Orthodoxy, amongst others.

Have things really become that bad? This is the moot point, one that I think the Children's Cross addresses with considerable relevance. From the perspective of those who would simply reject the relationship between Christianity and modernity, erecting the Cross in the first place was at best an act of mindless folly, at worst one of desecration – not of public space, but of the crucifixion. On this reading, the correct place for the cross is in church, from where it judges the world (good Johannine theology, of course). For those like myself, however, who are simultaneously fascinated and exercised by the relationship between Christianity and modernity, finding in it the moral obligation of the present generation, the Children's Cross is profoundly important. Why? because in a very real sense the distance which lies at the heart of the Cathedral plaza is the same as Lessing's 'dirty great ditch' of history. It is the distance we must leap, faithfully and imaginatively, if we are to make any sense of the cross (and thereby the Incarnation) in today's world.

I am not at all convinced that the Children's Cross successfully addresses this situation; in fact, I think it probably does not. But that hardly matters. The point of the Cross, on reflection, is to ask that question which is fundamental to the relationship between Christianity and modernity. It offers no answer, because there is no answer, apart from in faith, hope and love. What the Children's Cross achieves is to measure out the distance between the Church and the world, thereby identifying a gap which is both increasingly wide and increasingly narrow. Whether we pass through that gap, or stop in front of it, or step around it ('Not possible!'), or fall down before it, or turn our back on it, is not a question that can be answered by the Cross itself. It *can*, we hope and pray, be answered by the cross of Jesus Christ. But in making a distinction between the cross and the Cross – a distinction I have employed throughout this essay – I am asking the hardest question of all: is the Children's Cross actually *true*?

This is the question I want to address in the final part of this essay. Before I turn to it, however, I want to make one qualification. What I am about to write cannot ever constitute a judgement; it can only ever be a meditation. The point I have reached in my own spiritual journey is sufficiently confused without taking responsibility, however spurious, for those of others whom I do not know and have not even met. That said, I think it is a significant meditation; for the Cross asks us how we embrace the cross.

Violence, Memory and the Cross/cross

At the 1988 Lambeth Conference the then Archbishop of Canterbury, Robert Runcie, gave an opening address entitled 'The Nature of the Unity We Seek'. In it Runcie articulated a claim about the fundamental character of the Church:

> In and through such unholy conflict the Church eventually, and never without difficulty, came to a common mind. Through the initiatives of prophets and primates, the deliberations of synods, and the active response of the whole Church, the Holy Spirit has been at work. Conflict can be destructive. It can also be creative. We are not here to avoid conflict but to redeem it. At the heart of our faith is a cross and not, as in some religions, an eternal calm.

There are two important points here, leaving aside Runcie's position both within the Church of England and thereby the Anglican Communion (because I am not interested now in intra-Anglican church politics). First, Runcie makes conflict central to the Christian experience, because it is central to the historical character of the Incarnation and Christ's death. Runcie does not mention it here, but the corollary of conflict is violence. In redeeming conflict, therefore, the cross redeems violence; through specific violence – to Jesus – the crucified God redeems *all* violence. Secondly, Runcie relates the doctrine of the Holy Spirit to the redemption of conflict and violence. It is not simply, therefore, a matter of the cross being the moment of redemption, but of that moment being made continually anew through the sanctifying power of the Spirit. If I had more space here I might say something now about eschatological realism, and the openness of revelation in which we still find ourselves struggling for definition (for the story has yet to end). But it is enough to make the basic point: what began in Jesus Christ, continues now in Jesus Christ, in both cases in, by, and through the power of the Holy Spirit.

Two questions are thereby addressed to the Children's Cross in Chicago, both of them corollaries of Runcie's 1988 argument. First, does the Cross present the cross as the redemption of conflict and violence, not in terms of 'eternal calm', but rather in terms of recognizing the true nature of such conflict and violence? I think we can answer this question in the affirmative. The Cross is the *Children's* Cross, and it addresses their deaths realistically rather than sentimentally. The issues which centre themselves upon the Cross are not to do with the integrity of the people who erected it, after all, but rather its position and its signification.

Secondly, does the Children's Cross represent the work of the Holy Spirit? This is more difficult to answer. On the one hand, the Cross presents closure at just that point where I think the doctrine of the Holy Spirit intends us to think of openness, namely, the point of equation between the Cross and the cross. This is problematic, because it simply is not enough to state that the violent deaths of children is embraced by the death of Christ, without thereby also registering a massive shout of protest at the injustice of any such equation, however divine its initiative might appear. On the other hand, however, the positioning of the Cross, and the challenge it threw down to the way in which one understands the relationship between Christianity and society, should be regarded as the work of the Holy Spirit. And this, of course, is the inadvertent ambiguity of the Children's Cross: that it brings together closure and openness, completeness and incompleteness, and watches whilst the cross is crushed between the dimensions of late modernity and its attendant democratic capitalism.

Can a simple memorial, well-intentioned and sincere, carry the weight of such an interpretation? Unfortunately, it is simply a fact that any such memorial, particularly one that deploys the symbol of the cross, cannot avoid it. It is, after all, the weight of memory; or, perhaps, Lessing's ditch of history once more. For what is it that one remembers? And what *is* the constitution of one's memories? If one says that one *imagines* one's memories – because they cannot be retrieved objectively – then does this make all such religious remembering into an aesthetic process? I think it probably does, and this does not matter, as long as we remember that aesthetic processes are not *just* aesthetic processes (at least, they do not have to be just such things). They can also be acts of violence and conflict, and they can be acts of reconciliation, too. What makes the Children's Cross an important example of this idea in action is not its relative success or failure (such as it can be ascertained), but rather its thrusting of that moment into the midst of Christianity's relationship with society. This is not an apologetic moment. On the contrary, it is powerful, even if we do not know what that power is, or how it works. And that, finally, is why the Cross is both ambiguous and promising: because it challenges us to make something of *it*, or risk making nothing of *ourselves*.

Conclusion

Well, at this point I risk falling directly into devotional writing, rather than the kind of critical work that should characterize the academic's style. It's a writing style that comes more naturally when one works directly for the Church, when practical (that is to say, spiritual) questions and issues need to be addressed without qualification. That is what the Cathedral congregation did, of course, when they erected the Children's Cross. Their witness was and is devotional. The Cross's ambiguity has nothing to do with original act at all. It's ambiguity is found entirely in what the Cross symbolizes – violence, forgiveness, redemption – and *then* the way in which people interpret it. One cannot blame the congregation for this: it is simply the way things are, the way they always have been.

If all of this hints at incompleteness, then that is fortunate; for incompleteness is where I want to conclude this (itself incomplete) essay. Whereas previously I would have interpreted incompleteness philosophically, however, I now want to do so architecturally and in that way spiritually and theologically. It seems to me that there is an analogy to be drawn between the Children's Cross in Chicago and Gaudi's *Sagrada Familia* in Barcelona, started in the nineteenth century and 'due' to be completed in around 2025. I say 'due', because there is a school of thought that argues that Gaudi's cathedral should never be completed, because Gaudi never completed its plans. What one has, instead, is a work in progress: a continuing witness to an idea, an insight, and a conception.

The analogy, of course, is with the incomplete character of Jesus' cross, and therefore any witness to it. Or, as we should say: the analogy is with the incomplete because not yet completed *revelation* of our redemption through Jesus' cross. Like Gaudi's *Sagrada Familia*, the Children's Cross is incomplete, because it witnesses to something of which we can have no final knowledge. The fact that Gaudi's building is materially incomplete, whereas the Cross has been finished for years, is irrelevant; that is simply the outward and visible sign of something inward and invisible.

This, finally, is the point of the Cross, like *Sagrada Familia*: by depicting our sacramental reality, it somehow becomes part of our sacramental reality. And just as with every other part of that reality, it can be ignored or rejected, overlooked and passed by. To ask it to be anything more is to negate the constructive tension that exists between ambiguity and promise; i.e., the 'not yet-ness' of our Christian existence now. The true cost of discipleship, after all, is not to be found solely in the sacrifices Christians have to make in following Jesus Christ. It is also to be found in following Jesus Christ without knowing for sure *that* one follows him. It is a cost that the children of Chicago memorialized on the Cross perhaps never had the chance to pay. But the Cathedral chose to pay it on their behalf, not in erecting the Cross, but in the life to which the Cross makes witness. Like Janus, the Cross faces two ways at once.

And here I stop. I do not know whether or not what I have written is 'true', in the sense that it accurately portrays the intentions of some people in Chicago. But it does portray accurately the way in which I now think about the Children's Cross, and also the way in which I think about many other such memorials. There is much more that can be said, of course, and a lot of it has been said in the essays in this book. But there is virtue, too, in saying nothing more, because finally the cross is not about this world, but God's; its words are always simply reflections of one Word. And that must also be the final prayer said around the Cross, that its mute witness is truly the presence of something more than wood and nails and names:

I am dead to the world's bustle
And rest in tranquil space.
I live alone in my heaven,
In my love, in my song.

Notes

1 Ruckert's poem *Ich bin der Welt abhanden gekommen* was set by Gustav Mahler. I encountered Mahler's song, and therefore Ruckert's text, in a recording by Ann Sofie von Otter (Deutsche Grammophon 439 928-2GH). The translation from the German original is my own.

2 Since the first version of this essay was written, the Children's Cross has been taken inside St James Episcopal Cathedral, away from its public space. I have decided against altering the tenor of my piece, however. It remains an interpretation of the Cross as it was, rather than an intellectual autopsy. The reader can bear in mind the Cross's present fate (as outlined in the essays by Janet Campbell and Jule Ward and Jim Halstead earlier in this volume) as she thinks about the points I make.

3 As things turned out, I never returned to Birmingham: in July 1999 I was appointed to the chair in Christian theology at Christ Church University College, Canterbury.

4 This is obviously a complex question, and I do not think for one second that it can be reduced to any single issue, least of all the presence of Christian symbols in a secular world.

The Violated Body and the Nausea of Memory

Charles R. Strain

Chicago's Passion Narrative

On 21 March 1997 Lenard Clark, an African American boy, aged 13, was pulled from his bike and beaten by three white teenagers. Clark had ridden from his home in a largely black public housing complex on Chicago's South Side into the largely white neighbourhood of Bridgeport to play a game of basketball. Clark remained in a coma for over one week and suffered permanent brain damage. The severity of his beating as well as its racial motivation drew national as well as local media attention. The occurrence of the crime at the onset of Holy Week inevitably drew comparisons with the Passion narrative. The beating also coincided with my initial efforts to think through the meaning of the Children's Cross. In Chicago, as elsewhere, the violence against children goes on and on.

The violence directed against Clark may have been part of a recurring loop, violence masquerading as the snake that eats its tail only to generate itself anew, but it lost thereby none of its disruptive power. We are worldly bodies. As bodies we extend ourselves across fields of possibilities. Through our bodies we act to shape a world; we link ourselves with other bodies by means of words; we 'voice' our concerns. Intermingling with other bodies, we transgress the fixed boundaries of flesh. Pain drives us back within those boundaries, corrals us. 'In serious pain', Elaine Scarry argues, 'the claims of the body utterly nullify the claims of the world'.[1] If 'voice' is our most resourceful means of projecting ourselves beyond the limits of the fleshly body, pain cancels voice, renders us mute except for the most inarticulate of sounds. If memory, like imagination, is our worldly body extending itself in time as well as in space, severe pain destroys all psychological content. Experiencing 'blinding pain', we literally lose the ability to perceive let alone remember.[2]

For those days in which he remained in a coma, Lenard Clark was literally without memory or voice. He may even have been temporarily beyond pain. By situating his beating within the Passion narrative, the framework of Holy Week, we joined him to those innocents whose suffering is remembered as transformative. I too took part in this twin ritual of memory and voice but with a deepening unease. What was it about our assertion of moral voice that was both so shrill and profoundly self-congratulatory? Voicing our condemnation of Clark's attackers, we simultaneously inflated our own moral standing. *We*, in the *civilized* parts of the city, would never be tainted by such savagery. What was it about the way in which we remembered another's pain, about our haste to redeem it and to insert it within the passion narrative, that was both so soothing and so self-deceiving? Is there any way that we could have avoided betraying one who suffered violence when we spoke, allegedly, on his behalf?

I will address the issues raised by these questions in three stages. First, I will address the way in which both secular and religious narratives condemning brutal violence carefully isolate us (whoever the 'us' may be) from complicity with evil. Engaged Buddhism's application of the traditional Buddhist teaching of dependent co-arising, I will argue, provides one *upaya*, one skilful means, for transcending this spurious sense of moral superiority. Second, I will explore the problematic dynamics of giving voice to the voiceless, of speaking on behalf of those silenced by death or those who, like Lenard Clark while he struggled to regain consciousness, can only groan with pain. Finally, I will ask what kind of practice, attentive to the body, might redeem the narratives of witness and healing, whose banal repetition in the face of the enormities of mass murder or the relentless pounding of everyday violence drains them of all transformative power.[3] Though we cannot help but create narratives to resist violence, to reorient ourselves amidst moral chaos, and to redeem our lives, this process, I suggest, is perilous, involving as it does our own moral transformation.

Engaged Buddhism, Dependent Co-arising and the Transformation of the Moral Memory and Imagination

Time lapses. Read today, the earliest reports of Lenard Clark's beating in the *Chicago Tribune* seem positively surreal. While Clark's slow recovery would later capture the media, the first order of business apparently was to rehabilitate the neighbourhood and the city. A Chicago police spokesperson described the event as 'strictly a random act of violence based upon racial hatred'. The boy's father was quoted as saying that the beating was a 'senseless act' perpetrated by 'a few stupid people'. In the days that followed, that phrase 'a few stupid people' would be repeated, by the Mayor of Chicago among others, like a mantra to ward off evil. Bridgeport residents lamented that the beating was 'bad for the neighbourhood'. 'We have all kinds come in here', insisted a city official at the park where the beating occurred, 'and I've never seen any problems'.[4]

Subsequent articles probing the history of racial relationships in the neighbourhood made it harder to maintain this line but they did so none the less at the cost of a narrative riddled with contradictions. 'The attack on Clark was an aberration, according to dozens of blacks and whites in the area', an article entitled 'Unwritten Rules Remain in Bridgeport', maintained. Yet it immediately went on to say:

> Blacks said that racism in this part of town now usually manifests itself in more subtle ways: a steely glance from a distrustful merchant, the n-word shouted from a carload of youths and a snub at a fast-food stand packed with whites. Because of these experiences, many blacks continue to adhere to an unwritten code of conduct on how to avert problems around Bridgeport: Stay in the main streets and out of residential areas, get out of the neighbourhood before dark, and mind your own business.[5]

Similarly a graph showing the *decline* in hate crimes in Chicago in 1997 was contradicted by a statement indicating that the Bridgeport area had the second *highest* number of reported hate crimes. A statement by a Catholic Bishop lamenting the fact that all three assailants were current or former students of a Catholic high school and vowing to fight racism in that school was juxtaposed with a quotation from the school's president regretting the crime but praising his school for its commitment to racial diversity.[6]

What was going on here? It is as if the brutality of the beating was a contagion that threatened to engulf us all. To suggest that a racially motivated beating was simply the most recent eruption of a latent virus was unthinkable. The first narrative duty was containment. To this end journalists and their readers entered into complicity. *We* acknowledged the everyday violence of racism (the steely glances; the n-word flung from a passing car) but denied that it had anything to do with the violence directed at Lenard Clark whose beating remained 'an aberration', the act of 'a few stupid people'.

This narrative line reached its climax in a *Chicago Tribune* editorial on 25 March. Acknowledging that the 'sickening brutality' of the crime was 'a gut-wrenching reminder of decades past', it saw a 'heartening measure of progress' in the fact that it did not become the 'flash-point' for wider racial confrontation. Again, it repeated the mantra of 'a few stupid people' reminding us that 'every neighbourhood has them'. Lenard Clark's pain was not entirely forgotten; rather, it was seen as a 'devastating reminder of how far *some* of us have yet to go'. But it is the 'larger view', this 'testament to how far we have come', that prevailed.[7]

As the *Tribune*'s editorial concern about a possible 'flash-point' indicated, violence, indeed, is seen as a contagion. If it smashes the physical boundaries of an intact body, it threatens the social body as well. This strenuous narrative effort to isolate the criminals and to insulate the crime seems designed to heal the threatened social body by denying that the violence touches it at all. Steely glances and n-words notwithstanding, the brutal beating must remain a random, senseless aberration. It does not erupt out of a history of racial violence because that history is 'decades past'. The physical body of Lenard Clark might remain in a coma, but the moral health of the social body is intact. What arises, perhaps, out of a deep sense of unease about the possible endemic quality of racist violence culminates in a strenuous affirmation of the moral rectitude of the majority. Our moral rectitude is anchored through a narrative of progress. Our racial D-Days are behind us.

The *Tribune*'s telling of the story in the immediate aftermath of the beating of Lenard Clark performs one of the functions of a modern ideology, as engaged Buddhist Ken Jones sees it.

> As a relatively comprehensive explanation of social reality, [ideology] gives a stronger and more reassuring picture of reality to those who uphold it, and may legitimize their own place in the world ... Lionel Trilling, in his *Liberal Imagination*, defined ideology as 'the habit or the ritual of showing respect for certain formulas to which, for various reasons having to do with emotional safety, we have very strong ties but of whose meaning and consequences in actuality we have no clear understanding'.[8]

One striking consequence of the way we narrate stories like Lenard Clark's is that we employ the same kind of 'us versus them' formulas in our attempts to reassure ourselves of our moral rectitude that, presumably, Clark's assailants used to sanction their own violence. Only the referents of 'we' and 'they' are shifted.

I have found in Engaged Buddhism an analysis of this malaise and, perhaps, a way to escape it. 'Do not be bound to any doctrine, theory or ideology', argues Thich Nhat Hanh, a Vietnamese monk who led the Buddhist peace movement during the war in Vietnam and who now lives in exile in France. 'All systems of thought are guiding means. They are not absolute truth ... Peace can only be achieved when we are not attached to views.'[9] But how is it that we become attached to views? Ken Jones argues that we resolve the chaos of ignorance, doubt, moral ambiguity and, above all, the threat of difference by creating or adopting cognitive and emotional maps that confirm the self through a system of 'weighted polarizations'. That the myriad things are reduced to self-confirming polarities is the initial gerrymandering of reality. Weighted polarizations become 'socially amplified' through a process of 'antithetical bonding'. We choose sides. Rather, we create the very idea of 'sides'. In the context of modernity this is one of the tasks of ideologies. They are the means for demarcating social reality, for legitimating one pole over against another, for viewing boundaries and antithetical bonds as the order of things. The transformation of such an ideology into a 'master theory' capable of involving millions of people is, at the psychological level at least, an almost imperceptible shift.[10]

Engaged Buddhism seeks to dissolve the weighted polarizations by focusing upon the doctrine of dependent co-arising (Pali: *pattica sammupada*) as the basis for any mindful engagement, any expression of moral voice. In its most trenchant formulation in the Pali canon the doctrine insists: 'This being, that becomes; from the arising of this, that occurs; this not being, that becomes not; from the ceasing of this, that ceases'. At its core this teaching is not an abstract conceptualization of reality but a 'seeing which amounts to a reorganization of personality'.[11] Fully expanded, dependent co-arising redefines the moral self as a non-self whose three basic traits, according to Thich Nhat Hanh, are 'interbeing', 'interpenetration', and 'interdependence'. Interbeing 'because everything is made of everything else'. Interpenetration 'because everything contains everything else'. Interdependence because 'each thing depends on all other things to be'.[12] Through this redefinition of the moral self, engaged Buddhism reveals the extent to which the assertion of moral voice against, say, the attackers of Lenard Clark is covertly designed to establish boundaries between the self and the unholy other.

It is one thing to assert the theory of dependent co-arising as the antidote to the pathologies of modern ideologies and of public expressions of moral condemnation. It is another to apply it. In a poem that he has recited on many occasions Thich Nhat Hanh creates a new paradigm for social engagement, for the worldly extension of moral voice. 'Please Call Me By My True Names', like the parables of Jesus, permanently transforms the way in which we remember evil. The poem begins not with the remembrance of a traumatic past but in a sweet present. 'Do not say that I'll depart tomorrow / even today I am still arriving. / Look deeply: every second I am arriving / to be a bud on a Spring branch'. Reciting the poem, 'I' am identified with the arising and ceasing of all beings. With equanimity I say 'I am' a bird consuming the mayfly or a grass-snake silently approaching the frog. But in three abrupt stanzas Thich Nhat Hanh plunges us into a moral heart of darkness. 'I am', the narrator continues, a child in Uganda starving to death and the arms merchant whose deadly trade consumes the wealth of Uganda. 'I am' the inmate in a labour camp and the one who sentences him for 'crimes against the state'. In between these images of personal pain and systemic evil, at the very heart of the poem, is an image of arresting singularity.

I am the 12-year old girl,
refugee on a small boat,
who throws herself into the ocean
after being raped by a sea pirate.
And I am the pirate,
my heart not yet capable
of seeing and loving.[13]

Compare this poem with the narratives about the beating of Lenard Clark, with all their efforts to insulate the crime and isolate the criminals. Compare also the sense of time: Lenard Clark's story narrated as the unfortunate resurgence of a past happily (mostly) behind us versus a very precise event not fixed in the past but vitally constitutive of who I am. Dependent co-arising is the reorganization of the moral personality in ways that, initially at least, horrify. No wonder we hasten to bond ourselves over against those 'few stupid people' who bear the stigma of their violent acts.

Imagine a narrative that would acknowledge without flinching the full moral meaning of dependent co-arising. In 'Press Clippings', Argentinean writer-in-exile Julio Cortazar did just this by blurring the line separating fact from fiction. A sculptor, living in Paris, asks a writer who is a fellow political exile to draft the narrative for an exhibit whose theme is political violence. Cortazar's story is initially framed by an actual press clipping which records the litany of horrors experienced by one extended family at the hands of the Argentinean authorities in the late 1970s and early 1980s. Unlike the clippings telling the story of Clark which create a spurious sense of moral superiority, this clipping evokes 'the nausea of memories' in both the sculptor and the writer.

> 'You can see, all this is worth nothing', the sculptor said, sweeping his arm through the air ... 'I've spent months making this shit, you write books, that woman denounces atrocities, we attend congresses and round tables to protest, we almost come to believe that things are changing, and then all you need is two minutes of reading to understand the truth again, to – '.[14]

Engulfed in the horror of the clipping, the writer wanders the night streets of Paris. She is mesmerized by one detail, a mother's description of the loss of her daughter: 'All they would show me of my daughter were the hands cut off her body and placed in a jar that carried the number 24.'[15] Through a bizarre series of circumstances the writer witnesses the torture of a woman by her husband. Again, it is a single detail that transfixes the writer: 'Before understanding, accepting being part of that, there was time for the papa to withdraw the cigarette and bring it up to his mouth again, time to enliven the lighted end and savoir the excellent French tobacco, time for me to see the body burned from the stomach to the neck.'[16] The writer rescues the woman only to become complicit with her in torturing the torturer. Reality blurs and the torture session is interwoven with the memory of the events described in the press clipping. Later, the writer hands in the story of this confused night as the text for an exhibit on violence. Still later, the sculptor sends the writer another press clipping in which the events happening to the writer on the night streets of Paris are told in lurid detail as having happened in the suburbs of Marseilles. That, too, becomes another layer, another frame to the narrative for the exhibit on violence.[17] Bracketed by the 'press clippings', violence, real or imagined, gorges memory. Memory, for its part, ceases to be firmly attached to a single person with a distinct history. Memory ceases to appropriate what is properly mine, to give content to a bounded life. Cortazar intensifies the meaning of dependent co-arising: I can no longer cling to the memory of a distinct personal history in which I never tortured, never severed hands, never pirated, never raped, though I may well acknowledge the co-arising of the sea pirate or the Argentinean dictator with my action and inaction. Instead, the line between what I have done and what you have done dissolves. So does the line between what I remember having done and what I imagine as what I might have done.

Voice and the Inversion of the Structure of Violence

Cortazar's heroine may choke on her 'memory' but she must speak as well. However complex and ambiguous one's moral stance has become, it is equally imperative to tell the story, to give voice to those who are voiceless because they are either dead, imprisoned or silenced by their pain. So, Cortazar's narrative becomes layered, the convoluted story itself framed by successive press clippings, one presumably factual the other no less morally truthful for utterly blurring the line of fact and fiction.

I believe that we can understand the moral dynamics of giving voice to the voiceless better by turning to Elaine Scarry's treatment of what she calls the 'invariable' structure of torture as the paradigm for the acts of violence that we have been considering, whether we focus on state sponsored terrorism or on the 'everyday violence' experienced by Lenard Clark and the twelve-year-old Vietnamese refugee.[18] My thesis is this: the narratives that we create in response to such cases of rape, torture and murder are, ideally, the attempted inversion of the structure of violence.

According to Scarry, that structure is rooted in the perverse interaction of pain and power that is, in turn, grounded in the 'body [as] the locus of pain, and the voice [as] the locus of power'.[19] Recall what I said earlier about the worldly body extending itself interactively and powerfully remaking its world. Pain is a 'corporeal engulfment'. It forces us back into the confines of the physical body, shrivels our worldly extension, cancels language (voice). It unmakes our world.[20] It is, according to Scarry, the torturer's self-conscious intent not only to inflict pain on a prisoner but to use pain to unmake the prisoner's world. Actually aspiring to 'the totality of pain', the torturer creates a simulacrum of power. This sense of power derives from the dual nature of a weapon in the hand of the one who wields it, the weapon is a tool, an amplification of the body's power; at the receiving end the weapon creates pain, forces the self out of its world into the prison of the body-in-pain. Torture transforms all of the insignia of a human, civilized life-made objects such as rooms, chairs, lights, electric generators, forms of human interaction such as conversations and letters from loved ones, human emotions such as loyalty towards one's friends and love for one's family-into weapons.[21]

In the unmaking of the prisoner's world, the torturer finds his 'obsessive sense of agency' confirmed. Dependent co-arising is perversely twisted. The torturer's feeling of power and that of the regime that would be founded on this twisted ritual co-arise with the prisoner's feeling of pain. With the prisoner's terror of absolute vulnerability arises the torturer's illusion of absolute invulnerability.

> Now, at least for the duration of this obscene and pathetic drama, it is not the pain but the regime that is incontestably real, not the pain but the regime that is total ... Ultimate domination requires ... that the prisoner become a colossal body with no voice and the torturer a colossal voice ... with no body, that the prisoner experience himself exclusively in terms of sentience and the torturer exclusively in terms of self-extension.[22]

Torture expresses the simulacrum of power, power that can never create but only destroy because it is based on 'the dream of absolute non-reciprocity'. The prisoner's vulnerability hides the torturer's own vulnerability. To maintain this illusion of non-reciprocity requires multiple layers of self-deception, one of which is the denial of the inflicted pain that establishes the torturer's illusion of power.[23] 'This hurts me more than it hurts you' is not merely a sick joke; the compulsive expression of such thoughts in situations of torture is the precise index of the self-delusion that ensouls the simulacrum. In opposition to this cruel parody of dependent co-arising in acts of violence, Scarry argues that the full range of efforts to restore voice to the voiceless from words of support secretly communicated to political prisoners to the letter writing campaigns of Amnesty International 'become not only a denunciation of the pain but a partial reversal of the process of torture itself'.[24]

To illuminate Scarry's contention let us turn again to engaged Buddhism and Thich Nhat Hanh's attempt to invert the structure of violence. 'The Path of Return Continues the Journey', published originally by Nhat Hanh in 1972, focuses all of the horror of the Vietnamese war in a single incident, the murder of four young volunteers and the wounding of a fifth on 5 July 1967 in the village of Binh Phuoc. The young men were members of the School of Youth for Social Service, a non-violent organization begun by Thich Nhat Hanh to heal the devastation of war. The play begins within the hour after the death squad left the five bodies by the banks of a river. As with Cortazar's writer-in-exile, Nhat Hanh blurs the line separating memory and imagination. 'I remember when I first picked up my pen to write this play. I saw fourteen eyes looking at me [besides the four murdered men, the play includes two previously murdered women and a nun who had immolated herself for peace], fourteen eyes wide open. I have said that I guarantee the story to be true. But what does it mean to be *true*?'[25]

The heart of the play focuses on the conversation of the four murdered young men with Mai, the nun, as they row quietly up the river.

LANH: It's strange. I don't feel any sorrow, pain, or bitterness. Sister Mai, I thought we would bear those feelings even after death ... Now I see that the dead are calmer and more lucid than the living. We dead do not think about vengeance. We just feel compassion for the living, even for those who killed us ...

HY: Perhaps we dead are more forgiving because we no longer have to bear the heavy burden of our bodies, and their desires and angers. Desire and anger need a home, and now that we no longer have our bodies ...

MAI: But Hy, how can you say that we no longer have our bodies? How could I see you if you didn't have a body? Our bodies are no longer heavy, no longer a burden, that's all. See how small and delicate this boat is, and yet it carries all five of us with ease.[26]

Mai later explains what she means by the light bodies of the dead in a passage that reflects the Buddhist understanding of both dependent co-arising and impermanence.

MAI: If you set fire to a piece of charcoal, it burns red and becomes heat. When the fire dies, the charcoal is reduced to ash. Heat is the afterlife of the charcoal. From then on, the heat begins an uninterrupted process of influences, either in terms of energy or physical properties. And that process of transformation, like a chain reaction, takes place either directly or indirectly in relation to other processes of transformation ... Nothing can be lost; yet at the same time, nothing that remains static can keep its nature intact.[27]

'Are you saying to us, Nhat Hanh', asks Daniel Berrigan in his foreword to the play, 'that the Vietnamese dead will come back to us who murdered them? Will come, not as ministers of vengeance, but sacramental presences, angels, spirits of new creation?'[28]

While Berrigan speaks within the framework of a Christian narrative, there is also a Buddhist way of appropriating the story. We can place these 'light bodies' within the framework of Mahayana Buddhist teaching concerning the three Buddha bodies. In Nhat Hanh's rendition of the teaching, the *Nirmanakaya* is the actual, historical Buddha as one of a plentitude of historical embodiments in different cosmic and temporal realms. The *Sambhogakaya* is 'the body of bliss'. In traditional renditions these are the celestial Buddhas and Bodhisattvas. But each of these bodies is only a manifestation of the *Dharmakaya*, the ontological Buddha, Buddha as cosmos, cosmos as Buddha. 'If you are mindful', Nhat Hanh insists, 'the *Dharmakaya* is easy to touch'.[29] While the logic of Mahayana pushes towards a radical identification in theory and practice of the physical body of each sentient being and the ontological Buddha, it is common for Buddhists to talk of the physical body as of lesser significance.[30] Clearly the physical bodies of the murdered youth have been left behind on the riverbank in 'The Path of Return Continues the Journey'. They are barely mentioned and not described at all. The light bodies, radiating love like the heat of burnt charcoal, seem closest to the *Sambhogakaya*. Indeed, Nhat Hanh transforms these young relief workers into bodhisattvas of peace.

We might say that the fusion of memory and imagination at the heart of the play is a form of religious practice which transfigures a physical body into a celestial body. But transfiguration is not an ontological shift. All realities at all levels manifest the *Dharmakaya*; religious practice brings it to light. Here the students murdered in the dark of night are brought to light in their new modality of continuing presence as *Sambhogakaya*. 'Love enables us to see things', Nhat Hanh affirms, 'that those who are without love cannot see'.[31]

If we read 'The Path of Return Continues the Journey' in light of Scarry's analysis of the structure of violence, the play's underlying intentionality becomes clear. Memory/imagination lends a voice to those whom violence has rendered voiceless. The illusion of the regime's power signified by the speechless, inert bodies on the banks of the river is mocked and overturned. The bodies of the young men moving with the river are not only light but loquacious. The regime's voice, its system of meaning, is not so much pernicious as it is stupidly ineffective.

TUAN: When that man with the poncho brought his gun up to my head, I realized immediately, without being aware of it consciously, that he was not going to shoot *me*. He was going to shoot something else, but not me. How could he shoot me without knowing who I was ...?

THO: You are funny, Brother Tuan! He asked us over and over again to make sure that we really were Youth for Social Service, before he killed us. He shot you because he *knew* who you were. They wanted to kill the Youth for Social Service. Therefore they shot you.

LANH: Why are you smiling, Sister Mai?

MAI: Tho is speaking in terms of logic and the *Heart Sutra* is exactly the tool we need to shatter that kind of reasoning.

TUAN: I agree with you, Sister Mai. 'Youth for Social Service' is just a label that they pasted on the objects of their hatred or fear, an object that exists only in their perception ... They shot only at the object of their fear and hatred, but because they had pasted the label of this object on us, they ended up shooting us, and we died by mistake. They killed us because they truly did not know who we were.[32]

Memory/imagination restores voice and with it the sense that the young peace workers' radiant worldly power – the heat of the charcoal – has not been doused by torture or murder. Thich Nhat Hanh not only restores voice, he inscribes the voices of the dead within a narrative of the utter reciprocity of death and life, an inversion of the denial of reciprocity at the heart of torture. Oscar Romero's prophetic cry, 'If I die, I will rise in the heart of the Salvadoran people', is a similar, in this case proleptic, restoration of voice by inscribing it within a master narrative.

Consuming Fire: The Practice of Solidarity

Like Cortazar's heroine caught in the nausea of memory, however, I remain transfixed by the wounds in the bodies lying by the riverbank. Something in the work of resuscitation performed by Berrigan and Nhat Hanh in their equally compelling ways represents a movement of the religious memory/imagination that happens much too quickly for me to follow. Yet I must not forget both men's long history of solidarity with those who suffer violence. Other narratives by both Berrigan and Nhat Hanh express clearly what I take to be an ironclad principle for those who witness on behalf of those who suffer: No giving voice to the voiceless can be authentic which does not in some way arise out of a dark night of the soul.

In 'The Fire that Consumes My Brother', Nhat Hanh struggles with the memory of a young monk who immolated himself in the early days of the Buddhist struggle for peace in Vietnam. 'The fire that burns him/burns in my body', the poem opens. 'And the world around me/burns with the same fire/ that burns my brother./ He burns'. Here the body in pain does not disappear all-too-quickly. It sears memory. 'He burns'. Notice the use of the present tense which characterizes the whole poem. If the physical body is in pain, so is the entire universe. 'His figure dominates the mountain/and the giant torch of his body fills the jungle'. While the poet resuscitates the monk, 'Let me summon your young spirit from the shadows/ and give it life/ in the form of a flower,/ the first lotus of the season', the monk's pain becomes the poet's suffering. 'The fire that burns you/ burns my flesh/ with such pain,/ that all my tears are not enough/ to cool your sacred soul'. What is simply assumed in 'Please Call Me By My True Names' and in 'The Path of Return Continues the Journey', namely a religious practice of approaching another's pain, of not betraying the memory of that pain through religious amnesia, is developed explicitly here. 'Deeply wounded, I remain here ... / I will not betray you ... / I remain here/ because your very heart/ is now my own'.[33] No moral voice is authentic without this solidarity, so solidarity risks the nausea of memory.

Deep Memory and the Healing of the Body

Violence does more than deprive the victim of voice; it scars the body. Giving voice to the voiceless alone is not sufficient to invert the structure of violence. Those whose bodies have been violated know that narrative memory does not touch the core of pain. 'No experience is more one's own than harm to one's own skin', writes Roberta Culbertson,

> but none is more locked within that skin, played out within it in actions other than words, in patterns of consciousness below the everyday and the con- structions of language. Trapped there, the violation seems to continue in a

reverberating present that belies the supposed linearity of time and the possibility of endings ... The demands of narrative ... operate as cultural silencers to this sort of memory ... We lose sight of the body's own recall of its response to threat and pain and of the ways in which it 'speaks' this pain ... Charlotte Delbo ... asks us not to confuse her holocaust memories, rational, ordered and clear, with what she calls 'deep memory' ... 'I feel it again through my whole body which becomes a block of pain and I feel death seizing me, I feel myself die'.[34]

In the face of such deep memories even the profound narratives of our religious traditions seem unconscionably 'rational, ordered and clear'. Writing as a witness on behalf of those who suffer and die from AIDS, on behalf of friends whom he has cared for as they died, Daniel Berrigan empties himself of all illusions of having something to offer proportionate to what those who suffer are undergoing: 'He knew the only god we could mime in such circumstances was an inferior one, a ventriloquist's doll mouthing someone else's platitudes. So he kept quiet'.[35] Berrigan's fractured narrative, like Nhat Hanh's poems, like Cortazar's layered narrative are all attempts not to betray that deep memory.

To respect deep memory, however, is not to remain fixated in the nausea of memory. At the heart of each of Thich Nhat Hanh's works that I have examined is transmutation, the transmutation of the moral self in 'Please Call Me by My True Name', the transmutation of the murdered victims into light-bodied bodhisattvas in 'The Path that Returns Continues the Journey', the transmutation of the one who remembers, who speaks on behalf of the voiceless into a sacrament of their life and their pain in 'The Fire that Consumes My Brother'. In each case transmutation emerges from a practice that is rooted in awareness of dependent co-arising. In many of his talks about mindful practice Nhat Hanh begins with everyday activities, drinking a cup of tea or eating a tangerine. He sees these bodily actions, mindfully performed, as acts of non-violent resistance. 'These things are very important', he concludes. 'They can change our civilization'.[36]

It is easy to dismiss Nhat Hanh's suggestions as hopelessly sweet. What do they have to do with the systemic changes necessary to root out the structure of violence? Perhaps we need to think again. Think of Gandhi's daily practice of spinning yarn to clothe his body, his march to the sea to harvest salt or his refusal to consign to untouchables the duty of emptying the chamber pot each morning. Think of Rosa Parks' determination to let her weary body sit still when ordered to the back of the bus. The transformative power of these actions is rooted in their mindful care for the human body. These practices are counterweights to those which permanently scarred Charlotte Delbo and Lenard Clark. Nhat Hanh's practice of eating mindfully is a way of creating countervailing 'deep memories'.

I present two forms of practice centred on the body, one from an engaged Buddhist, one from the Jesus movement, as exemplifying this way of inversion. In the late 1960s Gary Snyder, poet, ecological activist and Buddhist practitioner, moved with his family to the Sierra Nevada and settled in a place they called Kitkitdizze. From this decision arose forms of practice which altered traditional monastic rituals. 'Sitting ten hours a day', Snyder argued, 'means that somebody else is growing your food for you ... Somebody has to grow the tomatoes'.[37] These new forms of practice were attentive to body and place, family and work.

> Practice simply is one intensification of what is natural and around us all the time. Practice is to life as poetry is to spoken language ... One of the first practices that I learned is that when you're working with another person on a two-person crosscut saw, you never push, you only pull; my father taught me that when I was eight ... We all have to learn to change oil on time or we burn out our engines. We all have to learn how to cook.[38]

In numerous places Snyder has argued for a specifically Buddhist sacramental consciousness built on the Hua-yen image of Indra's Net in which each node of the net is a jewel which reflects every other jewel. Nowhere is this deep memory more palpably present than in his compassionate eros for the body of his family. We do not simply remember; we enact this sacramental consciousness. In 'The Bath' Snyder washes his toddler son by the light of a kerosene lantern, smelling the sweet scent of cedar and feeling the nip of cool night air at the door.

> He stands in warm water
> Soap all over the smooth of his thigh and stomach
>   'Gary don't soap my hair!'
>   -his eye-sting fear
>   the soapy hand feeling
>   through and around the globes and curves of his body
>   up in the crotch,
> And washing-tickling out the scrotum, little anus
>   his penis curving up and getting hard
>   as I pull back skin and try to wash it
> Laughing and jumping, flinging arms around,
>   I squat all naked too,
>   *is this our body?*

The antiphon '*is this our body ... is this our body?*' becomes 'this is our body' as the family, clean from the bath, stretches out 'on the redwood benches hearts all beating/ Quiet to the simmer of the stove'...[39]

In 'What Happened Here Before' Snyder traces three billion years of ecological history in the Sierra Nevada, history that ebbs and flows while 'Turtle Island swims/ in the ocean-sky swirl-void.' The poem ends with the family at work:

my sons ask, who are we?
drying apples picked from homestead trees
drying berries, curing meat
shooting arrows at a bale of straw

military jets head northeast, roaring, every dawn.
my sons ask, who are they?

WE SHALL SEE
WHO KNOWS
HOW TO BE

Bluejay screeches from a pine.[40]

The juxtaposition of a technology geared towards violence with a family's patient labour, of the jet's roar and the blue jay's screech conveys all too plainly where the mindfulness that overcomes violence resides.

Body-centred practice as inversion of the structures of everyday violence is also the underlying message of John Dominic Crossan's portrayal of Jesus and the movement he generated. Ordinarily we focus on Jesus' preaching, on his prophetic voice. Crossan suggests that we attend more to the practices of healing and eating as enacting a politically explosive, alternative way of worldly being. If we see the gathering of humans around a table as a microcosm of the social order as Crossan does, Jesus' practice of 'open commensality' is openly transgressive. Not only do not kings go out to the highways and byways to bring in just anybody to a wedding feast, none of us would do this. Open commensality overturns 'the vertical discriminations and lateral separations' that are the structure of everyday violence.[41] Likewise a literally indiscriminate practice of healing reveals the rigid stratifications in any health care system, then or now.

> [Jesus'] strategy for himself and explicitly for his followers, was the combination of *free healing and common eating,* a religious and economic egalitarianism that negated alike and at once the hierarchical and patronal normalcies of Jewish religion and Roman power ... Miracle and parable, healing and eating were calculated to force individuals into unmediated physical and spiritual contact with one another. He announced, in other words, the brokerless kingdom of God.[42]

A short statement by a Venezuelan lay leader in a base Christian community captures the continuing power of this practice.

> Jesus was the first, he joined with people to see how they could get out from under ... Jesus came and celebrated, he got involved with people's problems. It's the same with us; a day's work always ends with a celebration. The two things. So you see, Jesus is here with us doing the same work.[43]

Both Snyder's mindful practice of everyday life and Jesus' 'free healing and common eating' and the narratives that they generate (Snyder's poems, Jesus' parables) transgress and thereby reveal the hidden structures of violence. In her treatment of torture as the paradigm of violence, Scarry argued that the hidden core of torture is 'the dream of absolute non-reciprocity'. That dream depends upon forgetting the body and its vulnerabilities. More precisely, it arises by creating the illusion of one's own bodily invulnerability through rendering someone else's body utterly vulnerable. Snyder and Jesus, like Gandhi, Rosa Parks and Thich Nhat Hanh, return us to our worldly bodies. They enliven the deep memory of another way of being. They enact a dream of mindful reciprocity.

Coda: Lenard Clark and the Violated Social Body

In its initial haste to restore a sense of communal rectitude, Chicago lost the opportunity to give voice to the complex moral implications of Lenard Clark's beating while he lay in a coma. As Clark's week-long coma wore on, Chicago's media shifted their attention from Clark as victim of racism to Clark as *patient* struggling to awaken.[44] A new narrative line focused on healing; its content became overtly religious.

Anyone who has ever sat with someone beloved in an intensive care unit can appreciate the importance of faith and prayer to Clark's family. Their voices, tempered by long days and nights of waiting, deserve our respectful silence and mindful listening. Yet the confident affirmations of God's presence in Clark's small room voiced by a parade of dignitaries and high profile ministers rang hollow, at least to my ears. I heard none of Berrigan's saving reticence nor sensed Thich Nhat Hanh's burning fire of shared pain. Or was it simply the bright glare of the media with its prefabricated narrative that blinded me to the genuine compassion of these designated spokespersons for our collective experience? Next to these religious interpreters, the cautious prognoses of Clark's doctors, who from the beginning suggested that Clark might never repair all the damage done to his brain, reflected a modesty born of long experience with human suffering.[45]

The *Tribune* followed Clark's struggle in the hospital and later in a rehabilitation centre throughout the spring of 1997. We *did* attend to Clark's body as it began to heal. We watched and read about his efforts to walk again. Clark, one article reported, had 'journeyed into a condition that is at once encouraging and, to the non-medical world, unfathomable. He walks and talks and at some moments appears to be almost like other teenagers. Yet he technically remains in a state of amnesia and coma, a mental limbo that is camouflaged by his emerging skills.'[46] Following in Clark's footsteps as he moved through this liminal state, we *did* get a sense of the persistence of his suffering and of the long and uncertain road ahead.

Yet the story of Clark's recovery was inscribed within a larger social narrative. It was proclaimed to be 'a symbol of racial healing'. While Lenard

Clark still remained in a coma during Holy Week, Reverend Jesse Jackson had outlined a new narrative: 'People should see us healing. They should see us throwing away the stone ... They should see us taking up a collection for Lenard Clark'.[47] This story had to be given a fitting climax. Healing was connected to the donations of toys and furniture that accompanied Clark as he left the rehabilitation centre for a new home in scattered-site public housing and 'a new chance at life, in a modest, middle class Southwest Side neighbourhood'. The new beginning was dramatically underscored by a resident of Clark's old neighbourhood who said, 'I'm so grateful to God for pulling him out of here ... because this is hell'.[48] Clark's salvation, apparently, was complete and we could conveniently forget what he himself said very soon after regaining his own voice: 'I am not the same as I used to be'.[49] Never mind that this master-narrative of healing and new beginnings might leave quite a few people in that particular hell, people like the children who were Clark's friends in the Stateway Gardens project who said that they wished that they had gotten hurt.[50] Such cruel ironies notwithstanding, *we* got the hope-filled ending that we wanted.

And then he was gone. Off our radar screens. Chicago awaited another child, a new chapter in its passion narrative. But this story refused to end. Lenard Clark's name was back in the news when his three assailants were brought to trial and convicted in autumn 1998. Only in the last few weeks, about three years after the initial incident, we learn that Clark and his family have become close to the family of one of the imprisoned attackers. The relationship began shortly after the attack. The father of one of the convicted boys has 'helped Clark learn to drive, taught him to ride a horse and helped him with his studies'.[51]

We are not told how well Lenard's body has healed but a boy who learns to drive, ride a horse and is back at his studies inspires hope. The news of a long-term relationship between the two families, however, draws scepticism and outright derision. The consensus among many in the law enforcement and African American communities is that these efforts at reconciliation are merely a ploy on the part of the attacker's family to gain early parole for their son.[52] No one presumes that the earlier rhetoric of reconciliation may actually have worked. Lenard Clark may be on the mend. There may even be some semblance of solidarity in suffering between two boys, once locked together as victim and assailant. The violated social body, however, refuses to heal.

Notes

1 Elaine Scarry, *The Body in Pain* (New York: Oxford University Press, 1985), pp. 32–3. I am indebted to discussions with Martin Ryan and to a reading of his senior honor's thesis for my understanding of Scarry. Ann Stanford, Roy Furman and Frida Kerner Furman carefully read this chapter and made suggestions for

revisions. I am grateful to Sr. Jane Gerard, C.S.J. for research assistance and for help in preparing the manuscript.

2 Ibid., pp. 8, 33–5, 52–4.

3 See Lawrence Langer, 'The Alarmed Vision: Social Suffering and Holocaust Atrocity', *Daedalus* 125:1 (Winter 1996), p. 56.

4 *Chicago Tribune*, 24 March 1997, p. 1 and back page.

5 'Unwritten Rules Remain in Bridgeport', *Chicago Tribune*, 26 March 1997, pp. 1, 26.

6 Jerry Thomas and Gary Marx, 'Bishop Vows to Fight Racism in His Schools', *Chicago Tribune*, 25 March 1997, pp. 1, 18.

7 'Editorial: A Quick Response to Racial Hatred', *Chicago Tribune*, 25 March 1997, Section 1, p. 16. Italics mine.

8 Ken Jones, *The Social Face of Buddhism* (London: Wisdom Publications, 1989), p. 92. For further introduction to engaged Buddhism as an international movement, see also Fred Eppsteiner (ed.), *The Path of Compassion: Writings on Socially Engaged Buddhism* (Berkeley, CA: Parallax Press, 1988); Christopher Queen and Sallie King, *Engaged Buddhism: Buddhist Liberation Movements in Asia* (Albany, NY: State University of New York Press, 1996).

9 Thich Nhat Hanh, *Being Peace* (Berkeley, CA: Parallax Press, 1987), pp. 89–90.

10 Jones, *The Social Face of Buddhism*, pp. 90–97, 100.

11 Joanna Rogers Macy, 'Dependent Co-arising: The Distinctness of Buddhist Ethics', *Journal of Religious Ethics* 7:1 (1979), p. 40.

12 Thich Nhat Hanh, *Living Buddha Living Christ* (New York: G.P. Putnam's Sons, 1995), pp. 183–4.

13 Thich Nhat Hanh, 'Please Call Me by My True Names', *Please Call Me By My True Names: The Collected Poems of Thich Nhat Hanh* (Berkeley, CA: Parallax Press, 1993), p. 72.

14 Julio Cortazar, 'Press Clippings' in *We Love Glenda So Much and Other Stories* (New York: Knopf, 1983), pp. 82–4. For leading me to this work, I am grateful to Lois Parkinson Zamora, 'Deciphering the Wounds: The Politics of Torture and Julio Cortazar's Literature of Embodiment' in Susan Van Zanten Gallagher (ed.), *Postcolonial Literature and the Biblical Call for Justice* (Jackson, MS: University Press of Mississippi, 1994), pp. 91–110.

15 Cortazar, *Press Clippings*, p. 85.

16 Zamora, 'Deciphering the Wounds', pp. 92–3.

17 Ibid., pp. 94–6.

18 Scarry, *Body in Pain*, pp. 19–28. My understanding of everyday violence has been enriched by a reading of Nancy Scheper-Hughes, *Death Without Weeping: The Violence of Everyday Life in Brazil* (Berkeley, CA: University of California Press, 1992).

19 Scarry, *Body in Pain*, p. 51.

20 Ibid., pp. 29, 38, 50.

21 Ibid., pp. 18, 27–9, 55–6.

22 Ibid., pp. 56–7.

23 Ibid., pp. 56–9, 80.

24 Ibid., p. 50.

25 Thich Nhat Hanh, *Love in Action: Writings on Nonviolent Social Change* (Berkeley, CA: Parallax Press, 1993), p. 10.

26 Ibid., p. 17.

27 Ibid., p. 26.
28 Daniel Berrigan, 'Foreword', *Love in Action*, p. 7.
29 Nhat Hanh, *Living Buddha*, pp. 40, 145–6; see also Thomas P. Kasulis, 'Reality as Embodiment', in *Religious Reflections on the Human Body*, edited by Jane Marie Law (Bloomington, IN: Indiana University Press, 1995), p. 171.
30 Kasulis, 'Reality as Embodiment', pp. 178–9.
31 Nhat Hanh, *Love in Action*, p. 10.
32 Ibid., pp. 29–30.
33 Nhat Hanh, 'The Fire That Consumes My Brother', *Please Call Me*, pp. 48–9.
34 Roberta Culbertson, 'Embodied Memory, Transcendence and Feeling: Reconstructing Trauma, Re-establishing the Self', *New Literary History* 26 (1995), p. 170.
35 Daniel Berrigan, SJ, *Sorrow Built a Bridge: Friendship and AIDS* (Baltimore: Fortkamp Publishing Company, 1989), p. 5.
36 Nhat Hanh, *Being Peace*, pp. 110, 115.
37 Gary Snyder, *The Real Work: Interviews and Talks, 1964–79*, edited with an introduction by William Scott McLean (New York: New Directions, 1980), p. 96.
38 Ibid., pp. 134–5.
39 Gary Snyder, 'The Bath', *Turtle Island* (New York: New Directions, 1974), p. 12.
40 Snyder, 'What Happened Here Before', *Turtle Island*, pp. 80–81.
41 John Dominic Crossan, *Jesus: A Revolutionary Biography* (San Francisco: Harper San Francisco, 1994), pp. 68–9.
42 John Dominic Crossan, *The Historical Jesus: The Life of a Mediterranean Jewish Peasant* (San Francisco: Harper San Francisco, 1991), p. 422.
43 As cited in Daniel Levine, *Popular Voices in Latin American Catholicism* (Princeton: Princeton University Press, 1992), p. 40.
44 For an analysis of cultural forms of betrayal entailed in this shift from 'victim' to 'patient', see Arthur Kleinman and Joan Kleinman, 'The Appeal of Experience; The Dismay of Images: Cultural Appropriations of Suffering in Our Times', *Daedalus* 125:1 (Winter 1996), p. 10.
45 Jerry Thomas and Nancy Regan, 'Jackson, Daley Pray for Beaten Boy', *Chicago Tribune* (26 March 1997), p. 26.
46 Graeme Zielinski, 'I Want to Go Home', *Chicago Tribune* (20 April 1997), pp. 1 and 12.
47 Gary Marx and Meg McSherry Breslin, 'Kids Make Their Feelings Known about Racial Hatred', *Chicago Tribune*, 27 March 1997 MetroChicago, p. 6.
48 Cindy Schreuder and Jerry Thomas, 'Clark in Spotlight of Old, New Neighbors', *Chicago Tribune*, 2 May 1997, MetroChicago, pp. 1, 6.
49 Zielinski, 'I Want to Go Home', p. 12.
50 Schreuder and Thomas, 'Clark in Spotlight', MetroChicago, p. 6.
51 Gary Marx and Noah Isackson, 'Lenard Clark, Attacker Reportedly New Friends', *Chicago Tribune*, 19 January 2000, MetroChicago, pp. 1, 7.
52 Ibid.

Memory, Memorials and Redemption

Denys Turner

It is sometimes said that the only thinker in the West before the modern period who attaches the importance Freud does to the place of memory within the construction of personal identity is Augustine. While this is far from true, as we will see, there is no doubt that Augustine's intensely personal exploration of his own memory in *Confessions* Books 1–9 combines with an extraordinarily acute conceptual discussion of philosophical problems about memory in Book 10 in a manner which must strike the modern reader as exceptionally prescient of our contemporary preoccupations. For Augustine it is memory which is the key not only, autobiographically, to who I am but also, philosophically, to what the self is. But if Augustine is by no means unique in his placing of memory at the centre of the problematics of selfhood and identity, it is true that to get at the significance of Augustine's thought on these linkages between oneself, selfhood, autobiography and memory, we have to acknowledge in him a conception of memory which is at once more dynamic, far richer, more complex, and at the same time in a role much more ambiguous, than any which is available in western thought in pre-Freudian times.

A revisiting of pre-modern conceptions of memory and identity is not irrelevant in a volume devoted to the subject of memorials and their place in contemporary urban society. Nearly every account of *collective* memory available to us today, and so of the acts of its exercise in the construction of social identity, draw upon analogies from – though it should not naively be thought they are mere replications of – models of *individual* memory and of its place within the construction of personal identity. It would be natural therefore if the pathology of the one had some bearing on the pathology of the other. And since, as other contributions to this volume witness, there is little doubt that the Children's Cross at the St James Episcopal Cathedral in Chicago is a deeply problematic memorial, or that its problematic character is also symptomatic of wider problems of social identities, there seems to be some point in attempting a pathology, and some appropriateness in the course of doing so in turning again to the question of the relations between individual and social psychologies of memory.

On the other hand, the prospect of revisiting pre-modern conceptions of memory in pursuit of such a pathology does not spontaneously entice the contemporary mind with hopes of fruitful outcomes. One could respond to this doubt with the reflection that such a priori dimissiveness of the relevance of pre-modern thought is already symptomatic of a contemporary malaise of memory, being evidence of a very contemporary incapacitation of intellect by means of the severing of its relations with the memory of our own intellectual culture, a preoccupation with an unhistorical 'immediacy' of thought and experience which cannot know itself because it denies to itself the knowledge of its origins. There is, I suspect, some truth in this: but if I do not choose to pursue this line of response, it is not because of any doubts about its being a characteristic of both our intellectual and popular cultures that they are characterized by a certain kind of 'denial' of memory, for, on the contrary, it is very much the purpose of this essay to explore that denial precisely as lying at the source of our problems with memorials as such, and with the Children's Cross in particular. As for drawing on Augustine and other pre-modern thinkers in the course of this exploration, I simply make no apologies: the thing will speak for itself, or not, as the reader judges.

Memory, Autobiography and Identity in Augustine

Augustine's *Confessions* is an autobiography. As such it is both record and construction. In both capacities it is an exercise of memory, first in the very plainest sense we have for the word, for it records the events of his life as he remembers them at the time of writing, some ten years or more after the latest of the events he recalls. But among the things he recalls when he is writing *Confessions* are memories which he had earlier in his life, memories of events, but more particularly of thoughts and feelings which he had had earlier still. So when Augustine remembers, among the things which he remembers are earlier memories.

Secondly, however, Augustine's writing of *Confessions* is not just an exercise of powers of plain factual recall, for it is also construction of the events recalled into a narrative, into a story of his life, into an identity, into the story of who he is. In this connection *Confessions* is not an account, merely, of events; it *is* the construction of that narrative which *is* his identity. For that, for Augustine, is what remembering always is: the construction of that narrative which constitutes what I now am. I *am* my story.

If that is the case, and if, within that narrative which is my present construction of selfhood is contained memories of former memories, then that present identity must consist in a construction of constructions. For those past memories which Augustine now recalls in writing *Confessions* were themselves, at the time, also constructions of the past which were then remembered and so, at the time, of a present selfhood. And those familiar with Augustine's *Confessions* will recognize the presence of this dynamic of overlapping and interweaving constructions and reconstructions of identity as providing the very tissue and nerve, and indeed the fascination, of the book itself. Punctuated as that narrative is by successive phases of crisis, emotional and intellectual, and by the revisions of memory forced upon him at each point of crisis, the account of his life, and so of his identity, is that of a personhood now achieved, but one which is constituted by layers of former identity once precariously constructed only to be soon deconstructed in emotional crisis and turmoil, and then requiring yet further, but still unstable, reconstruction. Conceived of on a geological, and so essentially static, metaphor, Augustine's present self, as he writes *Confessions* is a present landscape sustained by underlying strata, themselves formed by ancient upheavals now settled. Conceived of more dynamically, his present self is essentially a time-bound interaction of present memory with past memories, each constructing and constraining the other.

That said, we must not allow ourselves to be carried away by a post-modernist and faddishly relativist reading of Augustine's understanding of selfhood – tempting as that may be in view of his very platonist emphases on the contingency of our human powers of memory and judgement. When Augustine writes *Confessions* as autobiography, and so as self-construction, he does so because now he thinks that at last he can do so. There is a sense in which Augustine thinks that he *can* write a truthful account of who he *really* is only now, after his conversion. For only since his conversion can he occupy that stable ground from the vantage point of which his true selfhood can be seen for what it is. Only now can he recognize his earlier 'selfhoods' – in Carthage, Rome and Milan – as having been in some way 'false' appropriations of a selfhood: appropriations for sure, for of course, he really and truly lived as he did – among the 'hissing cauldrons of lust' in Carthage, in the arrogant self-confidence of the academic teacher in Rome and Milan; but 'false' none the less, because all that time what he *really* lived out was a *false* self-image. In short, until his conversion, his selfhood was, as after it he perceives his life to have been, a kind of *lived unreality*. Hence, no truthful account of it written from within that false selfhood could be anything but a false account even of its falsehood.

For when he wrote *Confessions* Augustine had found God. He had found God in and through the discovery of himself and he had discovered himself insofar as he had discovered God. 'For you were within me and I was outside myself, (*Tu autem eras intus, et ego foris*). Now that he has found God, he can re-read the whole story of his life as having been in fact a story of his 'searching for God'. In the same way as when, once it is reciprocated, one may discover that all the time one had been in love, little that one had known it, so Augustine can now see that the whole story of his life, all those vicissitudes of frustrated desire, of the pursuit of happiness and its unsatisfying outcomes, made sense as his desire for God, unable as he had been at the time to name it in those terms. *That*, for Augustine, is the recovery of memory, the realization that the pursuit of any and everything but God – looking for God 'outside oneself' – was 'all the time' but the desire for God who was within: 'all the time' because when God is at last found we can, truthfully, say: 'that *was* what I was looking for'.

In tension within *Confessions* are two contrasting emphases. As narrative, the book is dominated by Augustine's sense of the fluid, multi-layered, radically temporal, radically unstable nature of memory itself. And it is in just such terms of radical instability that Augustine conceives of our constructions of identity and selfhood. On the other hand, much as in this first connection Augustine is under the influence of the *platonici* and of their instinct for the precarious contingency of all created things, the other, contrasting side of this Platonism is revealed in his conviction, far less appealing to contemporary sensibilities, of the underpinning of that contingency in the 'eternal light of truth', in the 'beauty, ever ancient, ever new'. For that was what Augustine found 'within me' when, in the course of his painful and much frustrated exploration of his memory ever more 'within', he hit upon not some rock of perduring selfhood, but God: within him but not of him. In the end, for Augustine, I am what I am in God; that memory explored to its depths of inwardness is found at its limits to open out into the God who is 'above it', so that where I am most myself, most within, there am I most 'beyond'. Myself, I am at my core 'other', yet it is in this 'other' that I am to be found. In the discovery of that selfhood, therefore, but more particularly in that selfhood's relation to the 'other', lies the very possibility of autobiography as such.

The 'Magic' of Memory

What Augustine offers us is an account of the 'magic' of memory. My remembering is a present act *of mine*; yet the I which remembers is as much the patient of the action, *made* by my remembering, as it is the agent constructing her identity by means of the remembering she does. Remembering is a present act of my conscious agency, which *makes present the past*. Yet what I am able presently to recall is *determined by that past*, whether or not I recall it, by what that past permits me to recall, forms me to want to remember or to want to forget. It is easy, thus far, to find analogies with Freud, for whom what I consciously construct by way of an ego out of presently recalled experiences is very largely determined by those experiences which I do not recall, on the condition that I do not recall them, and thus by an anonymous 'other' which is at the same time within – the 'unconscious'. But the analogy can hardly be pursued any further. For in Augustine, that 'other' is not an alien force in which the self is trapped, not a causal constraint in which the freedom of my powers of action are gripped, but the source of my freedom; and, if it can properly be described as a cause, then it is the cause of all that I am, and so of my humanity.

The 'magic' of memory, then, lies in this, that though in itself a temporal, contingent thing, a sort of 'intertext' which draws a past and a future into a contingent, temporal present, itself instantly to become a past, none the less, it is precisely in the self-exploration of that memory that it passes beyond itself into the 'light of eternal truth'. Nothing in this could be further either from the pessimistic rationalism of a Freud or the pessimistic irrationalism of the postmodernist. Yet neither is there in Augustine any sign of that, as we sloppily like to call it today, 'Cartesian selfhood' of pure self-consciousness, in the denial of which both Freud and the postmodernists propose equally, if differently, to constitute themselves on epistemologically superior ground. Augustine's 'self' is no 'substantial subjectivity' underlying, but also the object of, pure consciousness, dualistically defined in contradistinction to 'body' and 'world'. The 'substantivity' of Augustine's self fades out, as it were, into God, but neither into a God whose substantival 'otherness' would displace and cancel my identity as a selfhood, nor one which would absorb it, but into the infinite, unbounded depths which are beyond substance, beyond identity, beyond the very distinction between sameness and otherness, the 'other', as Nicholas of Cusa put it in an essentially Augustinian phrase, which is the 'not-other' (*ly non-aliud*). That, then, is where Augustine's memory places our identity: in a selfhood constituted by its transcendence of selfhood, in the temporality of a memory which passes over into the eternal 'now' of the Godhead.

Memory, Sacrament and Church

Our contemporary philosophies are too little aware of Augustine's account of memory and identity even to know how to deny it. His is a conceptual world which those philosophies simply pass by. And yet the Christian inheritance of memory is profoundly influenced by it – or at the very least, by those theologies by which Augustine himself was influenced – most particularly in its sacramental theologies, and above all in its eucharistic theologies. For eucharistic theologies are essentially theologies of *collective* memory as redeeming and redeemed, they describe a community's act of remembering in bread and wine as a making present, in the contingency of that here and now, of the self-communication of Jesus in his body and blood. But that communication and presence is defined in its character of sacrament by reference to a double negation and absence which constitute it in a radical contingency: the body of Christ is not present in the manner in which it was to Peter and James and John in his and their historical existence, nor yet as it will be in the final Kingdom to all who have been raised. The body of Christ cannot be present as it was historically, because Jesus is dead. Nor can that body be present to us now as it is now, for it is raised, and ours are not. Therefore, Christ is present to us now in the Eucharist just as, and only as, a body which is raised – and so *is*, bodily, the Kingdom – can be present to bodies which are not raised, and so are, bodily, only that ambiguous, precariously, uncertainly communicating thing which is the Christian community or Church. The Eucharist, therefore, is an act of memory situated in times which are *defined by their 'betweenness'*, by a present whose nature and character as sacramental is constituted by its relation to a past and a future which it makes 'present' on a double condition of absence.

The Church, the community of those who thus 'remember', is therefore itself constituted in its identity by the character of its memory. For its acts of memory, which are its sacraments, both make the church to exist, for it exists as the community of those who thus remember, and are made to exist by the church, for the sacraments are the Church's institutional practices. Those sacraments are the site of intersection of past, present and future, a making present of what it remembers and, precisely as a remembering, witnesses to the absence of what it recalls. The Eucharist is, as it were, a kind of 'nostalgia for the future', it is the reality of the 'not yet' as it shapes and forms and defines the present. It is the future present by means of its absence: thus are all the Christian sacraments inherently eschatological in orientation.

Yet the acts of remembering which bear the weight of this significance are the paltry, ill-prepared, thoughtless acts of a half-attentive, partly reconciled, half-believing community which is at best, like Becket's women of Canterbury, but 'living and partly living'. You do not need the high Platonism of Augustine's concepts of 'temporality' and 'contingency' to get at this state of affairs, for this state of affairs is observable in every church every Sunday. Christian sacramental worship in its practice is shot through with ambiguity and contradiction within itself on the one hand, and its symbolism is unrecognized or ignored by 'the world' on the other.

False Memory, False Sacrament

As to this internal ambiguity and contradiction, let us typify it with a contrived, if, one fears, a not entirely fanciful, stereotype. Let us suppose a preacher delivering his sermon, as it were, from the height of his authoritarian pulpit, on the equality of all the people of God. Now it is easy to make a distinction between the formal message of the sermon and the secondary message conveyed by the conditions of its being uttered, for there is nothing novel in distinguishing, in general terms, between what a person says and what is being said by that person's act of saying it. If I utter the words 'I promise', I *thereby* promise. But what is being said by my promising is, for example, 'I realise that you don't trust me'. The distinction is easiest to see when the two locutions fall apart and contradict each other, as classically did the British MP, the late Enoch Powell, when he notoriously enacted a thoroughly racist provocation by means of utterances purporting to denounce its dangers. Such bastard locutions, we may say, enact a 'performative contradiction'.

But though we may properly distinguish them, we should not analyse the distinct elements which thus 'performatively contradict' each other into separate, unrelated factors, as, in our fanciful case, into the egalitarian communication and the fact that, as it happens, it is delivered from an authoritarian pulpit. For the point about authoritarian pulpits is that they are already sermons: actions, as we know, also speak, as does this pulpit, which communicates quite effectively enough within the words of the egalitarian sermon. We might suppose it is adequate to say that the pulpit is but part of the *materiality* of the preacher's act of saying, as if thereby to suggest that it can play no part in the total communicative act. But this would be to misdescribe the distinction. For the pulpit communicates too, it both internalizes and exhibits the character of the preacher's relationship with the congregation, and the significance of that materiality practices its own hermeneutic upon the explicit formal meanings of the preacher's words. Hence those words become the bearer of a condensation of conflicting meanings which, precisely insofar as it lies outside the intended communication of the preacher, exists independently of those intentions, while at the same time subverting them. The total result is a social reality constructed upon the contradictoriness internal to the communicative act.

For it is in the facts of this contradiction that the members of the worshipping community are socialized. They perceive their relationship to the act of worship via the condensation of contradictory meanings, for at one level they attend, perhaps with approval, to the egalitarian message of the preacher and *in so doing* they reciprocate the authoritarianism of his act of saying it. Consequently, the preacher and the congregation enact a relationship constituted by the contradiction in which they are jointly socialized. Thus as they live out their relationship with the egalitarianism of the preacher's message through the authoritarian structures of its communication, so they live out their relationships with the authoritarianism of those structures through mystified categories of egalitarianism. In short, what such rituals effect is a rupture between what the ritual signifies and what it effects. And when a ritual effects this rupture as a routine, when, in other words, it socializes the participants in this rupturing, then we can say that such rituals have the character which Marxists, (when there usefully were any to own the terminology) used to call 'ideological'. In more theological terms we can also say that they parodize the sacramental character which they are supposed to exhibit. For they are rituals whose social effects *contradict* what sacramentally they signify: thus do the participants, as Paul says, 'eat and drink judgment on themselves' (1 Cor. 11: 29).

Roman Catholic theology has traditionally protected itself against an excess of moralism which would conclude that such contradictory and bastard liturgies cannot be sacraments by supposing that the effect of the sacrament cannot be dependent upon the moral rectitude of the congregations which enact them: all that is required for the effect of the sacrament to be achieved is that the president intends what the Church intends. Of course, even if that minimum condition is met, the participants are not saved thereby from the consequences of their insincerities, thoughtlessnesses or plain hypocrisies; rather are they, as Paul says, all the more condemned for them. Nor will such ritual actions be saved from the contempt of those who stand outside the circle of belief and faith within which they get their significance. In any case, the point, more simply, is this: just because (and even if) the ritual does 'effect what it signifies', as ancient theological tradition has said of sacraments in general; and even if we concede that what the sacrament 'signifies' is entirely determined by what the community enacting it 'intends' to signify by it (and this must be controvertible), the matter is not settled thereby. For granted that the sacrament pulls off what the Church intends by it sacramentally; and granted even that the Church is guaranteed the efficacy of its sacraments by divine institution and authority, nothing in those guarantees can ensure that the concrete events in which those sacraments are enacted are not, in any particular enactments, fraught with performative contradiction, in which what is said and done *by the sacrament* is contradicted and subverted by what is said and done *by its enactment*.

And if this is a possibility in the case of sacraments – where on a concession to a 'high' theology their efficacy as sacraments can be thought to be divinely guaranteed – how much more possible will this be in the case of non-sacramental symbols, where on *any* theology, however sacramentally 'high', no such divine guarantees, whether of sacramental significance or of sacramental efficacy, can be counted upon. Which is why the Children's Cross is necessarily problematical and must be required to answer to an agenda of questions *not* of its own asking, about what that which it *intends* to signify actually *does*, and about what, in that *doing*, it actually signifies. For set firmly and statically within the precincts of a Christian Cathedral, drawing thereby upon that apparently stable repertoire of Christian significance, Christian memory and Christian symbol, it may seem to the Christian community of Chicago that it says and means what Christians say and mean by it. But that symbol, possessed in stability in Christian memory, is addressed to a public in hurried and preoccupied transit past it, whose transitoriness is itself a symbol of the conditions of instability and relativity of their *reception* of its significance, of a dissident memory, of a public which cannot, or in many cases positively wills not to, share in what that Cross 'says'. Think, just for one example, of what it says to Jews passing by, in its gallingly naive and insensitive association of child murder with the cross of Christ. In view of the paradigmatic Christian legends, all of them mendacious, which link these elements in reverse, to *whose* memory does this memorial speak, saying *what*?

Capitalism and the Denial of Memory

I do not wish, by these comments, simply and with no more ado to concede the argument to the politically correct who, like the Birmingham City Council, decreed out of some quite absurdly misplaced if well-intentioned sensitivity, to rename 'Christmas' Winterval. My concern in any case is not with how *Christians* in particular may communicate through their own symbols, invested as they are with, and sustained as they are by, the memories of their own history, to a pluralistic society which either does not or will not share in the historical memory which alone guarantees a meaning for those symbols. Rather, I wish to raise a more general question about whether *any* symbolic communication is possible in a 'pluralist' society and, more precisely, whether memorials can in principle have any significant role in a society ideologically constituted by its dismissal of memory.

For nothing more convincingly characterizes the urban community of Chicago than the ideologies of late capitalism; and nothing characterizes capitalism as such more precisely than Marx's perception that it suppresses history in the name of time, and so suppresses the reality of memory in the name of the instant experience, the immediacy of the present. It will not be surprising if, in such a cultural world, the very possibility of symbolic memorialization is problematic.

These displacements of a bourgeois ideology – and note the epithet 'bourgeois' is meant to denote precisely the *mores* of the *city* – have a long philosophical lineage which much predate historically its cultural and intellectual apotheosis in late twentieth-century postmodernism. Witness the potential subversion of memory's role in the constitution of personal identity contained in the very case Descartes presented for its establishment. The *Discourse on Method* demonstrated, as Descartes supposed, that my identity was founded with incorrigible certainty on the rock of the immediate experience of it: for any thought, he claimed, there must be an 'I' which thinks it. However it took but a couple of decades for Locke to note that the *continuity* of my selfhood could not be demonstrated thereby, since nothing was established by that argument to show that for any *series* of thoughts, there was just one continuous 'I' thinking the series: just for each thought *its* thinker. For what are acts of memory, but individual thoughts? So how can my remembering that it was this same 'I' now who thought of you ten minutes ago demonstrate anything but that there is an 'I' now, ten minutes later who has that thought? Who needs the deconstructions of the postmodernist, when everything they claim for themselves is already given in the very philosophical origins of 'modernity', when already in the seventeenth century Locke is reversing Descartes' prioritization of thinker as constructor and author of its thoughts in the name of the manifest implications of Descartes' own arguments, which is that it is the thinker who is constructed by the thoughts, the author the product of the text?

In such a cultural world in which agency is denied, the relations of thinker and thought, of author and text reversed, is found (on a paradox which is the very essence of Marx's critique of the bourgeois thought-world) a deeper ideological reversal. For the postmodernist, all is text, in no reality outside of the text is its meaning ultimately grounded: and yet, if Marx is right, just that *intellectual* conclusion is precisely what one could predict to be the ideological outcome of the social conditions of capitalism. Therefore, *if* Marx were right, the paradox of the postmodern would lie in the fact that its anti-foundationalism, its radical pluralism and relativism, its denial of extra-texual 'reality', are the precise and predictable outcome of those social conditions of capitalism on which it is founded;[1] hence that its character as an ideology would reside in the fact that it *cannot know*, that it *has to deny*, the very conditions which generate it; hence, finally, that it is intellectually and in essence a form of systematic *misrelation with reality*, as much at the social level, constructed out of the denials of ideology, as at the level of the neurotic individual, the Freudian ego is a construction of its self-deceptions.

That said, the analogy between Marx and Freud holds for more than that much. The neurotic individual may be, for Freud, an ego constructed on a misrelation with his own reality; none the less, it is in that 'unreality' that the neurotic individual really lives: he is *constituted by* his misrelation to his reality. So too – if Marx is right – is late capitalist society: insofar as its ideological denials are the product of precisely those forces whose reality it denies, it is *constituted by* that misrelation, it is a form of *lived unreality*.[2] And so if we live under the material conditions of a late capitalism whose culture is constituted by its incapacity to recognize the very conditions which determine it, this is not to say that those cultural conditions of misperception do not 'really' exist, for there is a very good sense in which the 'reality' of the late capitalist world *consists in* this unreality. It is no good, therefore, Christians supposing that they can simply shrug off, as it were, by merely intellectual gestures of rejection, the burdens of illusion imposed upon their cultic and symbolic activity by the relativistic cultures of postmodernity; for again, if Marx is right, given the shape and material form of capitalism, the shape of that postmodern culture is imposed as an ideological necessity of thought; in short, as he was so fond of putting it, you cannot abandon the illusions of an epoch until you have destroyed that epoch's *need for those illusions*.

And so I draw the obvious conclusion: if the ideology of our age subverts the conditions of the possibility of adequate symbolic activity – and if it does so it will be because it has subverted the conditions of the possibility of memory; and if that ideology is imposed upon us as the illusion required by the very nature of the material world of capitalism, then only a strategy – a *praxis* – of the critique of capitalism could adequately respond to the imperative of Christian witness; at any rate, all this would follow *if Marx is right*.

And as for that hypothetical condition, I present no argument for its truth. I merely suggest, counterculturally, that it *might* be true. Just suppose it were. Well, in that case, would not our present refusal (since 1989) to entertain that possibility, our complacent certainty of Marxism's falsehood and irrelevance, be just what is needed to sustain us in our illusions?

Notes

1   For a fascinating development of this argument, see Terry Eagelton's *The Illusions of Post-Modernism* (Oxford: Blackwell, 1996), Chapter 1.
2   For a development of these ideas, see my *Marxism and Christianity* (Oxford: Blackwell, 1983), especially pp. 24–51.

Part III
Memorializing Death and the Traumatic Pasts

Introduction

Isabel L. Wollaston

Memorialization is arguably emerging as one of the most widespread responses to violent death and the suffering of the innocent (or those remembered as innocent) today. The essays in this concluding section all reflect, in differing ways, on the forms such memorialisation can take and the questions they give rise to. Contributors focus on the African Diaspora's memory of slavery (Emmanuel Lartey); the variety of meanings attached to the Massacre of the Innocents (Martin Stringer); attempts to memorialise three very different examples of the death of young children (Kay Read); and three very different memorials in the United States (Frida Kerner Furman and Roy Furman).

What conclusions can be drawn from such a diverse series of examples? One recurring theme is the tendency to portray the dead as innocent (a theme developed at length by Stringer), or to rely upon idealised memories. Such idealisation is apparent in the way those who die in war are refigured as 'the fallen'. By emphasising the 'glorious dead's' suffering and sacrifice, our attention is deflected from remembering the fact that they died while often actively engaged in trying to kill others. Likewise, the 'Africa' remembered and celebrated by the Diaspora, particularly by African Americans is not necessarily the Africa that exists in reality (see, for example, Lartey's discussion of the representation of Africa in Eddie Murphy's *Coming to America*).

Such a diverse set of examples serves to indicate the purpose and function of memorials. As Theodore Evans notes, 'to remember means what the word itself suggests; to re-member, to put together again, to reconstruct.'[1] Building memorials or developing rituals of remembrance can be a practical response to an overwhelming sense of loss, particularly when that sense of loss is accompanied by a sense of injustice, either in relation to the ways in which the dead died, or the reasons why they died. Read makes precisely this point when she argues that the three examples she is discussing all attempt to transform the realities of a violent situation by building memorials and creating sacred space. The Furmans' discussion of some of the motivations lying behind the building of the United States Holocaust Memorial Museum (USHMM) and the Vietnam Veterans' Memorial (VVM) serves a similar purpose. Stringer's discussion of the roles both Herod and God play in the story of the Massacre of the Innocents focuses on the disquiet that this can provoke.

What is noticeable in many of these examples is that there is a deliberate focus upon the need to remember names. All three examples cited by the Furmans focus upon names. The VVM lists over 58000 names. Each panel of the NAMES Project AIDS Quilt incorporates a name (in 1992, the Quilt incorporated nearly 22000 panels). The USHMM includes two bridges of names, one listing 'lost' communities, the other the first names of those who died. Two of Kay Read's examples, the Children's Cross and the memorial to those killed by government troops in the village of El Mozote, El Salvador, in December 1981, incorporate the names of those who died. Why is the recording of names so central to memorialisation? Every war cemetery run under the auspices of the Commonwealth War Graves Commission incorporates a Stone of Remembrance, inscribed with the words chosen by Rudyard Kipling, 'Their Name Liveth for Evermore' (Ecclus. 44:14). Such a commitment to remember names stands in sharp contrast to the paradigmatic biblical curse against Amalek (Ex. 17:14; Deut. 25:17-9). The memory of Amalek's name is to be totally blotted out. Indeed, the Israelites are commanded to remember that they have to forget Amalek's name. This biblical injunction clearly points to active, rather than passive amnesia. By contrast, war memorials and Holocaust memorials and museums strive to embody active remembrance, primarily by provoking a response in others. The hope is that those who visit such memorials will participate in active remembrance of the dead, even if only to the limited degree of reading their names and recognising that they were individuals, as well as part of the statistics of mass death. Such memorials respond to a fundamental dislocation between name and body. Often the name is all that is left of the dead: there are no graves for relatives and other mourners to visit, either because there is no body, or because the place of death is unknown. As a consequence, such memorials 'are not about people, they are about names; the nameless names.'[2]

Memorialisation, particularly that which commemorates the 'missing', can be interpreted as an attempt to find meaning in the meaningless. Such 'meaning' can take the form of the legacy the dead left for the living or the 'lessons' that can be gleaned from the events being remembered, such as 'Never again'. Memorialisation is therefore as much, if not more, for the living as for the dead. The focus is as much on those left behind, coping with their grief and sense of loss, as it is upon the dead. The Furmans demonstrate how memorials such as the VVM or the Hall of Witness in the USHMM provide a focus for grief, particularly in cases where there is no known grave or date of death. Hence the significance of the decision to include the 'missing' on the VVM; this decision provides their relatives with a physical location, a substitute for a grave, where they can mourn and remember their loved ones.

Do such acts of memory embody popular collective memory, or are they primarily dictated from 'above'?[3] One only has to think of one of the most striking recent examples of memorialisation, namely the public reaction to the death of Diana, Princess of Wales. This certainly began as a spontaneous reaction, with flowers and messages being left and people gathering at Kensington Palace, as the news of her death filtered through in the early hours of Sunday morning. However, the Prime Minister Tony Blair can be seen as either capturing the mood, or influencing it, with his designation of Diana as 'the People's Princess'. He subsequently exerted pressure on both the Spencers and the Royal family to ensure that the funeral became a state occasion, rather than a private family affair. Although initially taken by surprise by the scale of public reaction, the media (and particularly the tabloid press) rapidly began to influence it, particularly in terms of the pressure exerted on the Royal family to make some public acknowledgement of the scale of this grief (for example, by breaking with royal protocol and flying the flag over Buckingham Palace at half mast). In this instance, we clearly have a popular reaction, but one that was also encouraged and influenced by politicians and the media. Memorialisation here developed its own momentum. How many people were genuinely paying their respects, acting out of a sense of personal grief and loss, or coming to be part of what was rapidly becoming a historical event and a tourist attraction?

Questions of manipulation and misrepresentation arise in relation to many acts of memorialisation. Is using the Massacre of the Innocents to commemorate the deaths of unborn children authentic or inauthentic, appropriate or inappropriate? Should there be a museum and memorial to the Holocaust in the heart of Washington DC, particularly when there is as yet no memorial to those who died as a consequence of slavery or involvement in the Civil Rights' Movement? Such questions highlight the fact that any memorial which is seen to be of relevance will often also be a source of controversy. Those memorials that cease to be relevant, either because we no longer notice them, or because we no longer remember those they are commemorating, in effect cease to be memorials and instead become part of the landscape. As Read notes, controversy surrounds the attempt to build a new church on the site of that burned down by government troops in El Mozote. For many who live their now, the past that is symbolised by the ruins of the old church and the nearby Catholic memorial is not their past. It is therefore something best forgotten. It is time to move on, to look to the future, as symbolised by the new church. For those who remember this past as their past, such forgetting exacerbates the pain of their sense of loss.

In the context of this discussion, the fact that the Children's Cross had a finite public existence and has subsequently been removed from its public location tells its own story. Such 'forgetting' raises the question of whether the deaths of the sixty-three children who died in Chicago in 1993 was of limited relevance: their memory is no longer a pressing concern of the membership or leadership of St James Episcopal Cathedral, and seemingly no longer deserving of public memorialisation.

Notes

1 Theodore Evans in Theodore Evans (ed.) *The Vietnam Reader* (London: Routledge, 1991), p. 250.
2 Geoff Dyer, *The Missing of the Somme* (London: Hamish Hamilton, 1994), p. 87.
3 For a more detailed discussion of the relationship between memorialisation and collective memory, see Paul Connerton, *How Societies Remember* (Cambridge: Cambridge University Press, 1989), pp. 1–71; Iwona Irwin-Zarecka, *Frames of Remembrance: The Dynamics of Collective Memory* (New Brunswick: Transaction, 1994), pp. 47-65; and Jay Winter and Emmanuel Sivan (eds), *War and Remembrance in the Twentieth Century* (Cambridge: Cambridge University Press, 1999), pp. 6–39.

Three Spaces Marking Child Sacrifice[1]

Kay A. Read

In 1454 in central Mexico, in the Mexica's (or Aztecs')[2] main ritual centre, an astounding ritual took place at the Templo Mayor (Great Temple). Forty-two children between the ages of two and seven, adorned in beautiful greenstone necklaces and turquoise mosaic pendants, had their throats slit. Their small bodies were sprinkled with blue pigment and buried with many water jugs in a rich cache dedicated to the rain gods.[3] The previous four years had brought disastrous drought and famine, and thousands of people had died of starvation and disease. Drastic measures were needed to end these dreadful conditions personified by rain gods who also were seen to be starving. Although the rains did return the next year, apparently the rite's cost was too high, for never again did the Mexica perform such a horrific and emotionally charged ritual.

In December 1981 in El Salvador, government troops massacred all but two people of the Evangelical village of El Mozote.[4] After brutally slaughtering many of the village's children, military personnel locked the remaining youngest in the church's sacristy and burned the building to the ground. One woman, who miraculously escaped the carnage, lay hiding in the bushes helplessly listening to the children's screams; her own crying out to her. At the time, El Salvador lay embroiled in a destructive and passionate civil war. The military leaders in power that day saw the peasant villagers – all of them – as potential enemies in this struggle, the children as future communists. After the town's extermination, just down a short hill from the church's remains, neighbouring Catholics built a memorial to the dead. Today a new village of completely different Evangelical inhabitants is rising from the ruins; and to the dismay of some Catholics in the region, the new inhabitants are building a new church on almost the same site as the old.

In August 1993 in Chicago, two men raped and strangled eight-year-old Bridget Rhynes and suffocated her grandmother; her two-and-a-half-year-

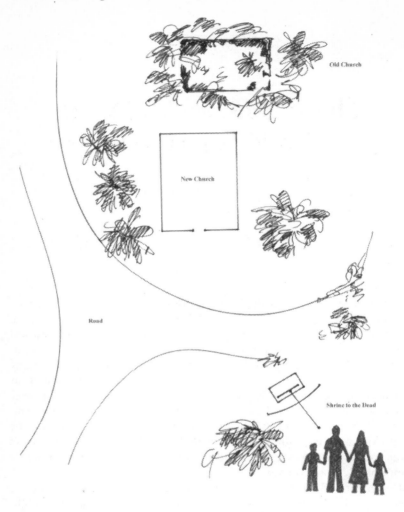

Figure 5: The Shrine to the Dead at El Mozote, El Salvador, in spatial relationship to the new church and the ruins of the old church (Drawing, Kay A. Read).

old brother watched the event.[5] The men, Marko Tomazovich and William Dukes apparently were looking for money, which Bridget's grandmother refused to give them. Bridget was just one of sixty-three children to die a violent death in Chicago that year, each of which the *Chicago Tribune* investigated in a year-long series of articles. In response to this exposé of the city's offences against its innocents, St James Episcopal Cathedral erected a simple wooden cross in its outdoor plaza adorned with all the names of the year's young victims, including Bridget's. Now, amid a variety of different voices offering contesting opinions, the Cross has been moved indoors and new plans are afoot for the plaza.

It is possible to view these three cases of violence against children as bearing sacrificial import, for each spatially marks someone's hope that the children's deaths might facilitate the transformation of an undesirable situation into a desirable one. At minimum, sacrifice always hopes that destroying something (taking its life) will lead to better conditions; at maximum it often (though not always) recognizes that death is linked inextricably with life, and destruction with creation. Beyond this, definitions of sacrifice can differ widely with differing contexts, from ritual exchanges of gifts to redeeming that which has been lost. Certainly these three cases each take their own particular sacrificial path. For example, in the first instance, an edible offering sustains living and necessary forces, for the rain gods needed to eat in the same way as people.[6] In the second, different sides of the Salvadoran civil war sometimes saw the many deaths of peasants as potentially leading to something better, although what they considered better differed radically. For the military, they were purifying the earth of communism's scourge; for the peasant Catholics who erected the memorial on the site, sacralized offerings would lead to peace on earth. This peasant definition also is found in the Greek basis for sacrifice, 'to make sacred', although the Salvadoran Catholic peasants probably also drew from more indigenous roots. Sacrifice's sacralizing element seems particularly clear, however, in the third example at St James Cathedral. By painting the names on a Cross, and inscribing on a companion plaque the biblical passage, 'All you who pass this way look and see: Is any sorrow like the sorrow inflicted on me', they directly compared the deaths of Chicago's children with the sacrificial death of Christ. Like Christ, the children now were sacred.

Other interpretations can arise from these events, spaces and objects; for these three cases do not exhaust all possible limits. Certainly not all the participants, either those involved in the acts themselves or those later commemorating them, necessarily chose to describe these events as sacrificial; some might even find such an interpretation repugnant. In fact, as will be seen, none of the three (not even the Mexica one) can be seen as strictly an 'active' sacrifice, or one in which its participants also are the ones calling it sacrifice. Nevertheless, sacrifice remains as one potential interpretation; and that is one of the points of this essay. Any given event is understandable in various ways by differing people whether they participated in the event or not, and this fact defines the spaces that border and contain these events as inevitably morally grey and often contested areas.

Given the multi-vocal and many-layered symbolic nature of these three spaces marking violence against children, I will ask two key questions: (a) how is space used to transform violent situations in the three examples described above; and (b) what can a comparison of these three different sites – Cache 48 at the Templo Mayor, El Mozote's church, and the Children's Cross of St James Cathedral – teach us about that question? To answer them, first I will discuss some of the theoretical issues and terms necessary for interpreting spaces such as these. Second, I will explore the spatially sacrificial and transformative natures of each of the above three cases. Finally, I will briefly draw out some of the ethical implications arising from this exploration.

Space: Full, Empty and Otherwise

Sacrifice is not the only thing defined differently by different people, space too can be understood in many ways. One continuing problem for Western theorists has been the temporal nature of the space, for its outward features must change through time. Both natural and human history alter and transform any physical structure: paint peels, walls crumble, and new participants create their own imprints by adding or removing things. In the process, a space's meaning can change. Even at any one moment, different participants will understand the same space differently, thereby offering the seeds for future change. As a result, almost all current theories about space also deal either implicitly or explicitly with its temporal nature. I will briefly summarize two of the most common approaches to understanding space in order to situate myself in a third.

Space's Sacred Fullness:

This approach suggests that some specially marked spaces, like the Templo Mayor, El Mozote's church, or St James plaza with its cross, are so full of sacredness that they cannot be integrated into the ordinary world. Their meaning has been fixed by transcendent powers. Thus people set sacred spaces apart from their ordinary profane world in order to provide an arena for controlled, extraordinary actions repeating some timeless ideal. Emile Durkheim was one of the first modern theorists to create a division between the sacred and profane, although he never thought anything other than the human need for social unity gave space its ultimate meaning.[7] Coming from a more faith-centred position, Gerardus van der Leeuw established a basic vocabulary for comparing sacred spaces. He noted the tremendous power of the sacred to manifest itself in ordinary space, developed an inventory of typical sacred spaces, and described how spaces create homologies that join many ideas at once.[8] Drawing on these and similar ideas, Mircea Eliade described the centre of a sacred space as an omphalos, a world axis at which the sacred irrupted into human experience, paradoxically manifesting transcendent realities in immanent everyday objects. He located common patterns of sacred space, viewing their differences as variations on fixed sacred themes.[9]

Following Eliade, others suggest that all sacred spaces provide 'symbols' that allow time-bound people to communicate with a timeless and infinite reality. Thus for Paul Ricoeur, the flux of history becomes the route to an ahistorical sacred. Sacred space is like a vessel that is too limited to contain the sacred's infinite nature, it overflows with meaning.[10] St James Cathedral with its plaza and cross may not be timeless in itself, but the sacred that bubbles out of it is. For more recent authors, the eternal fullness of sacred space does not preclude temporal clashes. Specially marked spaces become the sites of what David Chidester and Edward Linenthal called 'contest[s] over legitimate ownership of the sacred'. Space excludes as much as it includes, 'advances special interests of power', and can serve to 'dominate'.[11] Drawing from Ricoeur, they argue that it is not the people so much as the sacred that causes this cacophony; because the sacred always has a 'surplus' of possible meanings, 'no appropriation [of it] can ever be final'.[12] For them, different people could give different interpretations of El Mozote's church and memorial because no single, time-bounded person could possibly describe their infinite sacrality in full.

The Emptiness of Multi-vocal Free-For-Alls

Unlike the first approach, this second one suggests that no one fixed meaning can exist for any given space over all time, transcendent or otherwise. Because situations continually change, spaces like El Mozote's church or St James plaza embody an endless array of meanings. Pierre Bourdieu, for example, suggested that the practice of culture systematically changes through time. The ordinary patterns of life, which he called the 'habitus', are open to adjustment in order to meet the needs of particular conditions. 'In short, the habitus, the product of history, produces individual and collective practices, and hence history'.[13]

Following this Bourdieu-like ever-changing picture of culture, an image emerges of a never-ending column of different people parading through a space, all with their own intents upon it. Although any person or group may or may not argue for a space's eternal sacrality, most theorists in this category, like Durkheim, find space's import springing from more human sources such as politics, economics, class, race, or gender. Because of space's thorough integration with continually changing human activity, many theorists therefore describe space as an endlessly 'empty category' just waiting to be temporarily filled with significance.[14] Space becomes a vessel continually receiving new meanings like so many pebbles dropped into a bottomless chasm, thus meaning appears entirely arbitrary because it depends only on all those different people moving through it. Following this approach, one could say that the significance of El Mozote's church will necessarily change each time someone new takes control of the space. The Military saw it as a sign of perversion; the Catholics as a memorial to sacrifice; and the Evangelicals, who came in post-war times, as a new beginning.

Often following in the tradition of Foucault, Habermas, and Gramsci, many of these authors pessimistically view the situation as seemingly always resulting in conflict. Some authors like Dean MacCannel, however, take a more optimistic approach; seeing the multifarious babble as offering continually new possibilities for adaptation or even betterment. Spaces serve as 'empty meeting grounds', or 'free space' in which participants can explore possibilities for the 'future of human relationships'.[15] MacCannel might note that, unlike in the deeply conflicted Salvadoran case, the various voices at St James agreed to use its space to temporarily give new meaning to otherwise disturbingly meaningless violence. For MacCannel, contests occur, but they need not always end in battle, and this opens the way for a third option.

Fillable with Multiple, but Limited Possibilities:

A third position agrees with the multi-vocal folk in both camps, that spaces can be and are contested. But this position also suggests that: first, this is neither necessarily the result of infinite sacred possibilities, nor some arbitrary free-for-all; and second, such spaces as those at the Templo Mayor or St James are neither overfull nor completely empty, rather they are always potentially fillable. The question of change's origin is sidestepped because, whatever the source of ultimate reality (whether sacred or profane), humans are too limited by their particular contexts to understand it enough to make inflexible pronouncements. MacCannel calls this the 'uncertainty factor', in which we 'make no special claim on truth', but attempt to 'reach for a *possible* truth'.[16] Current interpreters of the Templo Mayor may argue that its significance lay in its sacrality, its ability to marshall great powers, unify heterogeneous groups, or control its populations with the fear invoked by violent rituals. But all of these arguments are no more than possible truths, for each interpretation rests on the particular circumstances surrounding its creation.

As with Bourdieu's habitus, the shape and a period's needs of a particular space must limit the range of possible interpretations people might give it.[17] The old dictum of the German Bauhaus school of design holds sway, that form follows function; as does its reverse, that function follows form. What needs containing will determine a vessel's shape, and vice versa. A leaky, shallow basket would make a poor container for orange juice; but it might contain pebbles or stamps very well. Similarly, different people may interpret the Christian cross in various ways; but it would be patently silly to think that anyone could suggest the cross means that checkers is an entertaining game. The two ideas have as little in common as does a basket with an orange juice container. And a cache filled with water pitchers adorned with the rain god surely had something to do with rain, not automobiles.

Because I will operate from this third position, it might help to define three key terms before discussing the three sacrificial spaces. First *space*, while linked to time, is necessarily visual, and therefore defined by concrete boundaries. Space contains things, whether they be the sacred, a cross, or water jugs; its borders mark where this containment begins and ends. Second, *marking* necessarily involves meaning – however shifting or historically bound. When people mark a space as special, they do so because it holds particular significance for them. A hotel room can contain a family for a night or two, but their home is where they properly belong. And its significance is conveyed by its forms, the rooms intended for different activities, and the furniture and objects therein. Likewise, El Mozote's space is bounded by the old Evangelical church and the Catholic memorial, and its significance is marked by its central position in town, the fact that the church is in ruins, and names of the dead appear behind a silhouette of a family at the memorial.

Third, *signs* convey significance among participants in a space. As MacCannel notes, a sign is that which 'passes among' the participants, it is that which allows people to think and communicate in whatever way they deem necessary: as friends, enemies, or perhaps not at all.[18] Signs are never arbitrary, but limited by their circumstances.[19] This makes space neither too full to allow any new meanings, nor so empty as to allow any meaning; instead it allows a limited range of meanings given the circumstances. And some of the interpretations with which Cache 48, El Mozote's church, and the Children's Cross could be filled include sacrificial intentions. After using this third approach to interpret the three sacrificial spaces, I will return to the other two approaches later to discuss their ethical significance because no interpretation is ethically neutral.

Three Sacrificial Spaces

The sacrificial interpretations of the three spaces intertwine with each space's physical and historical contexts. What happened, where, when, and who participated are all vital issues. And in each, the outcome indicates the transformative effect of past interpretations on the future.

Cache 48 at the Mexica Templo Mayor

The Templo Mayor rose from the middle of the eastern side of the main ritual district in the centre of Tenochtitlan, the capital city of the vast Mexica domain. Today, Mexico City lies upon its ruins, its centre rising from the same spot. Tenochtitlan lay in the Valley of Mexico, a high and dry mountain park with an elevation of over 2200 meters. Then as now, two seasons punctuated the valley, a wet and a dry one, and the altitude sometimes conspires with the climate to produce a skittish weather pattern punctuated by periodic droughts. Beginning with a great frost in 1449, and an even greater one in 1450, the valley entered a five-year period of starvation. Late snows and early frosts joined with severe drought to create enormous suffering; many died and many others were sold into slavery to those living in more fortunate lands. The children's bones in Cache 48 show signs of both pre- and post-natal malnutrition probably resulting from this famine.[20]

As a sign marking space, the Templo Mayor and its Cache 48 speak volumes on what can be called an 'eating cosmos'.[21] The signification of this structure was limited and bounded by its historical and topographical circumstances. Above ground the great temple rose like a giant mountain, its double staircases leading to two small houses on top, which belonged to the patron god on the south and the rain god on the north. The first marked the dry winter warring season, the second the wet agricultural summer; the space between marked the rising of the equinoctial sun on the eastern horizon. As the sun rose a bit further north each morning following the spring equinox, it entered the house of the rain god; for now the wet summer's season fed the plants, the food of earth's inhabitants. Moreover, beneath earth's surface lay the underworld through which the sun travelled each night. If the upper was dry, in need of rain's moisture, the lower was moist, the natural source of water. Here lay the rotting bones of the dead, food for the gods dwelling there. The rain gods dwelt inside the mountains, which were considered giant pots holding vast waters. Well sustained rain gods could tip these pots spilling some of their contents onto earth; if not well-fed, they would lack the strength to do so.

Annually, the Mexica sacrificed children to the rain gods during the dry season's worst period, although no text describes the exact ritual of Cache 48.[22] The Mexica believed that, because all things were alive, all things needed to eat in order to continue living. This meant that the rain gods also could starve; and without their moisture, people would starve. Sacrifice rested in a feeding exchange between humans and various other beings populating their world. The message was simple, if people were to have food, so too the gods.[23] Each being ate an appropriate living food; corn was the food of people, the blood and flesh of children the food of the rain god. In other words, some must die so that others could live. So they buried this most precious, youthful food with water vessels in the moist underground of their great ritual mountain. Cache 48 itself represented a vessel holding both the god's sustenance and people's existence, but its unusual nature indicates the desperate times.[24] Normally only two to seven children died, not forty-two. This was no ordinary godly meal, but one to feed the ravenous hordes.

Thus, the Mexica sought to transform a very nasty situation by controlling it through unusual sacrificial feeding. The ritual may have had at least some transformative effect, for rains returned in 1455, one year after the children's sacrifice. The meal must have been especially costly, however, for never again did the Mexica perform such a rite.

El Mozote's Church

Following decades of extreme social, economic, and physical repression of El Salvador's majority, civil war erupted in the late 1970s and early 1980s; it did not end until the United Nations brokered peace in 1992.[25] At the time, the bulk of the country's population lived in extraordinarily poor conditions. On the one hand, only 1 per cent of the population held 70 per cent of the land, and 8 per cent received 50 per cent of the national income; on the other, 20 per cent held no land, and received only 2 per cent of the national income. Furthermore, 70 per cent lived in absolute poverty, their wages not providing enough food to meet even minimum health requirements. By the time of the world recession of the 1970s, starvation had become a daily reality for many. So after peaceful demonstrations met with violent massacres, people resorted to civil war. In the war's early years especially, random massacres became a military tool designed to frighten the rebellious into submission by creating the impression that no one was safe at any time.

Unfortunately, the village of El Mozote imagined itself safe.[26] Because these Evangelicals did not align themselves with the largely Catholic opposition, they thought the army would leave them alone. But as Mark Danner noted, in those zones given largely to the guerillas, 'there was really no such thing as a civilian'.[27] Anyone, including Evangelicals, could find themselves open to the accusation of communism. The Army had begun 'killing by zone', and they wanted to make an example of all the villages in El Mozote's region.[28] So on 10 December 1981, its residents found themselves facing a battalion of the feared Atlacatl warriors. When they told the soldiers that they weren't guerillas, an officer responded: 'All you sons of bitches are collaborators ... You're going to have to pay'[29] Then the killing began. They decapitated the men, shot the women, raped and killed the young girls, and either slashed the very young with machetes or burned them alive in the sacristy. When some of the soldiers objected to killing children, the Major in charge growled, 'Which son of a bitch says that?' and grabbed a small boy, threw him in the air, and impaled him as he fell.[30]

What one makes of this atrocity depends on who one talks to, for certainly different sides explain it in very different ways. By and large, the Oligarchy or El Salvador's elite (who constituted only 1 per cent of the nation's population) fanatically fought a war of protection. A way of life stretching back to the Spanish conquest in the 1500s found itself under siege and the threat of annihilation. Living in almost total isolation from the populace, the Oligarchy believed themselves the builders of society without whom no one else could survive.[31] Those who threatened them threatened society's core. Hence, Colonel Domingo Monterrosa Barrios viewed operations like El Mozote as a 'draining of the sea', a 'cleaning' of those areas of El Salvador 'infected' by communism; and segments of the military described communism as a 'virus' or a 'cancer'. So they did not just kill guerillas, but everyone in their families to make sure 'the cancer [would be] cut out'. To do this, the leaders trained the Atlacatl warriors in a violent 'mística' or mystique, in which they shot practically anything that moved, smeared the blood of animals over their faces, and slit the bellies to drink the blood.[32] Certainly, many massacres did successfully kill Salvadorans sympathetic with the insurgents, but an implicit sacrificial imagery existed as well. By killing El Mozote's children, leaders of the Atlacatl warriors and many whom they trained believed they were purifying an infected land, and redeeming its previous good health.

Imagery of the popular Catholic Church paints a radically different picture. According to Anna Peterson, Salvadoran sacrifice continued the tradition of early Christian martyrdom. It demanded undesired but sometimes necessary actions in order to bring peace.[33] 'We know that we're not alone. Jesus Christ is with us and animates us to live and be faithful in the construction of the reign of God', explains a lay-oriented pamphlet on the ritual of the Stations of the Cross.[34] But to be 'animated' often seems to take on a culturally specific signification.

El Salvador's peasants can trace their folk heritage to the Pipil, a people closely related to the Mexica. In many Mexica sacrificial rituals, the offerings transformed into gods before they were sacrificed, as the children transformed into food for gods.[35] During the Salvadoran war, if the martyrs did not exactly become Christ, they came awfully close to that. 'Communion is union with God/ communion is union and truth/ our souls united forged together' asserts one song from the Nicaraguan Peasant Mass, which was very popular in El Salvador at the time. 'Like Christ they beat you with a ferocious rope/ with insults they whipped you to silence your voice/ You walked to Calvary like Jesus walked . . ./ the machine gun was your cross', asserts another. Jesus is like an ordinary person who 'sweats in the street', bears a 'weather-beaten face', and 'labors' with the people. Moreover, as among their ancient Mexica ancestors, Christ's sacrifice is repeated in every person who dies working for God's reign. And those who die remain 'alive' in those who continue fighting, for 'You are resurrected in every arm that is raised. . .because you are alive on the farm, in the factory, in the school'. For as with their ancestors, some must die 'to generate new life for the next generation'.[36]

From the point of view of this peasant Catholic theology, the children of El Mozote became unwilling sacrifices that eventually would transform the violence into peace. For the Catholics, they were sacralized as was Jesus. It did not matter that the dead were Evangelicals, or that they unwittingly participated in a communion prompted by people intent on evil. Anyone who died for the cause – willing or unwilling, believers or non-believers – had still been members of the community simply because it was dangerous to remain in a zone targeted for killing. Moreover, the Popular Catholic Church insisted that massacres were the result of human sin, not divine intervention;

the Military chose to kill these people just as the Romans killed Jesus. Because humans caused it, humans were compelled to resist it.[37] The sacrificer was evil. But that did not necessarily make his offering evil; for by dying, the dead now embodied the sacred.[38]

The church's burnt remains marked those evil acts because they offered a tangible sign of the youngest of those holy offerings. After the war, Catholics in the area built a modest memorial just down a small incline from the church's ruins, swearing that the ruins must never be replaced. A silhouette of a family stands against a wall inscribed with the dead villagers' names. But now a new church arises just a few feet in front of the old, blocking the spatial link between the memorial and the ruins. New Evangelicals have come to repopulate the town. They were not there during the war, knew no one who died in El Mozote, and do not share the same sacrificial imagery with the area's Catholics. Now that the war is over, they want to create a new life, and forget the old if possible. By hiding the old ruins with the new church, they hide the signs of past realities they don't want to mark or claim. They do so by creating the illusion of a new border on this space, thereby marginalizing the old. This 'forgetting'[39] has angered at least some of the local Catholics who remember only too well.[40] After all, certain circumstances necessarily define at least partially the space's significance, a significance which some do not want marginalized. Moreover, such forgetful marginalization becomes particularly disturbing in light of current post-war realities.

After the 1992 United-Nations brokered peace, some initial moves were made to reconstruct the country, but these have solved few of its ills. For, without the continued monitoring at first provided by the United Nations, the country has begun sliding through 'forgetting' into pre-war economic conditions. Enormous poverty and inequalities still infect the country, and the poor are as poor as ever. Moreover, the war's violence now has been replaced by street violence rivalling that of the war. El Salvador now probably holds the highest murder rate in Latin America, averaging 7211 per year.[41] War's sacrifices have indeed transformed the country, but whether for the better is yet to be seen.

The Children's Cross
In 1993, the *Chicago Tribune* front-page series touched members of St James Episcopal Cathedral, housed as they were in one of the city's richest sectors, which sits just a few blocks from one of the poorest and most violent neighborhoods.[42] What could they do about those sixty-three children and the violence that led to their deaths? First, they set up an altar in honour of the children, which among other things included a broken doll lying in a manger. They also met in regular prayer sessions with mothers who had lost their children to gang-related violence, and publicly called for gun control reform. Every year at Lent, however, the Sunday school children produced a

cross around some theme; so in 1994, they decided to dedicate that year's cross to the children who had lost their lives in the previous year.

A dozen or so primary-school children sawed and hammered together the wooden pieces, and shellacked the finished construction. They smashed mirrors and glued the pieces to one side of the Cross' surface. Finally, Sunday school teacher Dean Niedenthal painted the names of the sixty-three dead children on the other side. On Palm Sunday, the children struggled to carry the twelve-foot Cross up from the Sunday school into the Cathedral, out the front door, and one block along the side of the cathedral to its public plaza. Here, they and some of the adults raised the Cross and placed it into a planter situated on a busy corner, which marked a boundary between secular and sacred space.

The church's own tradition provided a limited pool of Christian sacrificial signs acquired by the cross through the millennia since Christ's death, and Niedenthal chose carefully from among those possibilities. By focusing on certain signs that could address particular problems, the explicit significance of the Children's Cross came to have more to do with memorialization, protest, and healing than the violence of sacrifice. Its adult producers were touched especially by the fact that many of the lost children's families were so poor they could not afford a grave marker, making the dead doubly lost to the community. The church also wanted to make a public statement on its disapproval of violence against poor children, and accomplish some healing of the sense of fear and hopelessness among its own members. With the altar, prayer meetings, call for gun control, and the Cross they hoped to come to some public and personal understanding of this 'new civil war'.[43] The plaques placed with the Cross in its plaza passionately called the public to action against the abuse of the city's children.

The mirror pieces marked this memorializing and redemptive intention for the children. Niedenthal said that the broken mirrors signified Christ broken on the Cross; likewise they mirrored back broken images of the school children gluing them onto the Cross, and of the city behind them. As Niedenthal explained, 'It is a remembrance that like Christ was broken on the cross so we are broken'.[44] Moreover, the night Niedenthal painted the names on the Cross, he felt the dead children's presence in the room with him. It seemed to him as though they were again alive, running around the room as his Sunday school children ran. He felt they were pleased because they could see their names appearing before them, and even leaned over his shoulder as he worked to make sure he had spelled them right.[45]

While memorialization, protest, and redemptive healing are clearly three of the intended significations of the Children's Cross, the Cross's visual messages and the participants' actions just as clearly marked its sacrificial messages. Created during the Lenten season, and carried by children on Palm Sunday who struggled to bear its weight, it ritually repeated Christ's sacrifice. Each dead child's name painted on its surface hangs there as Christ hung from the cross, and one plaque suggests that the children suffered as did Christ. The earlier altar with a broken doll in Christ's manger also linked Christ's death and suffering with the dead children; likewise, the mirrors signified Christ's, the children's, and the city's broken state. But salvific hope reigned, for just as Christ was resurrected, so too the children. Words offered on Holy Innocents Day 1993 prayed: 'They [the children] have passed from the sorrows of this world to risen life in your [Christ's] beautiful kingdom.'[46] The children even came alive for Niedenthal, and the very act of memorialization brought them back to life on earth. Like Christ's sacrifice, their deaths resulted in their resurrection, and the Cathedral hoped that prayer and ritually re-enacting those sacrificial deaths might result in some sort of salvific action for the city. As one of the leaders in the project, Phoebe Griswold, told a reporter, 'When we feel this pain as a corporate grief, as a family tragedy, then maybe we will know what to do'.[47]

In the fall of 1998, after some discussion of whether the now deteriorating Cross should remain outside or not, one of Chicago's infamous winds blew it over. Some took this as a sign from God. They decided to mount the Cross along with its accompanying plaques on a large wall leading down to the Sunday school, name side exposed and mirror side hidden. Later a women's group planned to construct a meditation labyrinth in the plaza space once occupied by the Children's Cross. Not all agreed with this new project, nor did all church members agree with making the Children's Cross public in the first place. Some, for example, objected to the crude, childlike style of the Cross; others objected to a labyrinth replacing the Children's Cross and wanted to see a more permanent and professionally designed sculpture commemorating the children in its place; and some of the children who helped make the Cross objected to this, because their role would have been diminished.

Finally, has anything been transformed by this sacrificial memorial? Some members have experienced personal healing as a result of its creation. By luck or divine intervention a small scholarship fund also was created to help inner-city school children as a result of the Cross' presence. Crime is down in the city, but no direct link between that and the Cross exists, although the Cross may be one small piece in the public puzzle that helped pressure for a solution. Both the Reverend Canon Janet Campbell and Niedenthal noted that perhaps the Cross sowed some 'seeds', which might have borne fruit later. Nevertheless, currently Chicago is the murder capital of the United States. In other words, some transformation has occurred, but as Campbell noted: 'The wound is always there. I mean the risen Christ always has wounds. . .So what is healing?'[48]

Ethical Murkiness

As fillable vessels containing shifting collections of signs, all three spaces mark sacrificial significance for someone, if not everyone. However, none of the cases are entirely examples of active sacrifice, in which the actual participants are also the ones who actually call it sacrifice. In the third case, members of the Cathedral – not the dead children or their killers – place these violent, destructive events into the context of sacrifice. In the second, while some of those who ordered and led the massacre used sacrificial language, Catholic peasants – not the Evangelicals who died – raised the memorial to the village's dead and gave them sacrificial signification. In the first, even though the Mexica rite might appear clearly sacrificial, contemporary historians call it so, not the Mexica. No word existed in classical Nahuatl (the Mexica language) that meant, for example, to make sacred (the root of the English word to sacrifice); only two words appear commonly used, one means to spread an offering (*uemmana*), the other debt payment (*neixtlahualiztli*).[49] Such a lack of participant interpretation in all three underscores the multi-vocality of these so-called sacrificial spaces. And multi-vocality itself raises important ethical issues, which are as murky as their sacrificial markings.

The Mexica appear to us now as the most unified of the three, but with a population of 300 000, Tenochtitlan must have encased a huge diversity of opinions. Only hints of those complexities come through the sources left to us, for our archaeological sources remain limited and all our non-archaeological were collected by their conquerors, the Spanish. Some Mexica may have objected to sacrificing the children, but unlike in El Salvador, we cannot know about them today. Now any original multi-vocal nature of Cache 48 can only be imagined, not demonstrated.

Nevertheless, the cache and other remains provide fodder for a huge spread of contemporary interpretational multi-vocality. All of these voices draw from the same sources, arriving at their differing conclusions by selectively highlighting some signs and ignoring others. This interpretational diversity ranges widely. Some wish to demonize the Mexica for their barbaric rituals (How could anyone slit the throats of two children, let alone forty-two?!!). This suggests that it is just as well that the Spanish conquered them. Others have sometimes denied sacrifice (Bodies, what bodies? The Spanish made up all those stories about sacrifice.), for some want to liken Mexico's ancient heritage to contemporary noble ideals of civilizing restraint, even if it was not like that. Such demonizing and ennobling images of the Mexica 'savages' have been with us ever since the Conquest, and they continue to serve colonialist agendas well. On the one hand, by focusing on the blood and guts of sacrificial rituals, demonic images help justify Western expansion (they deserved to be conquered). On the other, by creating noble images that deny sacrifice, one also denies both any actual nastiness, and the fact that the Mexica may not have seen colonialist ideals of morality as the same as their own. A more middle-of-the-road approach suggests that simply understanding sacrifice's reasoning need neither demonize nor romanticize it, for it should be self-evident that few today approve of slitting children's throats, although that nevertheless happened. By reaching for MacCannell's 'possible truth' in as many sources as one can, understanding might help both to come to grips with today's violence (We too kill children.), and mould a history that could prove ethically useful in spite of its nastiness (Are we missing something because we look at only the gore or what we want to see?).[50]

The obvious multi-vocality over El Mozote's church plays out larger issues of reconciliation and reconstruction. In this colonialist situation, the memories of hundreds of savagely murdered children pose a difficult dilemma. To remember is unutterably painful; yet to forget aids colonialism's continuance, and may even foster violence's return. And given the memories, how does one construct a better post-war life, especially when one may find the other side as close as one's own children? Reporting on a project to unite some 'disappeared' children with their families, Tina Rosenberg describes difficulties that echo the country's tensions.[51] These children emerged luckier than those of El Mozote, for instead of being killed, they were taken by the Military and placed for adoption to prevent their becoming communists. The emotional reunions inevitably raise all the horrific memories. Moreover, sometimes one finds one's child or grandchild now committed to the very government that caused those memories; yet somehow reconciliation must occur for the family members to function again. Not surprisingly, governmental agencies have been less than helpful in tracking down lost children. As one retired general said, 'Is it worth it to reopen wounds, when we have been able to throw some forgetting on them?' By denying the pain, the old establishment has been remarkably successful in returning to a version of their pre-war life.[52] But as Campbell said about the Children's Cross, the wounds are always there; how soon, then, before the next revolution?

As with both the Mexica and Salvadoran cases, selective 'forgetting' and remembering occurred with the Children's Cross, for certain signs of sacrifice were ignored in order to mark others. The prayer said on Holy Innocents Day begins with the words that, like Rachel, 'We cannot be consoled or comforted ... With helplessness, frustration, anger, and stubborn hope in our hearts, we turn to you [Lord Jesus]'. As with the church's children ritually repeating Jesus' struggle to carry his cross, members asked that Christ 'might inspire us to give ourselves for our children/ May we find bold witness in our city and our society'. Like the children of El Mozote, the Chicago children had become sacred by unintentionally dying at the hands of evil people, for they now resided in Christ's 'loving presence'. When parishioners prayed that 'the lives that have already been lost not be lost in vain', they stressed sacrifice's redemptive signs, while de-emphasizing the sacrificial necessity of destruction for that same redemption.[53] In contrast to the Salvadoran prayers, which focused sharply on violent sacrificial acts, this prayer selected memory, healing, and protest as its primary signs. Selective sacrificial language was used to give significance to the otherwise painful absurdity of the children's deaths. No one actually wanted to sacrificially kill children, but everyone desperately wanted their deaths to signify something.

Ironically, the only way for the Chicago prayers to do that, was to openly voice sacrifice's result, while using the Cross' sacrificial imagery to silently hint at the violence causing that result. Like the post-war Evangelical inhabitants of El Mozote, one reality needed marginalizing to create another; forgetting became a useful tool.

Other sacrificial interpretations are possible. The image of the Children's Cross by itself equates the children with Christ's sacrifice and therefore could mark them as so-many scapegoats taking on the sins of a city unable to control its violent nature; especially given that the Cross served in part as a kind of 'catharsis' for the Church's members, and the fact that it appears to have had little direct effect on the violence against which people raised their prayerful protests.[54] Yet to focus on that possible interpretation would be to overemphasize some of the historical evidence, just as it would be a mistake to overstress the children's role as sacrificial offerings, a signification at which the Cross barely hints. Church members did not originally intend to mark the children as sacrificial scapegoats. Of course with time, things could change. Should the Children's Cross fall into further disrepair, it might move to a storage room, only to be resurrected for some other purpose. In a couple of generations, the Cross might be reinterpreted as signs of the noble acts of the Church's ancestors, especially if the prayers or parts of the history or Cross itself are lost. These things have lives of their own, and any number of scenarios could be imagined. Outsiders could view the Cross quite differently as well. For example, a Salvadoran Catholic peasant interpreting the children who died in Chicago, might find it difficult to ignore the violence of sacrifice. Some might even choose not to use sacrificial imagery at all, for the Chicago children did not die in the midst of an organized struggle to make things better, but for horribly absurd reasons.

If spaces necessarily contain multi-vocality, they also necessarily hold murky moral issues, for no interpretation is neutral. The historically selective nature of marking and signification demonstrated by these three sacrificial cases also raises ethical issues for the three approaches to interpreting space discussed earlier. For the first approach, in which one subscribes to *sacred fullness*, the potential for suppressing multiple voices is enormous, for only one truth is possible. The space is already filled, allowing for nothing more. The implication exists that your truth is my truth, and if I have the power to mark the space and you do not, it will be my truth that is signified. In such an approach, a religious person who sees God as all-powerful might see the Mexica sacrifice as no more than faithful believers responding to the overwhelming power of their gods, thereby missing entirely the very human and rather humble nature of the rain-gods who can themselves starve to death. And if that religious person happens to be a well-known scholar and author, his/her voice may predominate. Even when multi-vocality is allowed because of sacred's infinite fullness, intense disagreement will defy its internal logic. If the sacred is ultimately a single unified entity, one would have a hard time suggesting that the children of El Mozote were simultaneously impure scourges who needed cleansing, and pure sacralized beings sitting at the side of Christ. Different people can make those arguments about the sacred, but not the sacred itself.

If one subscribed to the second, *multi-vocal free-for-all* approach, one might say anything about anybody because the space is simply waiting to be filled with anything. One moral judgement is as good as another; so again, whoever has the greatest power to speak will be heard. The interpreter might say of Cache 48 that Mexican indigenous history is a bad one, therefore it makes sense that the colonizer's history should set the standards. The events in El Salvador act out this same possibility. Slowly those in power are obliterating the symbols of sacrificial destruction through judicious 'forgetting'. At Perquin, only a few minutes drive, from El Mozote, the new conservative Catholic clergy in the area have already painted over murals honouring the war's redemptive power that used to grace their church's walls. And by ignoring the Chicago prayers, one would have the power to make the children whose names grace their Cross into no more than ineffectual scapegoats.

The third option – *fillable with multiple, but limited possibilitie*s – is as subject to self-interested interpretations as the other two, and therefore risks ethical murkiness as well. But unlike those two approaches, it incorporates some checks that can temper those tendencies, allowing some interpretations to fill the space because of their appropriateness, while rejecting more inappropriate ones. And by allowing for other interpretive voices, this approach more actively requires what the first way may gloss. Even if my god is all-powerful and I consider myself a weak but faithful human follower, other evidence can tell me that, in their need for food, Mexica rain-gods appear less powerful and more human-like. Therefore feeding, not propitiation, might make more interpretive sense. Historical evidence can always present a picture different from what one expected. Moreover, because circumstances can present contrary evidence, one cannot assume that anything is possible, as the second approach assumes. A fair consideration of the evidence makes the interpretation that St James parishioners viewed the Chicago children as sacrificial scapegoats very unlikely.

This third more centrist position also allows one to limit appropriately one's definition of sacrifice. Although the Mexica sacrifices appear to have been willing offerings in at least some sense, those at El Mozote and Chicago definitely were not. And their unwitting deaths and unwilling participation raises some disturbing ethical possibilities. One could accept, along with peasant Catholics, that El Mozote's children were indeed sacrifices because they shared in solidarity with all those who struggled for peace; their deaths then would not be in vain. Likewise, the St James parishioners view the deaths of Chicago's children as not being in vain. In their effort to share in solidarity with both the dead and their living relatives, the parishioners gave them the honoured status of sacrifice. In both El Salvador and Chicago, the living endowed the unwilling dead with deep and perhaps much needed significance. Yet, if one accepts the broad possibility that sacrifices can be unwilling, something these two sacrificial interpretations require, then one also opens the door for endowing ethnic cleansing, mass massacres, and military or revolutionary excesses with equally appropriate significance. However, if one finds the approval of such atrocities reprehensible, one might limit one's interpretation of sacrifice to only those who willingly offered themselves. One would probably deny, then, sacrificial status to the children of both El Mozote and Chicago. Instead, one might place their deaths among the evils that perpetrate social injustice, and therefore among those realities that cry for a different sort of transformation. At times, one needs to consider the appropriateness of one's interpretations historically, theologically, ethically, and socially.

But one last lesson these three spaces may teach us hides itself behind the signs themselves: moralistic denial alone will not eliminate violence. If sacrifice's oft-recognized link between death-dealing destruction and life-giving creation is ignored, then violence may actually increase for it remains out of reach of any kind of control. As nasty as the Mexica sacrifice was, at least they recognized that one cannot just forget about violence; to eat is to kill in order to live, a fact no one can avoid. And the unusual rite was never performed again, its violence curtailed. But 'forgetting' the sacrifices of the Salvadoran war is paving the way for new atrocities, while focusing on sacrifice's redemptive quality over its destructive necessity may gloss over the real violence Bridget Rhynes and the sixty-two other children experienced. Perhaps sowing small seeds is all one can hope to do, yet does that mean one should not openly recognize sacrifice's dark side? In January 1999 in both Mexico and the United States, the Pope fervently called for a religion based on life. But just as this twentieth-century society seeks to stress life over death, destruction's power creeps in through our television sets, hidden family abuse, inexorable pockets of urban violence, and economic structures that continue maintaining people like Bridget's family and Salvadoran peasants in poverty. And quietly lurking behind all this rests the ultimate dark power of the bomb. This inverse relationship between the marked focus on life over death, and death's unmarked force in the living world surely is no accident. And this should prove more than a little scary, for what signs one marks with remembrance or hides with forgetting do impact the world.

Notes

1 My thanks go to many members of the Birmingham crew who commented on the initial idea for this paper and read a draft. Werner Ustorf and Isabel Wollaston responded to the initial proposal. Charles Strain and Frida Furman both responded initially, and read an earlier draft. Special thanks go to my 'Sanity Group', Angelika Cedzich and Dennis McCann, for their consistent probing and prodding.

2 By the Spanish Conquest in 1521, the Mexica had not called themselves Aztec for several centuries. Indeed it is no accident that the Spanish City, which rose on top

of their capital Tenochtitlan was named Mexico City, or that the country also bore that name.

3 Leonardo López Luján, *The Offerings of the Templo Mayor of Tenochtitlan* (Colorado: University of Colorado, 1994), pp. 192–206, 347.

4 Mark Danner, 'The Truth of El Mozote', *The New Yorker* (6 December 1993), pp. 50–133.

5 Louise Kiernan and Gary Marx, 'The Boy Who Knew Too Much', *Chicago Tribune*, Sunday 15 November 1998, section 1, final edition.

6 Kay Read, *Time and Sacrifice in the Aztec Cosmos* (Bloomington, IN: Indiana University Press, 1998).

7 Emile Durkheim, *The Elementary Forms of the Religious Life* (New York: Macmillan Publishing Co., 1915).

8 Gerardus van der Leeuw, *Religion in Essence and Manifestation*, (Gloucester, MA: Peter Smith, 1933, reprint 1967).

9 Mircea Eliade, *The Myth of the Eternal Return or Cosmos and History* (Princeton: Princeton University Press, 1954), and *Patterns in Comparative Religion* (New American Library, 1958). Extending Eliade, Maureen Korp proposes a 'grammar of spatial organization' that offers a common, perhaps even universal, language of sacred space. *Sacred Art of the Earth: Ancient and Contemporary Earthworks* (NY: Continuum, 1997), pp. 25, 72–102.

10 Paul Ricoeur, 'The Symbol. . .Food for Thought', *Philosophy Today* 4 (Fall, 1960), and *Interpretation Theory: Discourse and the Surplus of Meaning* (Fort Worth: Texas Christian University Press, 1976), pp. 196–207.

11 David Chidester and Edward T. Linenthal (eds), 'Introduction' in *American Sacred Space* (Bloomington, IN: Indiana University Press, 1995) pp. 1–42, pp. 1, 8.

12 Ibid., pp. 18–19.

13 Pierre Bourdieu, *Outline for a Theory of Practice*, (Cambridge: Cambridge University Press, 1977), p. 82.

14 Anthony Giddens, 'Foreword', in Roger Friedland and Deirdre Boden (eds), *NowHere: Space, Time, and Modernity* (Berkeley: University of California Press, 1994), pp. xi–xiii, p. xii.

15 Dean MacCannel, *Empty Meeting Grounds: The Tourist Papers*, (NY: Routledge, 1992), pp. 3–4, 7. Although describing spaces as 'empty', MacCannel offers an interesting critique of the critical theorists subscribing to multi–vocal conflict.

16 Ibid., p. 6. Italics mine.

17 Bourdieu, *Outline for a Theory*, p. 95.

18 MacCannel, *Empty Meeting Grounds*, p. 7.

19 Classic semiology dating to Saussure has always maintained the arbitrariness of signs because they are fabricated by humans and not necessarily linked to their referents (e.g., Roland Barthes, *Elements of Semiology* (NY: Hill and Wang, 1964} pp. 31, 50–54). Yet because no sign can be fabricated outside of an historically defined context, a sign's meaning is necessarily limited by that context. Hence for all practical purposes of interpretation, at the very least, arbitrariness seems a less than useful concept. It may even be cognitively incorrect, for people cannot even think without their embodiment in a particular context, something at which Bourdieu hints (Bourdieu, p. 24, 90), and which Mark Johnson describes (*The Body in the Mind: The Bodily Basis of Meaning, Imagination, and Reason* (Chicago: University of Chicago Press, 1987)).

20 Luján, *Offerings of the Templo Mayor*, p. 200.
21 See Read, *Time and Sacrifice*, especially Chapters 5 and 6 (pp. 123–88), for an expansion on cosmological and phagocentric concepts of sacrifice.
22 Johanna Broda, 'Ciclos Agrícolos en el Culto: Un Problema de la Correlación del Calendario Mexica', in Anthony F. Aveni and Gordon Brotherston (eds), *Calendars in Mesoamerica and Peru: Native American Computations of Time* (Oxford: B.A.R., 1983), pp. 145–65, p. 151.
23 Read, *Time and Sacrifice*, pp. 123–55.
24 Luján, *Offerings of the Templo Mayor*, p. 206.
25 Anna L. Peterson, *Martyrdom and the Politics of Religion: Progressive Catholicism in El Salvador's Civil War* (New York: SUNY, 1997); Danner, 'Truth of El Mozote'; and Mitchell A. Seligson, 'El Salvador', *Academic American Encyclopedia* (Danbury, CT: Grolier, 1991), pp. 100–101.
26 Danner, 'Truth of El Mozote', p. 60.
27 Ibid., p. 62.
28 Danner quoting William Stanley, p. 62.
29 Danner, p. 70.
30 Ibid., p. 87.
31 Tina Rosenberg, *Children of Cain: Violence and the Violent in Latin America* (NY: William Morrow and Co., 1991), pp. 223, 242.
32 Danner, p. 67. In my own trips to El Salvador, I have heard similar.
33 Peterson, *Martyrdom*, pp. 79–80, 83, 85–88, 174. Although certainly Liberation Theology had a strong effect on peasant theology, it is too simple to attribute everything peasants said and did to that one source. As with any intelligent people, they could and did create their own imagery; for which they drew from both long-standing religious traditions, and their own cultural and personal experiences to interpret war's events.
34 Ibid., pp. 73, 87.
35 Read, *Time and Sacrifice*, pp. 144–47; Richard Townsend, *State and Cosmos in the Art of Tenochtitlan* (Washington, DC: Dumbarton Oaks Research Library and Collection, 1979), p. 28.
36 Peterson, pp. 76, 78, 82, 86–87.
37 Peterson, *Martyrdom*, p. 83.
38 It is important here to remember that the sacrificer need not be equated with the sacrifice.
39 Military people now use 'forgetting' as a noun. Rosenberg, 'What Did You Do in the War, Mama?', *New York Times Magazine*, 7 February 1999, p. 93.
40 In conversation with residents of Perquin, El Salvador (27 March 1997).
41 Ibid., p. 85.
42 See 'When Children Are Killed, What Do We Do' by James Halstead and Jule Ward in this volume for further background.
43 Halstead and Ward, pp. 38–39.
44 Ibid., p. 42.
45 Ibid., p. 42.
46 Janet B. Campbell, 'Intercessions' *Holy Innocents Service of Prayer*, The Children's Project, 29 December 1993.
47 Halstead and Ward., p. 39.
48 In conversation with Janet Campbell (3 February 1999).
49 Read, *Time and Sacrifice*, pp. 154, 157.

Three Spaces Marking Child Sacrifice 141

Ibid., pp. 194–98.
Tina Rosenberg, 'What Did You Do in the War, Mama?', pp. 52–93.
Ibid., pp. 59, 75–6, 80, 85.
Campbell, 'Intercessions'.
In conversation with Janet Campbell, 3 February 1999.

Celebrating the
Massacre of Innocence

Martin D. Stringer

On completion of the Children's Cross, and all the work and discussions which were associated with it, the staff at St James Episcopal Cathedral in Chicago chose the Feast of the Holy Innocents in December 1993 as the appropriate time to inaugurate the Cross and to commemorate that which it represented. The choice of date was partly fortuitous, the work that had gone into the Cross had taken place in the autumn and it was ready to be inaugurated during the Christmas period. Christmas itself would have been inappropriate. The Feast of the Holy Innocents, however, only three days after Christmas, seemed a highly appropriate and symbolic choice.[1] The Feast commemorates the story, found only in Matthew's Gospel, of how, following the visit of the Magi, and their return to their own country without informing Herod of the identity of the Christ child, Herod ordered the massacre of all the boys in Bethlehem under the age of two and how Joseph, having been warned of this in a dream, was able to take Mary and Jesus to Egypt.[2] This story tells of the innocent suffering of children at the hands of an oppressive authority and it was clearly the association of children, suffering and, perhaps most significantly, 'innocence' that attracted the Cathedral to this Feast. In this paper I wish to focus on the Gospel story, on the history of the Feast, and on the way in which children, innocence and suffering have become associated over the centuries. In the light of this history, I wish to suggest that the choice of this particular Feast to commemorate the 'innocent' suffering of 'children' in Chicago at the end of the twentieth century may not be as straightforward as it might first appear.

The Story of a Massacre

The story of the massacre of the holy innocents was first brought to my attention and 'problematized' at a day event I ran for a group of Methodist community workers from the Birmingham region in England. I vividly remember one woman suddenly beginning to talk very angrily about the story and the image of God that it clearly portrayed to her. Herod, she said, was about to kill all the children under two in Bethlehem and God warns just one family, that of His own son, leaving all the others to their fate. How could we accept a God who showed such callous favouritism and ignored the appalling suffering of so many 'innocent' children? Looked at in the light of contemporary massacres, and so called 'ethnic cleansing', this story clearly leaves a very bitter taste in the mouth. It is not an easy text to handle. Why, therefore, is it there, and what can be said of the story in its original context?

When looking at the birth narratives of both Matthew and Luke it is important to note that these two sets of stories, which look so different, probably have more in common with each other than either does with the rest of the synoptic texts. Each narrative aims to do two things: first to situate the story in a particular space and time with reference to important figures (either Caesar Augustus who initiated the census, or Herod the Great, King of Judea); second to emphasize the importance of the child being born by reference to supernatural events such as the presence of angels, the interpretation of dreams, or other signs and portents. The story of the massacre of the children, therefore, has to be fitted into a wider narrative which aims both to situate the birth of Jesus historically and to illustrate the special nature of that birth. For Matthew, both of these tasks can be achieved by reference to Herod and the ambiguity of the title 'king' as applied either to Herod himself or to Jesus. In more specific terms Matthew is trying to relate the events of the birth both to the prophecies which are assumed to relate to the birth of the Messiah, and to the person of Herod, whom he, for reasons of his own, is trying to portray in a very bad light.[3] It is this reference to Herod that was to be the most important element of the story for future interpretation and explanation.

Herod the Great was clearly not liked amongst the Jews of the first century. He had come to power under suspicious circumstances and was hand in glove with the Roman authorities. Matthew was not the only contemporary writer to give him a bad press. Like many rulers of his day Herod was accused of killing members of his own family and left the kingdom at his death in a state of turmoil. All the events which eventually led to the sacking of Jerusalem, later in the first century, could be laid at the door of Herod. Herod, therefore, was a particular *bête noire* of first-century Jews and fair game for any story of appropriate horror and cruelty. The massacre of the innocents fits easily into the kind of story that became associated with Herod even though there is no other reference to any historical event which can be linked to that described in this story.[4]

Much of the interpretation of the story over the centuries has also placed the emphasis on Herod. This is a story about the evil intentions and the actions of one particular King. It is Herod's cruelty which is at issue and not that of a God who allows such cruelty to happen. God, in terms of the narrative structure of the story, is seen to foil the evil plots of the king and to warn Joseph to get out. God has no more interest in the boys who are killed or their families than Herod, or, for that matter, the assumed reader of the text. These 'innocents' are bit players, they are nameless and featureless, unfortunate bystanders and observers of the action.[5] Some sympathy with their plight is encouraged by the inclusion of the quotation from Jeremiah to the effect of weeping in Ramah and Rachel's lamentation for her children. This, however, only serves to place these victims within a long line of such victims within the story of Israel and Judea, such that their death is associated with the exile and with other massacres by other tyrants of the past. This is the accepted fate of the nameless, powerless people of the Jewish nation, to be trampled on and massacred by tyrants and foreign powers. Herod is constructed, in this reading, as 'foreign' and as a tyrant to his own people, a view which is developed in some of the other literature of the period.[6] In the overall plan of the wider narrative, however, this particular massacre is a minor event and one which would not elicit any further comment except for the fact that it has been taken up time and time again by the Church and used for various different purposes throughout the centuries.

Martyrdom, Baptism and the Definition of 'Innocence'

It is clear that in the earliest centuries of the Christian Church the 'Holy Innocents', i.e. the children killed by Herod, were understood primarily as being 'martyrs'. Ireneaus, for example, says, 'since he [Jesus] was himself an infant he so arranged it that human infants should be martyrs, slain, according to Scriptures, for the sake of Christ'.[7] Or, as a later writer states, 'this death of the innocent prefigures the suffering of all martyrs'.[8] This is not a particularly surprising designation as many people who witnessed to the faith, or were killed because of some association with God or Jesus (including many Old Testament figures) were treated as martyrs by the early church. The term was used much more loosely in this sense, but much more exclusively in another, very different, sense. All members of the church in the early centuries were understood as being 'saints' and this title did not have the specific designation that it has today. The term 'martyr', therefore, took on some of the associations that we now attach to the word 'saint'. More specifically, a martyr was one who had achieved salvation through martyrdom as an immediate and automatic right. In these terms martyrdom was closely associated with the concept of baptism. In baptism the candidate was cleansed of original sin and achieved salvation through water and the prayers of the faithful. In martyrdom the martyr was also 'cleansed' of original sin, but this time in their own blood shed for Jesus or the Church.

In the light of this understanding, the problem of the innocent 'suffering' of the children of Bethlehem becomes irrelevant. Far from being a negative feature of the story, this suffering, for the sake of Jesus, leads to the immediate salvation of these children. The shedding of their blood is seen as their own baptism into Christ. What is more it is this suffering, this martyr's baptism, which establishes these children as 'innocents'. All people, according the earliest writing on original sin are born sinful and need to be baptized, to be cleansed of that sin.[9] The children killed by Herod, therefore, were sinful in and of themselves but it was their martyrdom, their sharing in the death of Christ, which made them 'innocent'.[10]

The next step was for the Church to set aside a specific day on which to celebrate this particular act of martyrdom. In the early church there were essentially two kinds of festival. In the East the emphasis was on the celebration of doctrines: the resurrection, the incarnation, epiphany, etc. In the West, however, particularly in Rome, the earliest calendars revolved around the feasts of particular martyrs.[11] Each martyr had their own feast, usually associated with their time of death (their 'birthday' in heaven), and it was not long before the list of actual martyrs was added to by celebrations of the more important martyrs of the New Testament, including the Holy Innocents.[12] It is this development which places the Feast of Holy Innocents on the third day after Christmas (following the first martyr, Stephen, and the Feast of St John the Evangelist, and so representing the Holy Innocents as proto-martyrs in their own right) rather than some time after the Epiphany which would be more reasonable if the event was celebrated in an historical context.[13]

Celebrating the Innocence of Fools

The next major development in the history of the Feast comes well into the Medieval period with the development of the Christmas period. The origins of Christmas in the west are largely a matter of guesswork, but it is clear that the time of year at which the feast was celebrated associated Christmas with other mid-winter feasts and celebrations of a more pagan nature such as the Satanalia in Rome.[14] While the official elements of the church constantly tried to play down these pagan associations many local communities continued to mix the Christian and the pagan in their local celebrations. One of the most significant and widespread of these celebrations within Medieval Europe was the Feast of Fools.[15] This Feast, like the Roman Satanalia and other pagan midwinter festivals, was rooted in a period of social licence and the usurpation of formal hierarchies, both within civil and ecclesiastical contexts. During the festivities 'Lords of Misrule' or 'Boy Bishops' were elected from among the lower echelons of society, or the clergy and a period of carnival and practical satire followed.

The exact dates of these festivals varied from place to place, but it was clear that by the fourteenth century they were an accepted part of many Christmas celebrations. In most cases the link with the ecclesiastical calendar was pragmatic rather than developed in any theological or symbolic way.

In a number of situations, however, some specific link was made between the Feast of Fools and the Feast of the Holy Innocents. This is, at first sight, a somewhat bizarre association. A Feast which aims to commemorate the death of children under the age of two is linked to a period of social and ecclesiastical licence with clear pagan, profane and even sexual overtones. The link, however, comes not from that which the feast of the Holy Innocents claims to commemorate but rather through the association of the name itself. Those who were chosen to be the Lords of Misrule, the leaders and prime movers in the festivals, were seen by the society at large as 'fools', or more broadly as 'innocents'.[16] This was particular true within monastic or ecclesiastical contexts where the figure chosen to lead the festivities was often a choirboy (the lowest order of ecclesiastical dignitary) who was crowned as the Boy Bishop for the period of the festivities.

The understanding of the fool in Medieval Europe is a complex, if interesting, one and there are clearly a number of subtleties and distinctions which I will have to overlook in this particular discussion.[17] What is important, however, is the distinction that was often made between the professional fool, those who 'played the fool' to earn a living, and the natural fool, or 'innocent'.[18] These natural fools were those who were slow-witted, had learning difficulties of one kind or another or who were disabled in some other way, either mentally or physically. Such natural fools were tormented by society at large but also treated with a great deal of suspicion, fear, and even awe. They were considered to be in some ways 'holy', closer to God, more open and trusting, more easily duped, and so on. It was in this way that such people were constructed by society as 'innocents'. What is interesting, however, is that in this designation the word 'innocent' no longer had its specific associations of 'lack of guilt'. Rather it comes to designate a whole group of people without the necessary social skills to act in a worldly way. Such people were often likened to 'children' who shared this same naivety and lack of social skills.[19] However, while children grew out of 'innocence' into full adult behaviour, the 'fools' or 'innocents' never did. It is this sense of 'innocence' that allowed the association of the Feast of Fools with the Feast of the Holy Innocents, especially when those who were given the guiding hand were real children, as in the case of the Boy Bishop.

The Feast of Fools was always opposed by the Church authorities for its pagan associations and its moral licence but it was not until the reformation that the Feast itself began to decline. With the decline of the Feast of Fools there followed a decline in the celebration of the Feast of the Holy Innocents. A number of the issues that it raised, however, particularly the association of the idea of 'innocence' to Christmas, and increasingly to children, led to some significant developments in the centuries which followed.

Celebrating the Innocence of Childhood

If we think of a contemporary Christmas, either in Britain or in the United States, then many of the elements which go to make that time of year special – presents, the tree, carols, Father Christmas and so on – can be traced back to the nineteenth century and in particular to the Victorian period in Britain.[20] It would not be pushing things too far to suggest that the contemporary Christmas is a Victorian invention. One of the significant factors of this Victorian Christmas, which distinguishes it from that of the Middle Ages, for example, is the great stress that is placed on the day itself. There is some memory of the 'twelve days of Christmas' and in well-to-do households the whole period from Christmas Eve to New Year was one of parties and celebrations. This 'twelve days', however, was a decidedly secular event. What had been lost was the series of Feasts which follow Christmas including that of the Holy Innocents. The other factor that is central to the Victorian invention of Christmas is the construction of the whole festival as a 'time for the children'. The primary image is one of the family, the log fire, the Christmas tree, the presents and, above all, the children in their sailor suits playing with their new toys.[21] Christmas for the middle class Victorian was focused in the family and was essentially a time for the children. It is this child-centred nature of Christmas, I would suggest, which maintains the link between the largely secularized Victorian Christmas and the medieval Feast of the Holy Innocents and the Feast of Fools.

Moving out from the festival itself, however, we can see the association of childhood and innocence being developed throughout the nineteenth century in a way that was essentially new and unique. It is within the same middle class, and increasingly nuclear, family who met around the tree on Christmas day that the modern conception of childhood began to develop and flourish. It is even possible to suggest that, alongside Christmas, 'childhood', as we currently understand it, is also a Victorian invention. Clearly, stated in such a stark fashion, this is a gross simplification. The origins of this concept of childhood can be traced back into the dawn of the modern era. The concept, however, probably reached its height, like that of Christmas, in the Victorian period such that our archetypal image of the 'child' still carries many associations of pinafores, sailor suits, nannies, tea parties in the nursery, spinning tops, lead soldiers and all the rest of it.

There are a number of elements associated with this construction of childhood which have a specific relevance to my own theme. The most important is the way in which this construction became intimately tied up with the notion of 'innocence'. The kind of 'innocence' that is being thought of in connection with the Victorian construction of childhood, however, is not the 'innocence and experience' associated with the fools of the middle ages, but rather, to use another literary allusion, the 'innocence' of paradise lost, a romantic, idealized, protected kind of innocence that had a great deal to do with the romantic, back to nature, noble savage kind of imagery from the early years of the century. Childhood was seen not so much as a time of social incompetence or preparation for adulthood, but rather as a space in its own right, a time of carefree fun and enjoyment. This temporal space also had a physical space in the image of the nursery and was further removed from adult life through the employment of the nannies and the general rule for children to be 'seen but not heard'. Towards the end of the century this space was developed by the growth of children's literature which, in many different ways, highlighted and celebrated the fanciful, romantic world of the child, whether through the fantastic imagination of Lewis Carol, the public school images of *Billy Bunter* and his equivalents, the Wordsworth-inspired romanticism of *Swallows and Amazons* or the Edwardian family imagery of Enid Blyton. This same set of images also came to be developed, in a slightly different way, but on the same principles, in the image of Tom Sawyer and Anne of Green Gables, amongst others, in the United States.

What is interesting about much of this children's literature, apart from its romanticism, and the construction of a space of childhood, is the relationship between good and evil that it develops. In some cases there are specifically 'evil' characters, although they are remarkably few and far between. The 'bad' is represented in many ways by the children themselves, none of whom are portrayed as wholly good. There is a 'naughtiness' or 'mischievousness' to many of these literary creations that portrays children as some kind of romantic 'free spirit', even in many cases as 'noble savages' (see, for example, Ransome, Blyton, and the role of the Indians in *Peter Pan*). This 'naughtiness' is in fact part of the 'innocence' that is being portrayed, an open-eyed excitement and naivety that is presented as being specific to children and as being lost in adulthood. *Peter Pan* is an excellent example of just this kind of 'innocence' in the way in which Peter refuses to grow up, he wishes to retain that sense of adventure, that mischievousness, that fascination and wonder at the world that is seen to be specifically associated with children.

It is at this point, and specifically with reference to *Peter Pan*, that the discussion comes back to *Paradise Lost*. It is in the very fact that childhood has to be put behind us and cannot be regained that sets it apart as a romantic Eden of youthful wonder. The adult can never return to this time and hence can never regain that 'innocence' which is inevitably lost during the transition between the child and the adult. Innocence for the Victorian image of the child is that which must be lost. The question, however, is how and when this innocence goes. This, with only a very few exceptions, is not a part of the story in any of the children's literature that I have been discussing. Some of the older children do 'grow up' or are on the verge of 'adulthood' (usually understood in terms of having to look after and have responsibility for younger children), but that significant step is never fully made in any of these texts. There is, however, a clear sub-text, in much of this discussion which associates the loss of 'innocence' with the discovery of sex.

Innocence and Corruption

The hidden (or even suppressed) sub-text of children's literature, concerning innocence and sex, is made explicit in other literatures of the Victorian period which were equally significant in the construction of childhood at the time. These were specifically focused on the campaign to 'rescue' children from the horrors of work, the workhouse, poverty and prostitution. With the construction of a distinctly middle-class image of childhood, which provided space for the child to be 'a child', it soon became clear that large sections of the population were denied any part in this idealized image. Children had worked alongside adults for centuries in the agricultural economy and this was always felt to be normal, the working unit was the family. In the early years of the industrial revolution this accepting approach to child labour was taken over into the factory. However, because of specialization, the family unit could no longer work as a team but rather the adult men worked in one part of the factory, the adult women in another and the children in another. It was some years into the century before this began to be challenged, primarily by middle-class women who felt that children needed space to be 'children'. This fight for the emancipation of children from industrial labour was associated with other campaigns for what today might be called 'children's rights' within and among the urban poor. Most notable among these was the fight against childhood prostitution in the inner urban areas of London. Large, essentially Christian, organizations were set up to rescue, primarily girls, from the corruption of prostitution and to provide them with a space to be 'girls'.

It is in the light of these developments that a very specific understanding of 'innocence' began to develop in relation to children. 'Innocence' was seen as something which was inherent in childhood, all people are born 'innocent' (a far cry from the original sin of Augustine and the early church's construction of the Holy Innocents). This innocence, however, can be, and in many senses must be, lost in the growth into adulthood. The only alternative to innocence, however, within what was essentially a protestant environment, was 'sin' and it was seen to be inevitable that eventually all people would 'fall into sin' and therefore lose their 'original innocence'. What is significant, however, is the fact that because of the particular construction of innocence in the popular discourse of the day, no child could actually discover 'sin' for themselves; however naughty they might be, children were not seen as being 'sinful'. Sin came from outside, from the adult world, and sin 'corrupted' the innocence of the child. Once corrupted, of course, innocence could never be regained. Corruption, therefore, was to be avoided at all costs and the corruption of innocents, particularly the leading of girls (always more 'innocent' than boys) into prostitution, was seen as the greatest of all evils in the moral hierarchy of the late Victorian world. Innocence, therefore, was constructed in distinction to, and in a necessary relationship with, corruption. Without corruption there would be no 'innocence' but 'innocence' existed as a state, or a space, beyond corruption.

The Sanctification of Innocence

Throughout the twentieth century the Victorian construct of childhood innocence has been retained, but it has been shorn of some of its more romantic associations and replaced with some kind of consumerist veneer. Children and childhood are now a 'market' and a very lucrative market for those who can milk it. More importantly, perhaps, the Victorian image has also been shorn of the concept of 'naughtiness' which enabled children to maintain some kind of less than entirely angelic stance. Children, as I have argued, were expected to maintain, within their own space, a certain licence which was not permitted in space that was defined as 'adult'. This backroom space (to use a Gofmannesque term) included the nursery within the home but it also spread out into a number of 'wild' and 'natural' spaces beyond the home.[22] This space, and the naughtiness or 'adventure' which was associated with it, was linked to the image of the child as 'savage', but more specifically to the child as a 'noble savage', essentially good and needing only to be educated.[23] With the slow removal of this space, I would argue, we have also lost the potential for the child to be adventurous, to be 'savage', to be naughty. This has occurred at one level with the expansion of the construction of childhood from the affluent middle classes, who had the money to maintain the space in terms of nurseries and country houses, to the population as a whole, and particularly to those who live in inner urban areas, where such space simply does not exist. It has also developed alongside the increasing perception of 'danger' within contemporary open space.

More widely, the shedding of the savage imagery of childhood has led to increasing difficulties within society in relation to violence among, and aimed towards, children. This has gone hand in hand with an increasing emphasis on the 'corruption' of innocence through a process of reification, such that the 'innocence of childhood' is no longer seen as a fictional construct but as some kind of real explanation of the 'nature' of children. As in the Victorian origins of these concepts the association of 'corruption' is still seen to lie with questions of sexuality and sexual practice and so, while the actual prevalence of sexual activity has increased among adolescents over the century, the expectation and the discourse surrounding sexuality among children and teenagers has become increasingly fraught. Both of these trends, the difficulties of associating children with both violence and sexuality, have led to a particularly virulent and impassioned discourse on questions such as sexual abuse, paedophilia and child pornography such that these are seen to be crimes (not 'sins' as such by this time) which put particular individuals beyond the pale. Behind all these discourses is the assumption that children are 'pure', are 'innocent', and that they should never be allowed to be corrupted by contact with the violence or sexuality of adult-hood.

Of course, there are difficulties with these discourses that tend to get overlooked. The first concerns a problem of definition. What exactly is a 'child' in the late twentieth century? The images are still there of the innocent, sweet-faced, six-year-old from the Pears soap advert, or the angelic, cherubic three-year-old of popular iconography. Any talk of the sexual abuse of 'children' therefore inevitably conjures up images of these very young, defenceless children, and the horror that is associated with the idea is the horror that is quite correctly associated with any abuse of children as young as this. Many of those that are actually involved, however, are considerably older than this, sometimes up to fifteen and sixteen and on the verge of adulthood. The damage that can be caused to these people by any form of abuse should never be underestimated, as abuse at any age can be damaging and destructive. The point I am making, however, is that the situation changes if we are discussing young children or if we are discussing teenagers and adolescents. The imagery and the associations are always those of young children, the practice is overwhelmingly, but clearly not entirely, concerned with teenagers, adolescents and young adults.[24]

Another area where the discourse of innocence and childhood starts to cause difficulties for contemporary society brings us back more fully to the Children's Cross. This concerns the possibility of violence, not just that which children suffer at the hands of adults, but that which children commit. Society finds it very difficult to cope with the idea of a truly violent child. The whole discourse of innocence suggests that children, while they can perhaps be naughty, cannot be truly violent or cruel, they cannot be 'evil', they cannot 'sin'. This is a very difficult area. If we go back to the trial of the two eleven-year-old boys who were found guilty of killing two-year-old Jamie Bulger in Liverpool in 1993,[25] the first reaction was one of denial. Children cannot commit this kind of crime. The second reaction was even more interesting, the suggestion that a child who commits this kind of crime must be truly 'evil', even more 'evil' than an adult who does the same thing. Children are by nature 'innocent', they are 'natural'; those who commit crimes of this magnitude have denied their 'innocence', there can be no other explanation, therefore, than that such children must be by nature 'evil'. It is society's construction of childhood innocence, I would suggest, that led to the sense of outrage and horror at what was just as likely to have been a childhood prank (a bit of adventurous mischief) that went tragically wrong. The discourse would not allow any other possibility to be voiced.

The 'Holy Innocents' of Chicago

This brings us back to the Children's Cross in Chicago. The Cross was set up to commemorate the 'victims' of gang violence from the South Side of the

city. In setting up the Cross, the children were portrayed as 'victims of violence'. They are implicitly portrayed as 'innocent' victims of violence. They
are also portrayed as innocent victims of 'violence' which is perpetrated by
adults. This is the portrayal that is offered by the nature of the memorial.
This is the portrayal that is reinforced by the fact that the date chosen to
commemorate these children is the Feast of the Holy Innocents. All the
associations of 'innocence' and 'childhood', from the nineteenth century on,
are brought in to focus specifically on these children killed in this city by acts
of ruthless 'adult' violence. This fails completely to take account of the fact
that a number of these children were themselves members of the gangs that
were involved in the violence, and that some at least were shot by other children of much the same age as themselves. Are these 'victims' really as 'innocent' as the construction is aiming to suggest?

Before exploring this further I need to mention one further twist to the
story of the Feast of the Holy Innocents which I also believe comes into
play in the choice of this feast to commemorate the victims of violence in
Chicago. If we go back to the original story, then we will note that part
of the aim of the story, whether implicit or explicit, was to show the violent and ruthless nature of Herod as an alien King to the Jews. It is Herod
who 'takes the blame' for the massacre throughout history. However, if we
go back to my original discussion, then it is clear that many modern com-
mentators are just as concerned about God's role in this story, and the
fact that God saved His own son but left the other children to die. Herod
it appears, has taken the blame and has been painted as the evil character
of the story, where perhaps that blame should really sit on God's shoulders for letting the situation develop in the first place. This line of thinking is particularly interesting when we look at two other uses of the story,
and more specifically of the Feast, that have been developed in recent
years.[26]

The first of these has been the choice of the Feast of the Holy Innocents
to commemorate the appalling suffering and mutations which have occurred
among a large number of babies who have been born within range of
nuclear test sites in the South Pacific. These children, and their mothers, are
the forgotten victims of the nuclear arms race and they have been neglected
by all concerned. There have been sporadic campaigns for decent health care
and for compensation, and it was as part of these campaigns that the Feast
of the Holy Innocents was chosen as a day to pray for, but also to publicize,
the cause. This all seems very straightforward and a sensible use of the
imagery concerned. Here we have a relatively straightforward case of children suffering 'innocently' at the hands of an uncaring and oppressive state.
The other case, however, is not quite so straightforward. In recent years local
branches of the Society for the Protection of Unborn Children (SPUC) have
chosen the Feast of the Holy Innocents as a special day for services and
prayers to commemorate the many foetuses aborted within Britain and to
sound a protest against what they see as abortion on demand. This is a

deliberate and clearly calculated decision. Given the Catholic roots of many of those involved in SPUC and related pro-life organizations, the choice of a special day to make their own seems reasonable. The choice of the Feast of the Holy Innocents, however, carries with it many different kinds of associations, most of which we have already explored. SPUC is constructing the aborted foetuses first and foremost as children, second as children that are innocent (again conveniently forgetting Augustine's doctrine of original sin) and third as innocent children who are being deliberately killed by the state.

What is interesting about these two uses of the Feast is that they both go back to the story itself for their core images and ignore much of the early church and Medieval (and even the Victorian and contemporary) images that have been associated with the story and its central concept of 'innocence' over the centuries. The story tells of a deliberate massacre of children by what can be seen as a totalitarian state, a massacre of the kind that we have become all too familiar with throughout the twentieth century. In both these cases, however, while the concept of innocence is important to the construction of the commemoration, it is the fact that it is the state that does the massacring that is perhaps the most significant element. Both commemorations are intended to be, in part, a protest against an uncaring and supposedly violent state. The perpetrator of the violence is as important to the construction as the representation of the victims. This is something new, and, I would suggest, gives another twist to the use of the Feast by the Cathedral in Chicago. Who is this Cross aimed at? Is it simply a memorial commemoration? Is it for the families of the victims? Is it aimed at pricking the conscience of individual gang members who might have carried out these murders? Or is it, like the use of the Feast by those protesting against the fall-out of nuclear testing, or those involved in pro-life campaigns, aimed primarily at the state who, like God in the original story, simply stood by and let this kind of massacre of innocent lives take place?

Notes

1 See Janet Campbell's discussion of the events surrounding the creation and setting up of the cross earlier in this book.

2 Matthew 2:13–18

3 There is also a suggestion that Matthew was deliberately developing a 'Moses typology' in these stories such that the events which happened to Moses, such as his birth at the time of the slaughtering of male children and his subsequent journey out of Egypt, also happen to Jesus. This, however, is not directly relevant to my own discussion. See D.A. Allison, *The New Moses, A Matthean Typology* (Edinburgh: T & T Clark, 1993).

4 See W. Hendriksen, *The Gospel of Matthew* (Edinburgh: Banner of Truth Trust, 1973), pp. 158–65 for a longer discussion of Herod and his reputation.

5 See Luz's brief notes on this theme in U. Luz, *Matthew 1–7: A Commentary* (Edinburgh: T & T Clark, 1989), pp. 147–8.

6 See Hendriksen, *Matthew*, p. 158.

7 *Against Heresies*, III, xvi, 4 quoted in Hendriksen, *The Gospel of Matthew*, pp. 180–81.

8 Rabanus Maurus (780–856) quoted in Luz, *Matthew 1–7*, p.148.

9 See H. Rondet, *Original Sin, The Patristic and Theological Background* (Shannon: Ecclesia Press, 1972) for a more detailed discussion of this issue.

10 Only Chrysostom of all the early church writers questions the designation of the title 'innocents' to these children and his argument is based on the assertion that there can be no such thing as 'innocent' suffering (See Luz, *Matthew 1–7*, p. 147).

11 See W.H. Frere, *Studies in Early Roman Liturgy, I. The Kalendar* (Oxford: Oxford University Press, 1930) for a more detailed discussion of this process.

12 Frere notes that the Holy Innocents are one of only two 'martyrs' within the calendar who are not linked with a specific 'stational church' and so they do not fit into the scheme as smoothly as many other local Roman or more important New Testament martyrs (Frere, *Early Roman Liturgy*, p. 25).

13 This sequence of three days after Christmas is one of the most consistent and fixed sequence of commemorations in the whole history of the liturgical calendar which must give it some kind of special significance.

14 For further details see E.O. James, *Seasonal Feasts and Festivals*, (London: Thames and Hudson, 1961), pp. 228–32.

15 See A.C. Zijderveld, *Reality in a Looking-Glass: Rationality through an Analysis of Traditional Folly*, (London: Routledge and Kegan Paul, 1982), pp. 58–70.

16 Zijderveld, *Reality in a Looking-Glass*, p.38.

27 See Zijderveld, *Reality in a Looking-Glass*, for a more detailed look at Medieval folly in all its forms.

18 Ibid., p. 35.

19 It should be noted that in this kind of discourse 'innocence' has lost its specific connection with sin. It is lack of social skills that makes a child 'innocent' not a lack of original, or any other kind of sin.

20 See J.A.R. Pimlott, *The Englishman's Christmas, A Social History* (Hassocks: Harvester, 1978), pp. 85–96.

21 Note the plot of the favourite Christmas ballet 'The Nutcracker' and the emphasis on Tiny Tim in Charles Dickens' *Christmas Carol*.

22 E. Goffman, *The Presentation of Self in Everyday Life* (Harmondsworth: Penguin, 1971).

23 See Taussig's reversal of this in his discussion of the 'savage', i.e. the Amazon Indians, as children in M. Taussig, *Shamanism, Colonialism, and the Wild Man: A Study in Terror and Healing* (Chicago: University of Chicago Press, 1987).

24 See L.A. Stanley 'The Hysteria over Child Pornography and Paedophilia' in J. Geraci (ed.) *Dares to Speak* (Swaffam: Gay Men's Press, 1997), pp. 179–206, for a particular response to these kinds of issue.

25 For a discussion of the Bulger case, see the two articles by Gitta Sereny for the *Independent on Sunday Review*, 'Re-examining the Evidence' (6 February 1994), pp. 4–10 and 'Approaching the Truth', 13 February 1994, pp. 4–11.

26 Each of these cases have been noted on Church notice boards over the last ten years or so. I am not suggesting that either has official sanction of any kind but the associations still remain interesting.

Black Memory: Commemorating the sacred and the traumatic in the African Diaspora

Emmanuel Lartey

In everlasting memory of the anguish of our ancestors:
May those who died – Rest In Peace
May those who return – find their roots
May humanity never again perpetuate such injustice
Against humanity.
We the living vow to uphold this.[1]

A fact which is not immediately obvious at the site nor from the records is that the majority of the slain children commemorated in the Chicago Children's Cross were African-American.[2] The African American community is one which has suffered unspeakable violence. The experiences of entrapment, 'the Middle Passage', and the life of slavery in America persist in the collective memory of African Americans. The re-emergence and re-discovery of slave narratives as collected in the Schomburg Center (New York) is evidence of this. At the same time African-American society today is a place of violence which paradoxically includes 'Black on Black' violence. It could well be that the majority of the children commemorated in the Chicago church were victims of such irony. The Children's Cross, then, could be described as an attempt to create what French historian Pierre Nora has described as a *lieu de mémoire* (site of memory). Here we find a sacred place where trauma is commemorated, which has particular poignancy for the African American.

For centuries Americans of African descent have been on a journey of self-discovery. First called *coloured* by their captors, then the pseudo-scientific '*Negro*' (with all the derogatory connotations carried by the term) later *Black* then *Afro-American* (reflecting a growing self-consciousness and self-definition or re-definition). They have generally now come to designate themselves as *African Americans*. As Magubane has argued,

Identity?

The combination of various factors – enslavement, denigration and contempt of Africa (and all it stood for), exploitation and white definitions of the black and his role in world history – created severe problems of identity. Was it possible for the black man to accept white definitions of the African character and to retain his integrity and self-identity?[3]

Magubane goes on to show how the 'Afro-American' image of Africa developed through the years into a dilemma involving 'ambivalence, embarrassment and a sense of possibility'.[4] Images of Africa throughout the nineteenth and early twentieth centuries tended to coincide with colonial and imperial interests. The reporting of this period placed great emphasis precisely on those aspects of African life known to be unfamiliar to Europeans and which were likely in their portrayal to cause horror. It is possible to demonstrate that this approach to Africa still persists in the western media and appears to be deeply embedded in the European psyche. The relationship between 'Black' Americans and Africa before the 1970s, as Hood has shown, 'has been complex and tortuous, complicated by the blacks internalising religious and popular views about the colour black and Africa'.[5] Hood is right in pointing out that the conversion of Black slaves to Christianity was informed by ongoing conversations among them with African traditions, retained or adapted to their strange new surroundings. The struggle for identity among African Americans could not be, and was not, divorced from Africa.

When Blacks created their first cultural and religious organisations in the eighteenth and nineteenth centuries, they consciously adopted the term *African* to identify and designate their activities. The first Black social service organisation established by Newport Gardner and others in 1780 was named the African Union Society. Richard Allen and Absalom Jones established a similar organisation in Philadelphia in 1787 and called it the Free African Society. Many Black churches self-consciously carried the name *African* in their titles. African Baptist Church, Lunenburg, Virginia (1758); First African Baptist Church, Savannah, Georgia (1787); Bethel African Methodist Episcopal Church (1794) and the African Methodist Episcopal Church (AME) founded by Richard Allen and others in 1816, are some notable examples.

The struggle for a distinct African identity is manifest in the emigration of Black Americans to Liberia after it gained independence in 1847, the founding of the Universal Negro Improvement Association by Marcus M. Garvey (1887–1940), Pan-Africanism and the work of W.E.B. Du Bois (1868–1963) and latterly (since the 1980s) Afrocentricity – the work of Molefi Kete Asante, and the African-centred Education movement, to name simply a few significant events and movements in which African Americans chose to name themselves and act on their own behalf. People who name themselves *African*-American clearly indicate a desire to be linked with their African heritage.

Alongside this naming has gone attempts to reconnect with Africa through study of African history and culture, the taking on of African names and pilgrimages to the motherland – the place of their origins. Large parties of African Americans are now to be found visiting the forts and castles along the coast of West Africa from where their ancestors were shipped, in an attempt to rediscover 'roots', commemorate their history or re-construct the steps of their ancestors. Robert O'Meally and Geneviève Fabre write, 'the desire to retrieve the past still endures. Threatened by a sense of discontinuity and forgetfulness, we seek new moorings and props, new means of reactivating the processes of remembrance as we reach toward a better sense of who we are and whence we have come.'[6]

African-Americans are not alone in this. There has been a discernible reassessment of Africa within the psyche of diasporan Africans in Britain and elsewhere in Europe. The image of the continent and its place in history has undergone a significant change for many who trace their ancestry to it. Africa, and especially the slave dungeons of West African castles – discussion of which will form an important part of this chapter – have for many indeed become *lieux de mémoire* 'where memory crystallises and secretes itself at a particular historical moment, a turning point where consciousness of a break with the past is bound up with the sense that memory has been torn – but torn in such a way as to pose the problem of the embodiment of memory in certain sites where a sense of historical continuity persists.'[7]

This chapter examines aspects of the memory of Africa within the African Diaspora in America and Europe. It will be argued that very much like the Christian symbol of the cross, Africa functions in the Diaspora as a sacred *place of origins which is both sacred and traumatic.*The approach adopted in the chapter will be to explore the co-incident themes of sacredness and trauma by examining some of the productions of Black popular culture in film and video, specifically Ethiopian film director Haile Gerima's *Sankofa* (1994) and Eddie Murphy's *Coming to America* (1988). By focusing on the African American celebration of *Kwanzaa,* I will explore Black efforts to commemorate the historical and cultural heritage of Africa and finally discuss the preservation of Ghanaian coastal forts and castles with their slave dungeons as world historical sites.

Sankofa

Sankofa is an Akan word which translated into English means 'go back and reclaim the past'. Although the reference is to the past, the force of the injunction lies in the present and the future. Sankofa is an act in the present of reclaiming the past, with the express purpose of enabling one to move forward into the future with understanding. Haile Gerima's film, *Sankofa* (1993) seeks to capture this sense of retrieval for the purposes of movement into the future. Murashige has argued that Gerima's cinematic sensibilities were forged long before he came to the US to study at Chicago's Goodman School of Drama in 1967. Born in Gondar in north-west Ethiopia, Gerima was exposed to the concept of art as a political tool by his father who was a writer, teacher, historian, priest and playwright. Gerima speaks of his father's 'plays of resistance' used to 'mobilise people during the Italian invasion of Ethiopia.'[8] It was his mother and grandmother who taught him the equally important storytelling traditions of Ethiopia. Gerima is convinced that the filmmaker is a storyteller who provides information, creates and explores vital aspects of social relationships, linking both historical and global dimensions of human experience.[9]

The film begins and ends in a slave castle in Ghana. An African-American young woman on a visit to the slave dungeons is transported in time and space through her ancestral experience of capture, enslavement, the middle passage, slavery in America and return to her African homeland as a visitor and tourist. The explosive theme of the horror of the trans-Atlantic slave trade is brought home to the audience through the medium of the psychic experiences of trance and vision; the merging of the historic experience of atrocity at the hands of slavers with contemporary circumstance and the interaction of diasporan and continental people through time.

Sankofa makes very clear the struggles of African peoples for their freedom. But perhaps what is most compelling about the film is that it demonstrates the importance of African people telling their own stories, seeking ways of expression which will capture and portray historic fact as it exists in the memory of Africans at home and abroad. The anguish and pain captured within the dungeons are experiences which no European historian can easily imagine or enter. There are dimensions of experience there which have to do with the African collective psyche which need to be conveyed from the depths of the African consciousness. This consciousness is not monolithic. Rather, as *Sankofa* makes evident, it can be glimpsed through the interaction of many African stories. The formation of underground meetings where the slaves attempted to re-create their ancestral rituals both psychic and festive are portrayed by bringing together present-day African actors, for whom some of these rituals are on-going living realities, and African American actors, who in a sense live the reality of the longing for lost names, rituals, understandings and beliefs. Such blending gives the film an air of reality tinged with palpable pathos which borders on the surreal. Gerima's storytelling ability, coupled with his African consciousness and spirituality, are evident in the weaving.

Sankofa spans time and space in a circular fashion. Here there are no individual heroes – only traumatized people who attempt to rise above their privations. In the end they all – living and dead – gather in the courtyard of the slave castle on the shores of the homeland in silent communal commemoration.

Coming to America

Eddie Murphy's *Coming to America* belongs to that category of films which Valerie Smith has described as seeking to recover 'respectable' images of Blackness.[10]

The film, however, seeks not simply a positive image for the Black in America, but rather by demonstrating the materially, culturally and spiritually rich heritage of Africa to inspire and motivate African Americans to rediscover and celebrate their 'African-ness'. Throughout the film glimpses of the splendour of Africa are portrayed.

Hakeem is an African prince who is prepared to work with his hands to earn a living. In spite of his status – indeed because of it – he tries to find love without reference to it. Hakeem embodies the values of humility and forthrightness which are to be emulated by all great African princes.

This is Africa – the American dream! Splendour, wealth, opulence, celebration, sunshine, laughter, sexual innuendo and fun. It is when the traditional values of ancient Africa are in conflict with the desires and wishes of emergent multi-culturalism that an air of realism is injected into what could be dismissed as Hollywood myth. In the end the charm and wit of matriarchal Africa wins out and coincides with the desire and wish of youthful African America. Such merging, though by all means desirable, leaves one wondering the extent to which the reality of struggle in both contexts is truly treated. Moreover the pain and trauma which is part of the African reality, especially in historical terms, is perhaps not sufficiently portrayed in *Coming to America*.

Nevertheless what is captured in *Coming to America* is the desire for a reconfiguring of the image of Africa in the African American and indeed Western mind.

It is an attempt to counter the historic denigration of Africa and to begin the process of creating more positive images which may have the potential of uplifting a humiliated people. Questions such as I have raised about the African American mythic dream of Africa while legitimate, miss the essential point of the text. Much that is horrible and negative can be and has been said about Africa in the west. It is time now to hear the other side of the story – the dignity, splendour and beauty which has been assumed to be absent. *Coming to America* seeks to do this.

Kwanzaa

Desires within the African American community for a stronger sense of community have been in increasing evidence since the early years of slavery. Following the Watts riots of 1965, Dr Maulana Karenga of California State University created *Kwanzaa* (first celebrated in 1966) as a celebration which would strengthen the African-American sense of togetherness and enable

African Americans draw on African values – values he believes enabled their ancestors to overcome the horrors of slavery, oppression and racism. It is currently estimated that at least eighteen million Africans celebrate *Kwanzaa* each year around the world with celebrants in the US, Africa, the Caribbean, South America (especially Brazil), Canada, India, Britain and other European countries. In Chicago, thousands of African Americans participate in the National Black United Front, Chicago Chapter's annual *Karamu ya Imani* (Feast of Faith) on 1st January, the final day of *Kwanzaa*. There is a growing number of Black British folk who likewise participate in some aspect of *Kwanzaa* observance either as families or organisations.

Karenga explains that *Kwanzaa* is based on ancient African harvest celebrations. The word *Kwanzaa* itself comes from the Swahili phrase *matunda ya kwanzaa* which means 'first fruits'. *Kwanzaa* is celebrated on the seven days from the 26th December to the 1st January, a period which represents the end of one year and the beginning of another. Karenga identifies five basic aspects of African harvest celebrations shared by *Kwanzaa*. These are: (1) the in-gathering of the people, (2) special reverence for the creator and the creation, (3) commemoration of the past, especially paying homage to the ancestors, (4) recommitment to a community's highest ethical and cultural values, and (5) celebration of the goodness of life, especially of family, community, culture, friendship and the human person.

Karenga explains that he created *Kwanzaa* to re-affirm the rootedness of African-Americans in African culture, to reinforce the bonds between them as a people and to introduce and re-affirm the value of the *Nguzo saba* (the seven principles) of *Kwanzaa*. These principles are formulated on the basis of concepts articulated in Swahili as follows: (1) *Umoja* (Unity) – to encourage a striving for and maintenance of unity in family, community, nation and race. (2) *Kujichagulia* (Self-determination) – to encourage self-definition, self-naming, 'creating and speaking for ourselves'. (3) *Ujima* (Collective work and responsibility) – encouraging mutual care and responsibility, shared work and togetherness. (4) *Ujamaa* (Cooperative economics) – encouraging African peoples to build and maintain their own stores, shops and other businesses from which shared profit accrues for the community. (5) *Nia* (Purpose) – the focused attention and effort at fulfilling the collective vocation to restore African people to their traditional greatness. (6) *Kuumba* (Creativity) – the desire to do as much as is possible in their own way in order to leave the community more beautiful and beneficial than was inherited. (7) *Imani* (Faith) – believing in 'our people, our parents, our teachers, our leaders and the righteousness and victory of our struggle'. Karenga refers to these as the 'Seven Principles of African American community development' which serve as a fundamental value system.[11]

For an African born and bred in the West African country of Ghana such as I am, there is much here of interest. What is of particular significance for me is the place accorded the ancestors in this. African religions were first described by European anthropologists in terms of 'Ancestor Worship'. So evident and striking was the reverence paid to illustrious ancestors by the African peoples that the European explorers could not help being struck by it. They were mistaken to have reduced African religions to this particular aspect alone. They were also wrong in dubbing what they saw 'worship'. Much ink has been spent especially by African theologians in attempting to correct this.[12] What is recognized now, with due regard to local variations of custom and belief, is that the more appropriate description is of 'high regard' or veneration paid to ancestors by African religionists. To discover an African American scholar and activist adumbrating and celebrating the African values of 'community, family and ancestors' is further evidence of the shift in valuation of Africa in the Diaspora. Commemoration of the past, especially of past illustrious persons – the living dead – who speak to us from beyond the grave, continues to be a hallmark of African spirituality.

The *Kwanzaa* celebration itself includes the traditional African ritual of libation in which family representatives pay homage to their foreparents in forms of words coupled with the pouring of water on the earth, the resting place of the ancestral bodies. A highlight of the ceremony is the lighting of *mishumaa saba* (seven candles) placed within the *kinara* (candle-holder). Like the menorah in the Jewish Hanukkah celebration, the *kinara* holds one candle for each day of *Kwanzaa*. There are three red candles (symbolizing struggle and the blood of those who have died in the struggle, with one each standing for *nia*, *kuumba* and *imani*) to the left of the central candle which is black in colour. The black candle represents Black people and the principle of *umoja*. To the right of the central candle are three green candles. The colour green stands for the hope and future that proceeds from struggle. The green candles represent the principles *kujichagulia*, *ujima* and *ujamaa* respectively.

One family's *Kwanzaa* celebration includes the recitation of the Black Family Pledge written by Maya Angelou.[13] The pledge is worth quoting in full:

BECAUSE we have forgotten our ancestors,
   our children no longer give us honor.
BECAUSE we have lost the path our ancestors cleared
    kneeling in perilous undergrowth,
   our children cannot find their way.
BECAUSE we have banished the God of our ancestors,
   our children cannot pray.
BECAUSE the old wails of our ancestors have faded beyond our hearing
   our children cannot hear us crying.
BECAUSE we have abandoned our wisdom of mothering and fathering,
   our befuddled children give birth to children
   they neither want nor understand.
BECAUSE we have forgotten how to love, the adversary is within our
   gates, and holds us up to the mirror of the world shouting,
    'Regard the loveless'

THEREFORE we pledge to bind ourselves to one another, to embrace our
lowliest, to keep company with our loneliest, to educate our illiterate,
to feed our starving, to clothe our ragged, to do all good things,
knowing that we are more than keepers of our brothers and sisters.
    We ARE our brothers and sisters.

IN honour of those who toiled and implored God with golden tongues,
and in gratitude to the same God who brought us out of hopeless desolation, we
make this pledge.

Embedded in this pledge are the stirrings of values which have traditionally
been associated with Africa. There is almost an over-playing of the illustri-
ousness of the ancestors in typically African fashion. There is clearly poetic
licence with causal links being drawn where they may not in reality be war-
ranted. Nevertheless the force is clear – we need to 'return and recover the
values of our ancestors' we need to return to the communitarian Africa.
Sankofa – we pledge ourselves today, to recover the communitarian values of
the past, in order to move into a better future. *Kwanzaa*, then, attempts to
fulfil the sacred injunction of the traditional Akan through ritual and commemoration.
    Recently the originators of *Kwanzaa* have found themselves having to
battle a growing trend to exploit and commercialize the festival. A 'National
Coalition to Preserve the Sanctity and Integrity of *Kwanzaa*' has been
formed. This coalition has successfully challenged food and drink companies, clothing companies and other stores for what are perceived as over-
commercialization and market re-definitions of *Kwanzaa*. The threat is
understood to be aimed at the sacred core values of what is a cultural, spiritual and communitarian act. This trend, which is evident in Christmas and
Easter festivities all over the western world, has to be resisted. The types of
questions posed include whether Black people should seek recognition for
Kwanzaa from entities outside the Black community and whether non-Black
businesses should be excluded from using *Kwanzaa* to sell products. In the
light of the US Postal Service's issuing of a commemorative *Kwanzaa* stamp
in which the colour symbolization of the ceremony has been altered, pointed
questions have been raised concerning the ownership of *Kwanzaa*. Who has
the right to change *Kwanzaa's* meaning, symbols or rituals?[14]
    The issues raised here have to do with the sacredness of the African her-
itage within the African American community. *Kwanzaa* has struck a chord
within that community and appears to be helping in education, commemoration, ritualization and participation in an African heritage lost through
years of slavery and de-culturalization. *Kwanzaa* has become the African
Americans' 'home-coming' without physical travel. Hannibal Tirus Afrik,
spokesperson for the National Council of Elders, argues that the *Kwanzaa*
tradition over the thirty years of its existence, 'became our symbol for (1)
reclamation of African traditions, (2) reverence to African ancestors, (3)
reinforcement and strength for family and community stabilization, (4)

intergenerational respect and adherence for African cultural values' the loss of which is to be resisted by a real coming together of African peoples. [15]

The struggle to preserve *Kwanzaa's* cultural integrity reflects how precious this sacred ceremony is for so many people. It is a struggle to save a sacred event from the profanity of commercialization. The sacred *Kwanzaa* in this sense has come against the reality of political economy in its American context. Ironically, this seems to re-echo the historical trajectory of the African presence in America. Africans would not have found themselves in America in the first place were it not for economics and politics. It was the pursuit by powerful white commercial interests of gain at the expense of African ability that first created the conditions from which redress is still being sought. The question remains to what extent this ceremony already to an appreciable extent participates in the inevitable Americanization of African reality. In as much as the participants share in an internalized American culture it remains a real difficulty to truly participate in an African experience. However, the point of all commemorative activities is to enable participants to enter a mythical space in which memories, experiences and symbols interact to create moods and images that inspire. In this respect *Kwanzaa* succeeds admirably in the commemoration of the trauma and the triumph which is the African diasporan experience of Africa.

Forts, castles and dungeons

One of the issues which has recently become fairly contentious is the extent of the involvement of Africans in the enslavement of their compatriots. It often comes as a sobering – indeed chilling – revelation to some African Americans to discover that Africans had any involvement whatsoever in the iniquitous trade. This fact is inescapable for any who examine the evidence closely or indeed who visit the shores of West Africa. The inscription on the plaque at the Elmina castle, reproduced at the head of this chapter, is an attempt by descendants of African traditional rulers to seek forgiveness for their part in the suffering of their own people. Many were the African raiders who captured fellow Africans for sale to Europeans on the coast.

It must be said, however, that those who would exonerate Europeans of blame by claiming that they were merely 'traders who bought what was offered them' by Africans must be suffering from a most disturbing form of guilt displacement or projection neurosis. That Africans were involved cannot be doubted. Africans, however, cannot be blamed for what happened to their fellows in the dungeons of the European castles nor for their treatment on the ships in the 'middle passage'. If one accepts, for a moment, the invidious argument of that day which claimed that the Europeans were civilized people on a mission to civilize the primitive and barbarian Africans, one is left wondering what form of civilization was on offer in the dungeons and on the slave ships.

The argument that slavery was a part of African culture and heritage which Europeans adopted is equally unconvincing. If this was so, why did the Europeans who rejected and attempted to suppress every aspect of African culture, not suppress this aspect also? Why did the 'civilized European' so readily single out this particular aspect of 'the barbarian African culture' to engage in with relish? It was European avarice for excessive profit through cheap labour that fuelled the trade. Racism, racist ideology and social Darwinism provided justification for the prosecution of the business. Africans, often unaware of what lay in store for their defeated, conquered or captured compatriots, traded them for European guns, alcohol or merchandise. The legacy of those three-hundred years of mass exploitation and humanity's inhumanity are the forts and castle that dot the coastline of West Africa, a majority being found on the shores of Ghana.

The government of Ghana is collaborating with UNESCO in seeking funds to construct a Slave Museum in Ghana as part of the Slave Route Project, a project which was adopted jointly by the World Tourism Organisation and UNESCO in 1991. The Cape Coast and Elmina Castles along with Fort St Jago have been declared World Heritage Sites by UNESCO. This development generated a wave of protests from Black people all over the world. Petitioners (over 3000 from the US, Jamaica, Italy and New Zealand), while generally in support of the restoration work on the former slave castles at Elmina and Cape Coast, emphasized the need for this work to be particularly sensitive to their primary functions as memorials to the dead. They were appalled that parts of the castles were to be used as gift shops, restaurants and tourist leisure spots and protested against the trivialization and commercialization of what, in their view, is a sacred space.

The dungeons are places of appalling memories. How are they to be preserved? To demolish them would be to attempt to wipe away a significant part of world history – a history which in part accounts for the presence of Africans in Europe, the Caribbean and the Americas. To commemorate the trauma of these places is a delicate balancing act. Money is clearly needed to restore and preserve them. Serious questions need to be asked concerning the means by which the needed revenue will be raised. To find monies in ways that mirror the slave trade or that reinforce the economic and political precursors and results of the trade is clearly repugnant. Opening the dungeons to tourists nevertheless means also catering for their creaturely needs. The quest for appropriate memorialization of evil acts is fraught with difficulty.

One such evil act that requires memorialization is the deaths of those who perished in the Middle passage. Given the nature of the acts being remembered, a fitting memorialization should take place at sea. There was in July 1999 such a memorial act. Nevertheless the quest for appropriate ceremonies to mark this occasion continues. Such ceremonies need to respond to the pain and unease felt by all people of good will, the sensitivities of the descendants of the Africans, who survived and the memory of those who died. For Africans the illustrious dead (ancestors) are a crucial part of the living community. They have a place and a part to play in the on-going life of the surviving community. Not to commemorate them in a fitting manner can result in psycho-social disturbance within the living community. The continued unrest in the African community, both continental and diasporan, could well be understood in African philosophical terms as reflecting the continuing collective trauma of the trans-Atlantic slave trade.

The Christian symbol of the cross is one which captures the trauma of the execution of an innocent young man. Upon this historic event have been constructed many doctrines of atonement which seek to centralize the death of Jesus Christ in the reconciliation of humanity with God. The adequacy or otherwise of these doctrines is not the purpose of this reference. What is striking to me is that there are parallels which may usefully be drawn by African peoples in our quest for an appropriate way of memorializing the execution of innocent African peoples in slavery. The Christian response to the cross has largely been to view it as a place of victory over evil. That the Christian faith continues to inspire in the face of the execution of its founder is mirrored in the recovery of Africa in the African-American experience in the face of the historic onslaught of forces aimed at the physical, cultural and spiritual destruction of the African.

The dungeons and slave ships were clearly places of execution for the African. This is a fact that needs to be recognized in any memorialization. Those who died were put to death. Second, human forces both White and Black conspired to place these people in this situation. Third, the motive was profit and it was White interests that overwhelmingly derived the benefit. Care must be taken to ensure this does not happen again in the guise of memorialization. Fourth, the cross as a symbol of trauma and victory can be paradigmatic for the dungeons. They can be preserved as places of trauma where we are able to see the victory of a people who rose above every privation to which they were subject to achieve greatness. As we enter into the unspeakable pain of the dungeons we can pause to allow the horror of the experience to have its full effect. As we leave them and enter upon the view of the expanse of sea which greets us in the courtyards above them, we can commemorate the victory of all Africans, wherever they may be, who attempt to keep alive the communitarian cultural values of a traumatized people.

Notes

1 Inscription on a plaque on a wall at Elmina Castle,Ghana, where Africans were placed in dungeons awaiting the slave ships. The President of the Ghana National House of chiefs apologized to the world for the part their ancestors played in the trans-Atlantic slave trade. This plaque was constructed to commemorate that apology.

2 It would be instructive to find out where their bodies were buried. Were they segregated in death as they were in life? Angelika Krüger-Kahloula observed that 'the categories of caste and class that affect the residential patterns of the living also touch the homes of the dead'. Angelika Krüger-Kahloula, 'On the Wrong Side of the Fence: Racial Segregation in American Cemeteries' in G. Fabre and R. O'Meally (eds), *History and Memory in African-American Culture* (New York/Oxford: Oxford University Press, 1994), pp. 130–49, p. 130.

3 Bernard M. Magubane, *The Ties that Bind: African-American Consciousness of Africa* (Tenton, NJ: Africa World Press, 1987), p. ix.

4 Magubane, *The Ties that Bind*, p. 37.

5 Robert E. Hood, *Begrimed and Black: Christian Traditions on Blacks and Blackness* (Minneapolis: Fortress, 1994), p.163.

6 Fabre and O'Meally, *History and Memory in African-American Culture*, p. 7.

7 Pierre Nora, *Les Lieux de Mémoire*, quoted in Fabre and O'Meally, *History and Memory in African American Culture*, p. 7.

8 See Mike Murashige, 'Haile Gerima and the Political Economy of Cinematic Resistance' in Valerie Smith (ed.), *Representing Blackness: Issues in Film and Video* (London: Athlone Press, 1997), pp. 183–203.

9 Ibid., p. 183.

10 Smith, *Representing Blackness*, p. 2.

11 See Maulana Karenga, *The African American Holiday of Kwanzaa: A Celebration of Family, Community and Culture* (Los Angeles, CA: University of Sankore Press, 1989).

12 See, for example, E. Bolaji Idowu, *African Traditional Religion: A Definition* (London: SCM, 1973) especially pp. 178–83; John S. Pobee, *Toward an African Theology* (Nashville, TN: Abingdon, 1979), and E.W. Fasholé-Luke, 'Ancestor Veneration and the Communion of Saints' in Mark Glasswell and E.W. Fasholé-Luke, (eds), *New Testament Christianity for Africa and the World* (London: SPCK, 1974).

13 Maya Angelou's 'Black Family Pledge' can be found at www.thecybermom.com/attic/issue1/family/angelou.html.

14 There have been debates within the Black community and discussions in which challenges have been put to the founders (who appeared to endorse the action of the US Postal Service in their unveiling of a Kwanzaa stamp) with questions concerning the role and ownership of the heritage of the celebration.

15 Hannibal Tirus Afrik, 'Preserve the Cultural Integrity of Kwanzaa', published at http://www.itskwanzaatime.com/usstamp.html, 1997.

Memorializing Collective Tragedy in Public Space

Frida Kerner Furman and Roy S. Furman

The Children's Cross at St. James' Episcopal Cathedral in Chicago seeks to address and memorialize tragedy at the local level using the medium of a traditional religious symbol. Seen as a text, the Cross is designed to communicate rage, sadness and loss to passers-by as it attempts to engage them viscerally through the names, photographs and pieces of mirror attached to it. In important ways, however, its impact is limited by its location on church grounds and its Christian associations in a city known for its ever-increasing religious diversity. None the less, the Cathedral's impetus has been to move from private to public space in memorializing collective tragedy. In so doing it joins company with a variety of recent memorials – monuments and semi-spontaneous happenings alike – that suggest a collective American impulse to bridge the individual and the collective, the private and the public and the religious and the secular in dealing with loss.

In this chapter we investigate the nature and function of three contemporary memorials in the US: the Vietnam Veterans Memorial (VVM), the NAMES Project AIDS Quilt, and the US Holocaust Memorial Museum (USHMM). All three, dedicated in 1982, 1987, and 1993, respectively, have been tremendously successful – considerably beyond their proponents' expectations. The Quilt grew from 1920 panels during its first national display in 1987 to 42,357 panels by March 1997; the VVM has become a standard for other memorials; the USHMM has literally been overwhelmed by visitors since its opening. The memorials have had a powerful influence on individuals' personal experiences – for the millions of 'pilgrims' to these shrine-like memorials in Washington DC – as well as on the culture at large. The periodic display of the Quilt on the Washington Mall, and the permanent location on or near it of the other two memorials, is not incidental but critical. For their location at the political centre of the nation has in part contributed to their remarkable impact on American consciousness. Our intention is to describe and analyse some of the key characteristics of these memorials that might account for their significance.

A drive into countless American small towns leads to a public square where one is likely to find a war memorial, usually dedicated soon after the First World War. Made of stone, a typical monument inscribes the names of those local men who died in service to the nation during one war or another. These monuments are often accompanied by a dedication that enlists God as the helping hand behind the glory and sacrifice revealed by the soldiers' death. In short, such memorials encode a narrative of devotion to God and country.[1] In this way they are quite predictable. In like manner, the other major monuments located in the Washington Mall – the Lincoln Memorial, the Washington Memorial, and the Jefferson Memorial – reveal a neo-classical architectural style that reflects heroic narratives of the American national consciousness.

By contrast, the three memorials under consideration might well be seen as anti-heroic: their compositions do not elevate their meaning into abstraction and grandeur but symbolically express the tragedies they memorialize. In addition, they celebrate, not the Washington/Jefferson/Lincoln triumvirate, but the great unsung: the dead and missing soldiers of an unpopular war, the casualties of AIDS, the victims of Nazi persecution. What is distinctive about all three memorials is their commitment to rescue ordinary individuals from oblivion by naming them, but not on behalf of a higher cause. In the case of the VVM and the Quilt, one could say that the names themselves constitute the very heart of the memorials.

Aside from their anti-heroic message, these memorials appear to be successful because they engage a developing American sensibility, one committed to emotional expressivity, personal experience, and the search for community. Instead of a single controlling narrative, they offer the viewer multiple stories and multivalent interpretive possibilities. All three are expressive – symbolically and functionally – of profound existential meanings; they also bridge certain long-standing social categories. We will argue, using sociology of religion categories, that these memorials support priestly as well as prophetic functions.[2] The priestly dimension is associated with the memorials' capacity to act as catalysts for the expression of grief connected with collective tragedies. In this regard, they facilitate emotional release, comfort and bring a measure of personal and sometimes collective healing, often mediated through implicit, if not explicit, religious meanings. While none of these memorials was self-consciously conceived to achieve political ends, we argue that all three serve prophetic functions: they constitute forms of public protest and critique, by – among other ways – challenging the epic narratives expressed and affirmed by traditional American memorials. This posture may have been facilitated by the fact that all three memorials were created with private funds.

The Vietnam Veterans Memorial:

The idea for this memorial was generated by a Vietnam veteran, Jan Scruggs, who along with others campaigned among veterans and in the private sector for funds before approaching the US government for a site for the project. In 1980 Congress gave the veterans two acres of land at the foot of the Lincoln Memorial. A few months later, President Jimmy Carter signed the bill into law. The Vietnam Veterans Memorial Fund made two stipulations for the memorial: it was not to be political, and it needed to incorporate the names of the deceased (and those missing in action and likely dead) veterans of the Vietnam War. The design by Maya Lin, then an undergraduate architecture student at Yale University, was selected from among 1421 entries.

The Vietnam Veterans Memorial was dedicated on Veterans' Day, 13 November 1982. Situated on the west end of the Mall, it is built into a shallow depression in the ground, its highest point measuring ten feet, rendering it invisible when approached from the north. It consists of two black, highly polished, symmetrical, triangular granite walls, each 200 feet long, which meet at a 125-degree angle and taper off at the ends. One end points toward the Washington Monument, the other toward the Lincoln Memorial, visually engaging with these monuments in a symbolic dialogue. Over 58000 names are engraved in white on the black granite walls. The inscription of names breaks with the symmetry of the walls in the following way: names are chronologically ordered by date of death or disappearance, but the list begins (with the year 1959) at the vertex of the angle formed by the two walls, proceeds to the right and begins again on the left wall, ending (with the year 1975) at the vertex. The only principle of ordering here is death; all other hierarchies and ranks are levelled – including those of race and education, which powerfully divided those who served in the war and those who were exempted.

The high polish of the walls makes them mirrors for onlookers, contributing, perhaps to the 'communion' with the dead experienced there. The colour of the walls, their horizontality, their seeming emergence from the earth, and their memorial function have been associated symbolically with graves. Indeed, the Memorial serves as a kind of graveyard to which people make pilgrimage, some on a yearly basis. The wall allows for powerful catharsis: for those who lost family members or army buddies during the Vietnam War, for those emotionally or spiritually touched by this war, whatever their political position may have been. Visitors of every stripe leave messages for the dead: from heart-felt expressions of personal loss – of a husband, a brother, a son, a buddy – written on pieces of paper or posters, or more artistically placed in frames, to more philosophical reflections on war, guilt, sacrifice, reconciliation and hopes for reunion in the afterlife left by familiars and strangers alike.[3] In this way the Vietnam Memorial has become the American analogue to the so-called 'Wailing Wall' in Jerusalem.

Other types of offerings abound as well: items of military garb – medals, shoes, jackets, hats; civilian clothes; teddy bears, model cars, and other toys; photographs of the deceased and of survivors; American flags; flower wreaths. In 1984 the US National Park Service formally began collecting these offerings at the tune of nearly 1000 items a month. As one author puts it, 'That this flood tide of artifacts and documents shows no sign of ebbing even as the war itself recedes into the past testifies to the insistent role Vietnam continues to play in the national imagination. As that role evolved, the memorial itself has become a combination of holy shrine and secular bulletin board.'[4]

Displays of pent-up emotion are commonplace at the Wall. Volunteers are always available to provide support for those overcome with grief. People reach to touch the names of acquaintances and beloved relatives. Many pilgrims to the Memorial take a piece back with them: they make a name rubbing. In these many ways the VVM has come to play an unexpectedly powerful priestly role in the experience of loss and sorrow. Despite its non-political intentions, the Wall has also played a prophetic role: it stands in indictment against all war. Its very powerful emotional impact has rendered the Wall the most effective tool of national reconciliation around the painful, and still unresolved, issues of the Vietnam War. Most particularly, it has brought social rehabilitation to the thousands who served in the war. Thus the Memorial both crosses boundaries and unites: it links the public and the private, the civic and the existential.

The NAMES Project AIDS Quilt:

Like the VVM, the Quilt was the brainchild of one individual, Cleve Jones, an AIDS activist in San Francisco. In November 1985 he asked participants to make placards bearing the name of someone they knew who had died of AIDS at a march held in memory of an earlier crisis in the city: the assassinations of Mayor George Moscone and Supervisor Harvey Milk. The placards, hung on the facade of the federal building, reminded Jones of a patchwork quilt handed down within his family and used to comfort those who were ill or housebound. Based on the traditional American association of quilts with 'cosiness, humanity and warmth', Jones conceived of the AIDS quilt as a public metaphor of national unity, a means to convert a 'gay disease' into a shared national tragedy.[5] While addressing the grief of the AIDS epidemic was a central goal of the Quilt, a political agenda was also part of the picture: to critique the government for inaction in dealing with AIDS and public indifference about the loss of gay lives. Interestingly, Jones repeatedly denied having political motivations: 'We're completely non-political, we have no political message at all.'[6]

The NAMES Project was formally organized in June 1987. A few months earlier, Jones had made the first panel, which became the model for other panels. Each panel measures three feet by six feet, the size of a grave. For major displays, eight panels are linked together with grommets into 12-foot squares according to colour and area of the country. When the Quilt has been displayed at the Mall for a weekend, panels take up an area the size of multiple football fields, evoking a kind of symbolic graveyard (in 1992, nearly 22,000 panels were displayed; because of its increasing size, 1996 was the last year that the Quilt in its entirety was displayed at the Mall). Panels are individually conceived and executed and then sent to the Names Project; only standard size and the writing of a name are required. Contributors include relatives, friends and lovers of persons who have died of AIDS; strangers, gay and straight, male and female; quilting groups typically composed of heterosexual women who are otherwise unconnected to the gay community.

The panels reflect the choices of the quilters, but often also the individuality of the deceased. Personal missives are frequently stitched into the design, as are descriptions of the deceased, some serious, some playful, some erotic; much of their substance is secular, some is religious. Many panels function as witness to a life lived and to a painful death. Some panels are testimonies about the person who died, but many are about the panel-maker's relationship to the deceased; some ask for forgiveness, expressing guilt and regret. Materials used vary widely. Items of clothing belonging to the dead – such as a shirt, necktie, or hat – are frequently sewn into the panel. Photographs abound. Objects such as teddy bears are evident as well. As in the VVM, there is no hierarchy or ranking here; it is a quintessentially democratic memorial. In death, both memorials declare, there are no differences that matter.

The Quilt serves as a site of pilgrimage for the many who have lost loved ones; for those who are HIV positive; and for those who want to stand in solidarity with the dead and the survivors. Public displays of the Quilt are accompanied by moving rituals, including the reading of the names, candlelight vigils and singing. There are places interspersed among the panels for visitors to leave messages. Those who have not been involved in the actual composition of the Quilt panels have an opportunity to connect or 'commune' directly with the dead as they contribute to the collective memorializing. What is distinctive about this memorial is the centrality given to individual identity. As Peter S. Hawkins suggests, 'Private identity is held up as monumental; the intimate stretches as far as the eye can see. In fact, by overdramatizing intimacy, by taking small gestures of domestic grief and multiplying them into the thousands, the Quilt makes a spectacular demonstration of the feminist dictum, the personal *is* political.'[7]

Expressions of loss and sorrow are encouraged, hence both personal and collective grief is facilitated through the Quilt's priestly function. By emphasizing the magnitude of losses due to AIDS and utilizing the Mall as a site of protest, the Quilt has also helped to effect a prophetic function: to shift mainstream understanding of AIDS as a gay disease to AIDS as an American crisis. The Quilt has bridged several social categories in this process – between gays and straights, between femininity and masculinity. The latter devolves from the fact that most of the panels memorialize gay men, yet the medium is a traditionally feminine craft in the US. The Quilt actively expresses non-dominant notions of manhood through its often tender representations of male love. Such expressions throw into relief, especially, the absence of heterosexual men among the makers of the panels, which are done largely by gay men, lesbians and straight women.

The US Holocaust Memorial Museum:

The Holocaust, the Nazi murder of eleven million European civilians, among them six million Jews during the Second World War, is frequently held up as an unquestioned metaphor for human evil. Claims to its absolute uniqueness among historical events suggest to many that utmost caution be exercised in describing, evaluating and memorializing its horror. As Michael Kernan puts it, 'This event must be spoken of – yet must remain unspeakable'.[8] Indeed, it is often referred to in near transcendent terms, as if it were sacred in its power, its awe, its challenge to those who proclaim the presence of God in the world and, paradoxically, His (or Her) absence. No wonder that the process of developing an American national memorial to the Holocaust and its victims was accompanied by an unusual degree of political and emotional 'fear and trembling'.[9]

Initially the idea of American Jews, especially Holocaust survivors, the USHMM emerged from a commission established by President Jimmy Carter in 1978 and charged to develop 'recommendations with respect to the establishment and maintenance of an appropriate memorial to those who perished in the Holocaust'.[10] (Not coincidentally, Carter's charge came within two weeks of the television screening of the mini-series, *The Holocaust*, whose viewing figures of 120 million undoubtedly stirred the conscience of the nation.) The commission ultimately rejected the idea of a Holocaust monument in favour of a historical museum, a 'living memorial',[11] which would have a 'Hall of Remembrance' adjacent to it. The museum, opening in April 1993, has become an enormously popular institution, with the number of visitors, especially those who are not Jewish, far exceeding even the most optimistic predictions. It is always a crowded place.

As with the VVM and the Quilt, the Museum serves both prophetic and priestly functions, the latter in more subtle though clearly intended ways. Indeed, it is the Museum building, along with its permanent exhibition, which has proven to be the 'living memorial' in ways that the beautifully designed 'Hall of Remembrance' does not functionally approach. For it confronts visitors with what the building's architect, James Freed, calls 'a visceral language of architecture', designed to reduce the emotional distance that many bring with them in approaching the Holocaust.[12] In fact, a visit to this museum is akin to participating in a religious ritual, one that allows participants to experience that which is awesome through the intentional reenactment of the 'sacred' narrative of the Holocaust, thus commemorating collective memory.

While the Museum, located just off the Washington Mall in close proximity to the Washington, Jefferson and Lincoln Monuments, presents an exterior that seems to harmonize with nearby federal structures, that public presentation is a cleverly constructed façade – actually an enormous limestone and concrete screen – beyond which lurks a spatially and emotionally disconcerting interior: the facade is an architectural analogue to Nazi efforts to camouflage the true nature of their genocidal intentions. In entering this memorial structure, the visitor enters 'a different reality', far removed from that of official Washington and contemporary American society.[13] Indeed, Freed, a Jew who emigrated as a child from Germany in 1939, sought to introduce the Museum visitor into the 'universe' of the concentration camp. According to historian Raul Hilberg, Freed succeeded in creating a 'concentration camp on the Mall'.[14]

And so the journey begins, from the imposition of selected entrances for groups, school children, the elderly ('to the right') and other individuals ('to the left'), to the necessary passage through the Hall of Witness. With brick walls and exposed steel bands suggesting to the more knowledgeable the patterns and structures of crematoria or the open area of a railway platform, the space is virtually sealed off visually from the outside. This is not a place for leisure (there are no convenient resting places); indeed, visitors experience a vaguely ominous tone within such a 'tectonic' environment, a feeling that is hardly alleviated by a required and intentionally crowded ascent to the permanent exhibit in large, dark grey metal elevators. From that point on, visitors need to follow a set path, walking through the entire exhibit, four floors down. As Freed puts it, 'There is no way of backing out of it. . . . The elevators won't take you back. They deposit you, close their doors, and go back for more.'[15]

For the visitor, the exhibit moves inexorably from life to extermination. Deprived of civil rights and legal guarantees, Jews are depicted uprooted from their normal lives, as Nazi Germany moves down its increasingly racist and anti-Semitic path. Brutality and forced expulsions move those 'undesirables' who come under German military and political control into ghettos, and by trains to camps, and then to gas chambers and crematoria. As one observer noted, 'As visitors enter the world of the death camps, the space becomes tight and mean, heavy and dark. Indeed, walls are not painted, pipes were left exposed . . . there is [seemingly] no escape.' Exhibit artifacts, he adds, 'allow museum visitors to "touch" the physical reality of the Holocaust: to smell the pungent doors of victims' shoes, to stand next to an Auschwitz fence-post, to walk through a German rail car of the type used to transport people to their deaths.'[16] Such a journey creates memory, and, for some, allows for an experience of loss and grief, opening the way for an authentic memorialization. Beyond that, a prophetic function is in greater evidence through the values expressed by the Museum's exhibit and the structure that houses it.

This can be seen in the material portraying America's relative lack of concern for Jewish suffering at the hands of the Nazis, the seemingly callous decision not to bomb railway tracks that took Jews and others to their deaths in Auschwitz-Birkenau, and the refusal to allow the Saint Louis and its desperate Jewish refugees from Germany to enter US waters off the coast of Florida. The prophetic impulse is also evident in the implicit charge to guard against the erosion of civil rights and liberties given by the Museum's chronicling of Germany's descent into a fascist and racist society. The presentation of such a message within the heart of America's governmental centre, amidst those memorials to leaders committed to America's democratic values, and within a city where racism is, in part, manifested in impoverished African-American communities, is a powerful moral challenge.[17] Such a critique will also bear particular significance as world situations again cry out for American intervention on behalf of imperilled civilian populations.

In the centre of the Hall of Witness is a reflective black granite wall inscribed with Isaiah's prophetic challenge, 'You are my witnesses.' As Freed notes, one must make a choice which way to move past it, left or right[18]: another selection process perhaps, but one of one's own choice. Which way does the witness go? What does she do with her testimony? What is the appropriate response to the Holocaust, or to a 'living memorial' in its name? Perhaps the more than six million visitors and the tens of thousands of school teachers from around the United States who have 'entered' the Holocaust have already begun to write the answers.

From Metanarrative to Multiple Vocalities

Traditional monuments implicitly or explicitly communicate what are perceived to be shared social values, often, as we have suggested, through cultural metanarratives. The breakdown of social consensus, most dramatically demonstrated by the cultural eruptions of the 1960s and beyond – the civil rights movement, the Vietnam War, the women's movement, the gay liberation movement – undoubtedly complicates the task of memorializing. A variety of complex questions come to mind: For whom are memorials created, and to whom do they belong? How does a memorial define who or what is remembered and who or what is forgotten?[19] Whose memory counts? How is it accessed?

The absence of a single story in each of the three memorials acknowledges a multiplicity of stories, hence affirming inclusivity, while recognizing, in a postmodern manner, the impossibility of a unified telling. The tensions surrounding the planning of the VVM mirrored the social divisions regarding the war between supporters and opponents. Some opponents of the

Maya Lin design argued that the grave-like nature of the Wall failed to appropriately honour, in a traditional manner, the memory of those who died for their country. A compromise was reached by the addition of a flag and a representational statue by Frederick Hart of three American soldiers in fatigues, intended as a balance to the non-representational Wall. We find persuasive the conclusion of Carole Blair *et al.* that this compromise results in the two sides of the conflict – over the war and over the Memorial – 'being endlessly articulated rather than transcended. The presence together of the wall and the statue allows them to "question" one another's legitimacy indefinitely.'[20] Since alternative interpretive possibilities are available at the VVM, given both the Wall and the additions, visitors may 'read' either priestly or prophetic messages – or both – inscribed there.

The NAMES Project also had detractors. Some decried the Quilt for its priestly functions, calling, instead, for a more militant use of time and energy in combating AIDS. Others criticized it for appealing virtually exclusively to white, middle-class, gay men.[21] In assessing the merits of the Project, Hawkins argues, 'Rather than "fixing" the NAMES Project . . . it seems wiser to acknowledge the necessary plurality of responses to the epidemic, no one of which can possibly work for all'.[22] The panels themselves inscribe this kind of plurality since some reveal cathartic motifs, while others raise a condemnatory prophetic fist.

The controversies surrounding the planning of the USHMM were multiple. Should the museum be located at the Mall, in Washington, in the US, even, since its intent was to memorialize a European event? Should the Jewish story be the only story told, and if not, should it be at the centre of the narrative? Should human hair be displayed as part of the exhibit? Should survivors' feelings in this regard be decisive (they were: no hair is currently on exhibit, but a photo of human hair from Auschwitz is on display), or should designers' sense of the dramatic prevail?[23] Choices were made along the way, but no single voice dominated others. Contested meanings about the Holocaust remain in place at the Museum today.

Memorials as Conceptual Bridges:

In this age of deconstruction, traditional social categories are often contested, given the recognition that they mirror cultural constructions as opposed to eternal truths. The three memorials, along with the responses of their respective audiences, are occasions for the bridging of several traditionally distinct social 'realities.' The success of these memorials may well be related to their elasticity in their ability to cut across these social dimensions. We have mentioned several instances of such border crossings along the way. Here we consider the memorials' bridging functions in the assumed dichotomy between the individual and the collective, the private and public, and the religious and the secular 'spheres' of life.

The Individual and the Collective:

The pronounced individualism of contemporary American society explains in part the turn away from the collective, heroic narratives of previous eras. America as 'the culture of narcissism' has surely not changed dramatically since Christopher Lasch coined the term in the late 1970s.[24] But along with the individualistic, self-referential orientation of American citizens, there is evidence today of a hunger for community, a desire for belonging, and a search for common values.[25]

Richard D. Mohr suggests that, as a text, 'The Quilt is a map of classical liberalism operating at its best . . . it asserts the individual, not groups, classes, or society in toto, as the locus of human value.' He later adds that there is 'no social theory here to read or tell. The panels do not together make a picture. Collectively, they have no meaning. . . . The Quilt keeps the named safely both from merely being a heap . . . and from being or telling some larger multicharactered tale.'[26] On the one hand, Mohr is correct, insofar as each panel does celebrate the individuality of the person memorialized. On the other hand, his reading misses the social process involved in patchwork quilting: quilts are stitched together from multiple sources and traditionally done by groups. In addition, the Quilt needs to be understood as more than a text, for texts come alive only as they are read and responded to by people. The ritual acts, both formal and spontaneous, that have developed around the Quilt reveal a response not only to individual lives and losses, but a recognition of the immensity of the tragedy of the AIDS epidemic precisely because a whole population of people – people with AIDS – have been neglected. It is this recognition that fuels the Quilt's prophetic power – that more needs to be done to combat AIDS, and it is a collective responsibility to do so.

Maya Lin also reveals an individualistic perspective when she reflects on her design of the VVM. As she thought about a memorial's purpose in the twentieth century, she concluded that it is about individuals and their need to deal with their loss. Seeing death as a 'personal, private matter', she intended the Wall as a quiet place for individuals to go for personal reflection.[27] Indeed, the Wall does function in this way, as people quietly stand before a name, touch it, make rubbings of it, deposit offerings, weep. The tactility of these moments allows for a deeply personal, experiential encounter that some people find stirring, others, transformative. But experience at the Wall is often communal as well, sometimes formal in nature, as in special ceremonies and vigils, but more frequently spontaneous. Victor Turner's notion of 'communitas' characterizes the erasures of hierarchy, heightened bonding ('communion') among strangers, and engagement in a shared enterprise that are clearly in evidence at the Wall.[28]

Veterans connect not only to this or that buddy who died in battle, but also to their associations with the war in toto, from their fighting in the jungle during an unpopular war to their social rejection upon their return home. Part of the reported healing pertains to the symbolic power of the Wall to heal those social scars. Even for those who were conscientious objectors during the Vietnam War, the Wall appears to be awe-some.[29] Hence collective reconciliation, not only personal healing, is at work here.

The USHMM chose to humanize the Nazis' victims by personalizing their experiences in a variety of ways. In what has been called the Tower of Faces, thousands of photographs depicting the faces and lives of the pre-war Jews of the Polish town of Ejszyszki, almost all of whom were murdered in the Holocaust, form a distinct and particularly moving part of the Museum display. Given the prescribed route that visitors must take through the exhibit space, all must pass through this 'village of the doomed'. Bridgeways connecting different sections of the Museum – reminiscent of bridges connecting sections of the Warsaw Ghetto – are, on one Museum level, lined with the first names of victims and, on another, the names of towns and villages whose Jewish populations were decimated. Visitors also carry 'identity cards', each representing an individual who passed through the Holocaust. The attempt here is to move the narrative from the numbing world of statistics ('the six million') to embodied realities. Even the video depiction of Nazi doctors' experiments on Jewish men, women and children, however horrific, functions to communicate the actual suffering experienced by individual human beings. It thus enhances the dignity of the victim as it engages the empathy of the observer.

While the USHMM seeks to individualize the victims and survivors of the Holocaust, it also aims to uproot the visitor from the reality of contemporary America, disorienting and reorienting individuals into a collectivity as they are 'herded' together through the designated exhibit passages. Each elevator-cohort of visitors collectively experiences the Holocaust narrative, thereby identifying with those the Nazis sought to dehumanize: Jews, Gypsies, Russian POWs, Poles, Slavs, homosexuals and other 'degenerate' and 'inferior' categories of people who were swept up into the Nazis' genocidal world.

The tendency to stereotype those who experienced the Holocaust into such broad categories as victim, oppressor and 'innocent' bystander is averted, as the exhibit culminates in a wall of names honouring those individuals, groups and, on occasion, towns that risked their own safety in aiding and rescuing Jews and others during the Holocaust. Thus the message emerges that moral decision-making is ultimately individual in nature, an indictment of those who denied that this was possible 'under the circumstances' and a challenge to departing museum visitors to consider the actions of Holocaust-era rescuers as models for their own moral behaviour.

The Private and the Public:

In *The Ordeal of Civility*, John Cuddihy contends that the US, as a modernizing society in the late nineteenth and early twentieth centuries, 'civilized' the immigrant European masses by curtailing their public display of emotion.[30] Jackie Kennedy was widely lauded for her grace in maintaining composure in the hours and days following the assassination of her husband. While contemporary television talk shows may well reflect a changing sensibility about public displays of emotion, American society as lived by most Americans is still ordered by a firm separation of emotional expressivity allowed in public – in the corporation, the university, or the halls of government – and that permitted at home and among family.

Both the Wall and the Quilt repeatedly contest such separation. Indeed, the private and the public often blur, as individuals grieving quietly are publicly lent emotional support by relatives, friends, or even total strangers, who hug them, commiserate with them, cry with them, or, together, construct emotionally charged, spontaneous ceremonies. When visitors to the Wall leave favourite toys or clothing of the deceased, they open the latter's private life to strangers.

The bridging of private and public is more dramatically evident in the Quilt, where 'intimacies are everywhere confided to strangers. The panels betray a delight in the telling of tales, revealing in those who died a taste for chintz, for motorbikes or drag shows. It is as if the survivors had decided that the greatest gift they could offer the dead would be telling everything, breaking the silence that has surrounded gay life long before the advent of AIDS.'[31] The negotiation between what is revealed and what is concealed on the part of panel makers reflects the ongoing risks encountered by homosexuals in American society. Ten per cent of the names in the Quilt omit surnames in an attempt to mask identity. Those panels that reveal an individual's full name may be seen as a kind of coming out, especially for the families of gay men.[32]

The USHMM in its own way deconstructs the separation between the private and the public. It is generally not in the nature of museums to demand a high investment of emotional energy. At this museum, by contrast, the visitor is exposed to trauma and required to make an offering of personal feelings, typically conceived as personal and voluntary. It is through this process that the viewer of artifacts, videos, narratives and Museum architecture may be challenged to engage in a process of inner transformation.

The Religious and the Secular:

None of the three memorials was constructed with a specifically religious goal in mind as understood from a confessional perspective. The fact that all three address massive death and loss, however, places them within the traditional purview of religion. The memorials are intended to raise questions about death; they certainly did not anticipate the multiple religious but generally non-denominational gestures and rituals that have spontaneously arisen in response. Among others, the following religious acts and themes arise from these contexts: silence, spontaneous prayer and ceremonies, 'communion' with the dead and with other mourners, contrition, healing, pilgrimage, communitas, witnessing.

The cathartic experience revealed by many at the Wall and at the Quilt suggests that perhaps traditional mourning rituals are not adequately responding to the needs of survivors for comfort and healing.[33] Many of those who died of AIDS were cremated and their ashes scattered; the Quilt may thus provide a 'place' for mourning otherwise unavailable to family, lovers and friends. Unlike the Wall and the Quilt, however, the USHMM sees itself as part of the effort to engage Americans – especially non-Jews – in the events, losses and overall tragedy of the Holocaust, thus promoting emotional engagement rather than assuming already present but unresolved emotional tensions in need of catharsis and healing, as is the case in the other memorials.

Religions have frequently used master narratives to give meaning to death, to rescue human beings from 'dying in vain'. None of these memorials raises these master narratives as explanations or legitimations. In fact, rather than following the usual Western religious tendency to separate spirit from body in order to transcend the ugliness of an early and violent death, the memorials attend to the embodied dimension of the victims they honour, thus resisting the urge to spiritualize it away. The VVM encodes the reality of each veteran's death in stone, a traditional medium for signalling finality. The Quilt more emphatically tells the individual stories of embodied lives, typically within the context of pre-AIDS narratives. Relatives and friends engage in telling a larger story, one that extends the name into a face, a body, a favourite toy, or a piece of clothing. Both of these efforts link the themes of death to life; symbolically they may be asserting the healing moment when mourners themselves begin to turn toward renewed life. John Wheeler, a Vietnam veteran who was a chairman of the Vietnam Veterans Memorial Fund, talked of the presence of the sacred that surrounds the Wall, suggesting that the Wall 'is not just a sign that healing is taking place in the nation. . . . It is the centre of that healing – a power spot where Americans can come to renew a sense of national unity and belonging.'[34]

The planners of the USHMM struggled over an appropriate end to the exhibit, some wanting a hopeful conclusion, given the optimism of American society. In the face of the incomprehensible evil of the Holocaust, such a conclusion was thankfully not chosen; instead, the exhibit of rescuers during the Second World War provides a measure of hope and a compass to take the visitor a step away from despair in the direction of moral responsibility and accountability.

The actual ending of the exhibit is a small amphitheatre with filmed accounts of Holocaust survivors sharing their individual stories of survival. This space, which architect Freed calls the Memory Room, effectively invites the viewer into the lives of those for whom the Holocaust is an abiding memory. The parting message to museum visitors is that, in a way, they too are survivors of an encounter with the Holocaust; and like those on the screen before them, they are also mourners for those who perished, unable to resume their post-Holocaust lives without carrying the memory of the Holocaust with them.

It is only after being intellectually, emotionally and existentially challenged by his or her journey through the permanent exhibit and the building in which it is enveloped, that the USHMM visitor encounters the specific memorial to the victims of the Holocaust, the Hall of Remembrance. In some ways it is a striking counterpoint to the architecture and exhibit from which the visitor has just emerged: it is tall and quiet; its symmetricality provides not so much a focus as an absence of one. Here visitors may sit on stone steps in quiet contemplation, though no particular ritual acts are apparent, aside from the voluntary lighting of candles. Left to oneself and one's own resources after hours of immersion in the Holocaust world, there is, perhaps, a sense of not knowing what to do or how to appropriately respond to the experience. And if this memorial space restores 'a sense of order and calm and comfort' for some, it is not a little disconcerting for others, intentionally withholding any sense of hope, redemption, or resolution of tension.[35] Freed himself suggests that 'the void in the middle of the room becomes the core of remembrance. It is the place where those who are not should have been. It's the absence of people – the absence of six million. The absence is what we look at. We don't look at anything solid. The absence is all, I think, that you can have here.'[36] Fittingly, the space incorporates a black granite panel similar, in Freed's thinking, to that of the VVM, as if to say that the essence of both memorials is a confrontation with the reality of loss and the sheer horror of its magnitude.

Ironically, if the success of the AIDS Quilt and the VVM lies in their capacity to make symbolically present those being memorialized, the success of the USHMM's Hall of Remembrance is its capacity to symbolize the absence of those murdered in the Holocaust. This makes it far more difficult to mourn adequately such losses and to promote anything like the sense of healing, community and closure that mark the Quilt and the VVM. If anything, new wounds are opened by the USHMM – any search for healing is left for the future.

Beyond this, the very nature of a museum, with its internal space and carefully controlled environment, presents barriers to the kind of access and openness to spontaneity so evident at the Wall and The Quilt. The spontaneous public and private rituals that have emerged at these other memorials, which allow them to function so effectively on a priestly level, are not evident in what may be perceived as the more daunting and inhibiting official space. This is not to say that further priestly possibilities are necessarily precluded by the structure of the Museum and its Hall of Remembrance. Indeed, the USHMM can enhance its priestly functioning by encouraging the same type of individual and group initiatives found at the Wall and the

Quilt: personal reflections of loss, perhaps incorporated within some folk art, offerings of Holocaust memorabilia, and acts of communion at the memorial lamp within the Hall of Remembrance. On the other hand, the extension of the Museum's prophetic role through regular symposia on Holocaust-related and often controversial topics presents a model that other memorializing efforts, including the Wall and the Quilt, may wish to emulate.

Conclusion:

The three memorials we have studied have had a significant impact on American society. They have also succeeded in responding to those most directly affected by tragedy and loss. We suggest that this is the case due to the way in which each implements its priestly and prophetic functions. The fact that *both* functions are addressed by each memorial is important; so are their postmodern uses of inclusivity, ambiguity and multivocality, which allow the memorials to meet the individual and collective needs of late twentieth-century Americans in ways that traditional symbols and credal structures, classical monuments and national metanarratives seem no longer able to accomplish as effectively.

It is no wonder that strictly political motivations were denied by the memorials' designers and advocates, even where politically critical stances clearly inhere in the nature and location of the memorial. Politics, especially in Washington, is perceived as necessarily partisan and therefore exclusionary. It is, rather, the more ambiguous but inclusive prophetic messages of the value of human life, the need for people to care for and nurture one another, the primacy of tolerance and justice as personal and national values that allowed each memorial to transcend the barriers to its establishment. It is also the inclusive nature of the memorials' priestly efforts, the facilitation of emotional expression, comfort and healing, that allows for their broad and powerful attraction to so many who make 'pilgrimage' to their sites.

The memorials' capacity to bridge social categories – the individual and the collective, the private and the public, the religious and the secular – recognizes the fluidity of personal and collective identity experienced by postmodern individuals but seldom articulated in more discursive mediums. The memorials, but also the tremendous response to them, suggest places and moments that capture and mirror, in a profound manner, important aspects of contemporary American sensibilities. These opportunities for crossing boundaries allow for the forging of community, however fleeting. They assist the mourner in ways reminiscent of traditional mourning practices, when social distance diminishes and human beings pool their resources for the sake of a common end – the existential confrontation with loss and the imperative to pick up one's life and move forward.

Notes

1   For a useful discussion of 'metanarratives' and public memorializing, see Carole Blair, Marsha S. Jeppeson, and Enrico Pucci, Jr., 'Public Memorializing in Post-modernity: The Vietnam Veterans Memorial as Prototype', *Quarterly Journal of Speech* 77 (1991), pp. 263–88.

2   For an insightful application of the priestly/prophetic categories to American civil religion, see Martin E. Marty, 'Two Kinds of Civil Religion' in Russell E. Rickey and Donald G. Jones (eds), *American Civil Religion* (New York: Harper & Row, 1974), pp.139–57.

3   For a poignant photographic treatment of visitors to and offerings at the Wall, see Larry Powell, *Hunger of the Heart: Communion at the Wall* (Dubuque, IA: Islewest Publishing, 1995).

4   Leslie Allen, 'Offerings at the Wall', *American Heritage* (February/March 1995), p. 94.

5   Peter S. Hawkins, 'Naming Names: The Art of Memory and the NAMES Project AIDS Quilt', *Critical Inquiry* 19 (Summer 1993), pp. 752–9, p. 757.

6   'The Quilt: Stories from the Names Project', *Publishers Weekly* (19 February 1988), pp. 41–3, p. 43.

7   Hawkins, 'Naming Names', p. 777.

8   Michael Kernan, 'A National Memorial Bears Witness to the Tragedy of the Holocaust', *Smithsonian* 24, No. 24 (April 1993), pp. 50–62, p. 51.

9   Edward T. Linenthal, 'The Boundaries of Memory: The United States Holocaust Memorial Museum', *American Quarterly* 46, No. 3 (September 1994), pp. 406–24, p. 424.

10 Edward T. Linenthal, 'Locating Holocaust Memory: The United States Holocaust Memorial Museum' in David Chidester and Edward T. Linenthal (eds), *American Sacred Space* (Bloomington, IN: Indiana University Press, 1995), pp. 220–61, p. 224.

11 Linenthal, 'Locating Holocaust Memory', p. 232.

12 James Ingo Freed, 'The United States Holocaust Memorial Museum – A Dialogue with Memory', *Curator* 38, No. 2 (June 1995), pp. 95–110, p. 102.

13 Freed, 'The United States Holocaust Memorial Museum', p. 103.

14 Cited in Linenthal, 'Locating Holocaust Memory', p. 249.

15 Freed, 'The United States Holocaust Memorial Museum', p. 104.

16 Linenthal, 'Boundaries of Memory', p. 428.

17 Linenthal, 'Boundaries of Memory', p. 429.

18 Freed, 'The United States Holocaust Memorial Museum', p. 104.

19 Marita Sturken, 'Conversations with the Dead: Bearing Witness in the AIDS Memorial Quilt', *Socialist Review* 92, no. 77 (April–June 1992), pp. 65–95, p. 66.

20 Blair *et al.*, 'Public Memorializing in Postmodernity', p. 277.

21 On these issues, see Sturken, 'Conversations with the Dead'.

22 Hawkins, 'Naming Names', p. 779.

23 Linenthal, 'Boundaries of Memory' and 'Locating Holocaust Memory'.

24 Christopher Lasch, *The Culture of Narcissism: American Life in an Age of Diminishing Expectations* (New York: W.W. Norton & Company, 1979).

25 See, for example, Wade Clark Roof, *A Generation of Seekers: The Spiritual Journeys of the Baby Boom Generation* (New York: Harper San Francisco, 1993).

26 Richard D. Mohr, *Gay Ideas: Outing and Other Controversies* (Boston: Beacon Press, 1992), pp. 107, 111.

27 Freida Lee Mock and Terry Sanders (producers), *Maya Lin: A Strong Clear Vision* (American Film Foundation, 1333 Ocean Ave., Santa Monica, CA 90401, 1994).

28 Victor Turner and Edith Turner, *Image and Pilgrimage in Christian Culture: Anthropological Perspectives* (New York: Columbia University Press, 1978).

29 See, for example, John K. Simmons, 'Pilgrimage to the Wall', *Christian Century* (6 November, 1985), pp. 998–1002, pp. 998–99.

30 John M. Cuddihy, *The Ordeal of Civility: Freud, Marx, Levi-Strauss, and the Jewish Struggle with Modernity* (New York: Dell Publishing, 1974), p. 13.

31 Hawkins, 'Naming Names', pp. 770–71.

32 Sturken, 'Conversations', pp. 70–71.

33 Mary Murray Mayo, *A Cultural Analysis of the Meanings in the NAMES Project AIDS Memorial Quilt* (Ann Arbor, MI: UMI Microform, 1996), p. 121.

34 John K. Simmons, 'Pilgrimage to the Wall'.

35 Kernan, 'A National Memorial', p. 60.

36 Freed, 'United States', p. 110.

Epilogue

Martin E. Marty

The authors in this collection have a clear sense of space and time and a love of the concrete. As they tell the story of the Children's Cross and similar adventures with public place and sacred intentions, they have at times used the language of the detective novel. As in, 'at 11:59 a.m. on the corner of Main and Through, under a gray Chicago sky, there appeared'. And there is a certain detective story character to what they are telling.

Who done it? We have met Phoebe Griswold and other well-intentioned citizens and church members. On the other hand, we have met equally concerned citizens who, out of a variety of motives, counter her efforts, with a cathedral congregation, to identify with and empathize with children who have fallen victim to violence. Was the whole venture ill-conceived? Do the critics have a case? If the faithful cannot find the form of identification, empathy, and stimulus to their and others' awareness, should they do nothing? What else should they do? How to trace back the actions and the motives to the Griswolds, the church-and-state separationists, the cross-haters? And, if we trace these back, how account for them?

One theme that courses through the book, whether pressed by authors or not, has to do with symbols and symbolism. It is not hard for seniors to remember that a third of a century ago thoughtful analysts foresaw the decline and fall of myth and symbol. In the 'secular city' people were going to move beyond mytho-symbolic expression and be breezy pragmatists, concerned with the practical side of life but hardly being attentive to symbols.

Hardly. Supreme Court Justice Felix Frankfurter liked to quote Oliver Wendell Holmes: 'We live by symbols'. He was speaking of the United States flag in a 1940 decision. Some Jehovah's Witnesses children were forbidden to salute the flag in the classroom, even where it was governmentally mandated. America was on the verge of war and was mounting patriotic sentiments and appeals. How could they resist?

They did. In that decision the court ruled that since we live by symbols, we had to privilege the national symbol, the flag, and compel assent to its being revered. Jehovah's Witnesses thought that doing so gave obeisance to another God than Jehovah. After the decision some Americans, 'living by symbols', persecuted, castrated, violated Witnesses and children taunted their children. In 1943 the court reversed itself. But by then we had learned what the St James Episcopal Cathedral people relearned in our time: symbols are potent.

Fly the Confederate flag over the South Carolina capitol and you evoke strong responses. Some Confederacy leftovers and racists live by that symbol and dare any one else not to bow. African-Americans and others who see it as a symbol of anti-civil rights efforts and pro-racist activities when it began to be bannered there in 1962 engage in boycotts and turn their backs on the state over which it flies.

The cross can be an eloquent symbol of human hope in the churches of the Mexican-American poor in America's Southwest or on the wall of a terminally ill patient in a hospital. It can be bejewelled and dangling from a chain into the décolletage of a celebrity who looks for decoration, not inspiration. The cross can be removed from megachurch auditoriums, a.k.a. sanctuaries, because the market-oriented church leaders do not want to have *any* religious symbols on view as they set out to attract the unchurched. 'Hold Thou thy cross before my closing eyes' calls for the symbol to have central place in the imagination of those on the verge of sleep – or death. We live by symbols.

As some of the authors here point out, even among Christians the cross comes across as an ambiguous symbol. In most centuries it had unquestioned place. But today thoughtful believers look back and recall it on the shields of Crusaders, killers-for-Christ who, living by symbols, wanted to retrieve the Holy Land from the Infidel. They know that it has often been painted on the armament of military forces on both sides of battles, both having had their cannon blessed by the priesthood.

And they know that even within the originating stories, in the New Testament, the meaning of Jesus' cross is ambiguous. There is no single, consistent, insisted upon 'theory of the atonement' connected with the story of the cross within the biblical canon. And through many centuries of elaboration in the history of the church, the meanings of the cross have never been reduced to a dogmatic clarification or insistence. One might almost say that there are as many crosses as there are believers — or unbelievers. Each individual makes up his or her mind about what the cross means, when it is presented appealingly or jarringly, as was the case at the cathedral. Or we make up our mind in groups.

So it is that an author or two reaches for readings of the symbol that suggest that it is offensive for anyone who seeks identification, empathy, and motivation to change the circumstances in which children get killed. In their choice of readings, the cross suggests sadism and abuse and victim-creation on the part of a divine Father against his divine-human Son — hardly a lesson for children who suffer abuse and are victims.

That there is warrant for such interpretations is clear to anyone who has read the history of atonement theories, which have included 'substitution-ary' and 'penalty-paying' views. But to others such psychologically reduc-tionist theories will sound like the kind of thing tenured academics and comfortable people can come up with — far from the abuse and victimized sufferers who use the cross as a sign for countering misery, a signal for God's triumph in a world that does not know it.

So if it was hard for the Cathedral people to reach out to the victims across the boundaries of class and areas of town and circumstance, so it is difficult for their critics to find the posture from which to criticize. What the critics are not clear about, sometimes in this book, is this: should the Cathe-dral folk not notice the plight of the children? Should they be indifferent? Should they insist that their class and precinct should stand above and apart from those who are in the line of fire in bereft parts of the city? Should they sell the Cathedral and turn over the profits to welfare programs, which would get a few extra days' or weeks' worth of financial boost from the out-come? Should they move into the ghetto and be themselves in the line of fire? One detects, in this detective story, that this is less a story of 'who done it?' than 'what should anyone do?'

Even more, *where* should they do it? For if this is an essay on the ambi-guity of symbols and intentions, it is also a collection of pieces that quicken us to the sense that space and place are as much at issue in our profane world as they were in worlds marked by the sacred.

Profane: the word does not connote obscenity in speech but, at its root, that which is *pro + fanum*, outside the temple. Let Christians do anything they wish behind the walls that would enclose them from the jamming sig-nals of the secular and pluralist society of passers-by and the city at large. Just don't move the symbols outdoors. Oh, all right: we can't get you to take the cross down from that steeple or out of that window. That is still part of the *fanum*, the set-aside holy space. But we can't let you bring it out into the open at ground level.

Valid issues are at stake here. The public space *does* belong to the public, which has developed and lived with certain ground rules for the use of its grounds. Intense religionists who would like to preempt that space for their particular symbols resent the fact that profane sub-publics get to put up their banners, some of them of the sort that violate expressions of human dignity. Why cannot they put up particular religious symbols that promote it?

Therefore: why not have the Ten Commandments on the court room wall; the Nativity crèche on the court house grounds; the cross on the pavement outside a cathedral? So heated have been arguments over religious symbols around Christmas, that people can write at book length about *December Wars*. Efforts at peace-making do not achieve much. One wonders whether efforts to plant the cross — not this Cathedral instance, it is clear! — are not sometimes motivated by a desire to say, 'We belong here! We were here first [or second]! Take your symbols into your private places. We built this country and want to win it back.'

Or the symbols can be so surrounded on public space that they lose their potency and get transformed into the trivial. The United States Supreme Court did agree in the 'Pawtucket case', that one can have the crèche on public grounds so long as it is surrounded by menorahs, Christmas trees, bells, santas and enough other images that Jesus comes into view as one more secular symbol. We call this the 'two plastic reindeers and one baby Jesus' policy. It is hard to picture worshipers being satisfied with that kind of trivialization as the price for using public space.

When vigilant ones and vigilantes on the church-state front spoke up against the very modest, hardly obtrusive, signal of repentance and identification on the cathedral grounds and, once, some inches into non-cathedral public space, opponents became agitated. They did a public service. Something valid *is* at issue when particular religious symbols, moved from the *fanum* to the *pro + fanum* space, make their appearance. And they called some members of the Christian community to rethink their understanding of witness and appeal to passers by who do not share their commitment.

This Children's Cross case is worthwhile for these and other issues that it raises, far beyond its own intrinsic value. What puzzles the reader, or at least this reader, is this: it is an instance that can quicken Cathedral parishioners and the writers of this book to deal with profound concerns. It inspired legal action and made front pages. Yet in the course of time support faded, Cathedral members stopped showing care, the public just passed the Cross by. Is this the case of a symbol losing its valence and power because too many people attached too many sentiments and opinions to it?

Will that ever happen at the Western Wall, where the Pope's wearing of a cross as he prays there in Jerusalem offends the Orthodox guardians of that wall? Will the cross lose its power to offend after years and years of its appearance on the grounds of Auschwitz? Or was the Cathedral Children's Cross such a muted, ambiguous witness from the first, placed by Christians who do not want to offend, that it stopped attracting?

One must observe how hard it is for anyone to present satisfying symbols on public grounds. We read above of the Vietnam Veterans Memorial in Washington. It is a highly successful presentation, revered by millions. Yet it was born in controversy and had to be matched by a different, more literal, representation before the controversy was muted. Must every public space have two kinds of monuments, plastic reindeers plus plastic baby Jesus, to satisfy the interests of pluralist society?

Behind all such questions lurks another, not developed much in this book. (Watch for Volume Two?) Are *any* profound public symbols really non-religious? Define religion as having to do with ultimate concern, sacrifice, myths and symbols, rites and ceremonies, metaphysical assumptions, behavioural correlates, and issuance in community, and it is hard to see the flag as other than sacred. Try burning one, or resisting a Constitutional amendment to protect it? You can destroy a cross as part of a chancel drama by a youth group, and no one resists. You cannot destroy a flag.

Objects in trophy cases, diplomas, judicial robes, dollar signs, get to be perceived as sacred objects. Only the traditionally recognized religious symbols come into firing range of critics. The Cathedral Children's Cross supporters may have played their own small part in forcing more of us to think through the legal and inter-religious implications of 'religion' as currently defined by the courts.

I have a friend who has observed how difficult it is for Americans to develop mourning rites or places for grieving. He has studied some European postmodern cemeteries and their artful use of space and asked whether analogues here might be of help. Thus, why not have on public school grounds some equivalents of the Vietnam Veterans Memorial engraving of names? Let there be a passage into a labyrinth in the atrium of a public high school, where students on the way to a special classroom would pass ponds and peacocks and other symbols of the living and the lifecycle. *En route* they would confront the names of their near-contemporaries who died in gang warfare, from substance abuse, or from other violent means.

The idea has enough value to quicken curiosity about its possibilities. Of course, planting a cross in that atrium would be offensive, presumptuous, preemptive, and violating. But would not-planting it mean that all the other symbols and rites that would go on in that passageway would not have a sacral and, yes, religious dimension?

How to celebrate the achievements of the civil rights struggle without remembering a host of 'Reverends' who brought religious symbols onto the bridges of Selma and the highway to Montgomery? Does one finally look for public spaces to be devoid of symbols? (I am only half kidding when I say that emptiness also has sacred symbolic value; ask your friendly neighbourhood Zen Buddhist.)

I find myself having used many question marks in this chapter of response, because the authors served us well by leaving so much up in the air.

What I take from the experience has to deal with basic issues of human encounter. Just because it is difficult to associate across boundaries of class and precinct and ward does not mean that one should not make the effort. After reading all the criticisms I have to say at least 'Two cheers for Phoebe Griswold' and those who made a genuine, sincere, necessarily limited effort to identify with children who do not and cannot know their world. Martin Buber taught us that 'all life is meeting'. Meeting through symbols, prayer, being mindful of the other, has to be a somehow positive signal in an indifferent universe and a warring world.

Contributors

Janet B. Campbell
A priest in the Episcopal Church. At the time of the Children's Cross Project, she was Canon for Liturgy and Outreach, St James Cathedral, Chicago. She is now Director of Liturgy and the Arts at St Mark's Cathedral, Seattle.

Frida Kerner Furman
Associate Professor of Religious Studies, De Paul University, Chicago. Her research interests include the social construction of identity and cultural values, feminist ethics, feminist theology, the sociology of religion, and cultural representations of the self and the body. Recent publications include *Beyond Yiddishkeit: the Struggle for Jewish Identity in a Reform Synagogue* (State University of New York Press, 1987) and *Facing the Mirror: Older Women and Beauty Shop Culture* (Routledge, 1997).

Roy S. Furman
Instructor in Comparative Religion and Jewish Studies, Department of Religious Studies, DePaul University Chicago. He is also Adjunct Faculty member in Jewish–Christian Studies at the Chicago Theological School. Ordained rabbi at Hebrew Union College, Cincinnati, Ohio (1971), and holder of a Masters Degree in Clinical Social Work (University of Southern California, 1975).

James Halstead
Associate Professor of Religious Studies and Director of the Program in Catholic Studies at DePaul University, Chicago. He holds a doctorate in moral theology from the Catholic University of Louvain. In addition to his work at DePaul, Fr. Halstead has been actively involved in ministerial education in Chicago for more than a decade.

Gareth Jones
Professor of Christian Theology, Christ Church University College, Canterbury. His research interests include modern and systematic theology, theology and aesthetics, and theology and social theory. Recent publications include *Critical Theology: Questions of Truth and Method* (Polity Press, 1995) and *Christian Theology: A Brief Introduction* (Polity Press, 1999).

Emmanuel Lartey
Senior Lecturer in Theology, University of Birmingham. His research interests include pastoral theology, pastoral care and counselling, intercultural studies, and third world theology. He is editor of the journal *Black Theology in Britain* (Sheffield Academic Press). Recent publications include *The Church and Healing: Echoes from Africa* (Peter Lang, 1994) and *In Living Colour: An Intercultural Approach to Pastoral Care and Counselling* (Cassell, 1997)

Martin E. Marty
Faifax M. Cone Distinguished Service Professor Emeritus, University of Chicago. Recent publications include *Modern American Religion: Under God, Indivisible, 1941–60* (University of Chicago Press 1999), and *Politics, Religion and the Common Good: Advancing a Distinctly American Conversation about Religion* (Jossey-Bass Publishers, 2000).

Dennis P. McCann
Wallace M. Alston Professor of Bible and Religion, Agnes Scott College, Atlanta/ Decatur, Georgia. He is Executive Director of the Society of Christian Ethics. At the time of the Children's Cross Project, he was Professor of Religious Studies, DePaul University. Along with Charles R. Strain, he co-authored *Polity and Praxis: A Program for American Practical Theology* (Winston/Seabury, 1985, reprinted by the University Press of America, 1990). Other publications include *Christian Realism and Liberation Theology* (Orbis, 1981) and *New Experiment in Democracy: The Challenge for American Catholicism* (Sheed and Ward, 1987).

Kay Almere Read
Associate Professor of History of Religions, Department of Religious Studies, DePaul University, Chicago. Her research interests include pre-Conquest religious traditions of Mesoamerica, comparative ethics, and religious imagery. Recent publications include *Time and Sacrifice in the Aztec Cosmos* (Indiana University Press, 1998), and both with Jason J. Gonzalez on *A Handbook of Mesoamerican Mythology* (ABC-Clio Press, 2000) and *An Encyclopedia of Mesoamerican Mythology* (ABC-Clio Press).

Charles R. Strain
Associate Vice President for Academic Affairs and Professor of Religious Studies, DePaul University, Chicago. He is the co-author (with Dennis P. McCann) of *Polity and Praxis: A Program for American Practical Theology* (Winston/Seabury, 1985), and editor of *Prophetic Visions and Economic Realities* (Eerdmans, 1989). More recent work in the area of socially engaged Buddhism includes 'Socially Engaged Buddhism's Contribution to the Transformation of Catholic Social Teaching on Human Rights' in Damien Keown, Charles Prebish and Wayne Husted (eds), *Buddhism and Human Rights* (Curzon, 1998).

Martin D. Stringer
His research interests include anthropology of religion, ritual, Christian worship, the popular articulation of faith, and sexuality and theology. Recent publications include *On the Perception of Worship* (University of Birmingham Press, 1999)

Denys Turner
Norris Hulse Professor of Divinity, University of Cambridge. His research interests include political theologies, medieval theology, medieval and modern mysticism. Recent publications include *The Darkness of God: Negativity in Christian Mysticism* (Cambridge University Press, 1995) and *Eros and Allegory: Medieval Exegesis of the Song of Songs* (Cistercian Publications 1995).

Jule D. Ward
Department of Religious Studies, DePaul University, Chicago. She is also a research consultant to the Religion, Culture and Family Project at the University of Chicago. Her research interests focus around ethical issues of family life. Recent publications include *La Leche League: At the Crossroads of Medicine, Feminism, and Religion* (University of North Carolina Press, 2000).

Isabel L. Wollaston
Lecturer in Theology, University of Birmingham. She is Editor of the journal *Reviews in Religion and Theology* (Blackwell Publishers). Recent publications include *The Sociology of Sacred Texts*, co-edited with Jon Davies (Sheffield Academic Press, 1993) and *A War against Memory: The Future of Holocaust Remembrance* (SPCK, 1996)

Index